Live on the Margin

Learn to Love Risk, Profit from Fear, and Retire Tomorrow

Nick O'Kelly & Patrick Schulte

Two Old Goats Publishing

Live on the Margin
Learn to Love Risk, Profit from Fear, and Retire Tomorrow

Cover design by Antonio Souto
Book designed by Nick O'Kelly & Patrick Schulte

ISBN 978-0-578-11664-8

Visit our websites:
www.liveonthemargin.com
www.bumfuzzle.com
www.nickokelly.com

For Ali, Lowe, Megan, and Ouest.

Table of Contents

Introduction

Everyone has a dream, but unless you're set-for-life financially, you know that pursuing that dream today will require tradeoffs—at least two: (1) you'll have to trade the routine you know today for an experience and outcome you can't know ahead of time, and (2) you'll have to trade the money not made—and instead spent—today, for the money you think you'll need to have in the future.

To make those trades, you have to evaluate the risks—pursuing your dream now means trading the *certainty* of your current situation (low-risk) for something *less* certain (higher-risk). Regardless of your choice—you're already a trader—but are you taking the right risks and making the right trades?

This book is going to show you how to find the right risks, choose the right trades, and use those profits to make your dream happen, sooner rather than later—maybe even tomorrow.

Learn to Love Risk

Most people choose to trade uncertainty for certainty, and give up the opportunities for adventure they have now for ones they think they'll have later—they set their dreams aside in the "someday" files. We think these trades and risks are wrong—dead wrong—and based on two fundamentally incorrect assumptions: people think they'll live forever, and they think that sacrificing earned income now means delaying or even jeopardizing their financial future.

We believe that the greater risk lies in *not* pursuing your dream today. Money can appreciate and grow—time does not—it just gets spent. Waiting for "someday" to come guarantees one thing with absolute certainty: you'll have less time to live your dream, if you get to do it at all. Waiting a lifetime to do what you really want to do is a very high-risk proposition. We believe it was the philosopher-poet Eminem who said it best: "You only get one shot." Slim Shady had the right idea.

Financially speaking, there are alternatives to earning money from a job, and there's no reason you have to burn through all of your savings to do what you really want to do. In fact, why do you have to give up the pursuit of income just because you're crisscrossing the globe doing anything but the usual? Is there a law somewhere that says that being a "Slacker" means you have to sit around on the beach all day sipping beers while you burn through your net worth? We don't think so.

Profit from Fear

Fear is natural, and making your dream happen by stepping into an unknowable future for a life of adventure takes courage, decisiveness, an unwavering belief in yourself, and the willingness to take 100% responsibility for the outcome. Those happen to be the very same traits that define the successful trader. Why?

Greed and fear govern market behavior. Greed is just the fear of missed opportunity, so in the end, it's fear that moves the financial markets both up and down. Slacker-adventurers understand and confront their fears in a way that the average person doesn't and can't, and that gives us an advantage over the frightened masses in the stock market. When the market is being irrational and chasing its own tail, it's the courageous and decisive that profit. This book is about finding those opportunities.

Retire Tomorrow

People often appear astonished that we've done what we've done and do what we do at such a young age. *How in the heck are you "retired" in your 20s and 30s? How have you sailed around the world and RV'd tens of thousands of miles by the time most people are just beginning to pay off their student loans?* We get the sense they're not just envious, but also a little suspicious: *must be trust fund kids, must have struck it rich in a tech startup, must be drug dealers!*

Let's dispel those ideas right off the bat. We are a couple middle-class guys who started our professional lives just like most everyone else: student loan debts, mortgages, ramen for lunch, pizza and beer on Wednesday nights, and a week or two of vacation every year. Neither of us took the express elevator to the top of daddy's company nor did we hit the Megalotto Jackpot. We started our financial lives as workers, as people who live off of the fruits of their labor.

Our freedom has come about by utilizing the strategies you will find in this book, and it's going to become clear that we are not "retired" by the classic definition—in fact we don't even like the classic definition of retirement. We've discovered that freedom comes from *living on the margin,* and that's not simply a personal finance system; it's values and lifestyle choices.

We think you can live the same way, and we don't think you need to start with a million bucks. $10,000 just might do.

Ride the Wave, Bradda!

Retire on $10K? Make big promises—now that's how you sell books! If that sounds ridiculous, consider this: how much cash did you put down on your last house?

Let's go back to the glory days of 1998 when the average home price in the U.S. (adjusted for inflation) was just over $100,000 and you could easily get a first and second mortgage with a job and a small down payment. Even with conventional financing, you could put down as little as $5–10K and end up servicing the debt for less than a comparable rental property. Even if you rented the property to someone else, you broke even or had positive cash flow. So for $10,000, and the ability to service the debt, you could buy a $100K house.

By 2006, the average home price in the U.S. was over $200,000. So let's do a little math: if you timed the market just right and sold that house near the top, you turned a $10,000 investment into $110,000 in eight years. With a little fuzzy-math, rounding down and carrying the 1...that's about $1,000 a month! So your $10,000 made (very, very approximately we realize) about a 120% annualized return. Now who couldn't live on that kind of investment performance?

Bubbles and Markets

Of course consensus thinking today is that the housing bubble of 1998–2006 was an anomaly; it was an *exceptional* situation created by overzealous lenders, dubious appraisers, and even outright fraud. Well, maybe, partially, but those were simply the *market conditions* of that time; those were the rules as we all understood them.

You personally weren't out committing mortgage fraud to buy and sell houses, were you? We hope not. On a day-to-day basis, most people were simply playing by the rules, trying to buy assets that were going up in value. We were all just trying to make money. We weren't making ethical decisions—we were all selfishly trying to profit; doing our best for ourselves and our families.

Later, the housing market proved to be a market like any other, and market conditions changed...demand waned while supply increased, just like it has many times before. If you got in and got out at the *right* times, you made money—perhaps a lot of money. If you got in and out at the *wrong* times, you lost money—possibly a lot of money.

Winners and Losers

So ask yourself: who were the biggest winners and who were the biggest losers during the housing bubble? Did it help or hurt to buy into the marketing and nostalgia of home ownership? Did it help or hurt your position to see a home dispassionately as an asset with a value that could go up and down? The answers are pretty clear aren't they? Financially speaking, the losers bought the perfect place to nest and raise a family. The biggest winners dispassionately bought and sold assets.

How about timing? Did it help or hurt to sit on the sidelines until housing was "hot," a "sure thing," or a "can't lose" investment? When signs began to appear that the market was nearing a peak (of which there were many over the course of many months), the investor was saying: "These assets are about to lose value." They sold. They won. The people with the emotional attachment to their home? They held. They lost.

Vocabulary

The stock market is really no different than the housing market—only the vocabulary is different. It's easy to get confused by the Wall Street jargon and say, "This is too complicated to understand." It isn't. Instead of city or state housing numbers, you are looking at things like global market indices. Instead of neighborhoods, you are looking at market sectors. Instead of the other houses on the block, you are looking at individual companies doing roughly the same types of things. Price per square foot is somewhat akin to the price to earnings (P/E) ratio; analyst sentiment is analogous to neighborhood reputation, etc.

Read a couple books and do some googling, and you will have most of the vocabulary down within a week or two. Believe us, learning a foreign language is a much bigger undertaking.

It's Always the Same Game

Trading one thing for another, whether cash for a house or cash for a stock or bond or derivative of some sort is always about *perceived value* and *market conditions*. The same old rules hold true: the fundamental idea is that you want to buy things that people are going to want more of in the *future*. You sell things that you think people are going to want less of in the *future*. It really is that simple.

But of course that's only part of the story.

Risk

"Buy low and sell high" is easy enough to understand, but risk is where the profits and losses are. In the housing market, there was always a risk home values would fall; it's just that most people didn't understand that risk—they thought, "Houses always go up in value." Looking back, you can see how irrational that previous sentence is...how in the world can a house continue to appreciate infinitely unless people are making more and more and more money to pay their mortgages? Clearly that was not happening—there is no huge jump in logic required to see that.

So, looking back—the general public, "the herd," was acting irrationally and did not understand the risk that home values could fall. The banks understood that risk a little bit better. That's why they were willing to lend you $90k on a $100K house—they knew you would lose your $10,000 investment before they lost any of their $90K. (Now granted, it turns out that the banks underestimated their downside risks as well and were willing to lend up to 100% of a home's value, so they had their own dumb herd mentality, but that confuses our point, so just play along.)

Using your 10% down payment to purchase the house, you were able to expose yourself to risk in a market. If you kept your eye on that market and dispassionately looked for signs that the market was changing, you probably did OK. If you followed the crowd, always waiting for the masses to decide when it was right to get in or right to get out, you probably didn't do so great. If you listened to your paid experts, the realtors you were giving 6% to for, "unbiased advice," you may have been royally screwed both ways.

Captain Your Ship

Most of the time, independent thought and first-person analysis are worth more than blind faith in any "expert" opinion, and that's the case in every area of life. In our experience, the keys to success in any endeavor, whether we are talking about trading or quitting your job and untying your dock lines to sail across vast oceans—or whatever—it all boils down to this:

- Dispassionately understand the real risks and avoid getting confused by fear, discomfort, and opinion.
- Have the courage to expose yourself to good risk when others are unwilling or unable to do so.
- Maintain personal responsibility; never rely on the crowd—or anyone else for that matter—to make up your mind for you.

Live like Gates, Ellison, and Buffett

In life—as in the market—the higher the risk, the higher the reward. We go further in this book; we think that a linear relationship between risk and reward isn't good enough. We aren't satisfied risking X in hopes of making a fraction of X. Instead we want to risk X for the potential of receiving 2X or 5X or 10X. We want to leverage our assets to increase our reward disproportionately to the risks we are taking.

With our mortgage analogy, the borrower leverages his one dollar to control the bank's nine dollars. It's a good deal for him and it's a good deal for the bank. The borrower gets higher risk exposure with higher upside potential, and the bank gets paid less (your interest rate) for their lower exposure to risk. This bargain—this agreement to share risk disproportionately—is at the crux of this book, because we are going to show you how to risk that one dollar in the equities markets to control $10 or even $100.

This is the same game that every extremely successful and wealthy entrepreneur plays, whether they are building companies or financial portfolios. They are masters of identifying risks worth taking. They find an opportunity to use their one dollar to control ten dollars; but instead of buying a house, they buy a delivery system, a software patent, stock, or perhaps an entire company. No matter what the opportunity is, they are always looking for leverage; they are always looking for places where their money can *work*; where the potential payoff is disproportionately high compared to the risk. Risking X to make a fraction of X isn't good enough for them either.

That's how the big guys do it. But that's only part of the reason why the rich stay rich.

Living on Less is the Key

Think of the money in your bank account like electricity in a battery. It has the potential to do work; to accomplish things. Every dollar and every cent can be used in one of two ways:

- To support you, your family, and lifestyle.
- As a tool for making more money.

Wealthy people use a small percentage of their net worth to live on. Warren Buffett is one of the wealthiest people in the world but lives a very modest lifestyle in Omaha, Nebraska. Bill Gates spends a tiny fraction of a percentage of his net worth on living day to day in any of his many high-tech homes that he can fly to in any number of his jets. Even very opulent bazillionaires like Larry Ellison, with his 453-foot mega yacht, use virtually zero percent of their wealth to cover personal expenses. The risks they take then have very low impact on their lifestyles—if any impact at all.

We know what you are thinking: *hey guys, it's easy to live on very little of your money when you have a lot of it.* True dat, friend, but you can play the same game as Larry, Bill, and Warren. You, too, can live on less money compared to your total net worth and it will change the way you invest and the risks you take. In fact, living on less changes <u>everything</u>. When living on the margin, the money you spend on your lifestyle may even be more important than what particular investments you choose to make.

Think about it this way: let's say to maintain your lifestyle costs you $5,000 per month. We are talking about your "nut," or the total sum of all the bills that have to be paid every month or bad things happen. Let's also say that you have $100,000 in the bank that you want to invest with a return high enough to cover your nut. Without getting specific and rounding some numbers, you'd have to see an average annual return of 60% to cover your nut. That's a very high return—so you have to take really big risks to try and make that much money. Realistically, you will lose sometimes—so your wins will have to be even bigger. Losing even a small chunk of $100K is going to hurt.

Now let's say you have the same $100,000 cash in the bank, but you are living in a small house on the beach in Guatemala and your nut there is more like $1,000 per month. Now your $100K has to make just 12% per year. That's *very* doable. You still have to take risks, but they don't have to be as big. You will still lose; but hopefully less often, and your wins don't have to be as big. It is much more likely that you will be able to live on that $100K for a lot longer.

One last what-if: let's say that you have $10K that you can risk. To cover a $5,000 monthly nut, you would need a 600% annual return—that's not going to happen in this lifetime. But let's say that you were able to get your monthly nut down to $1,000 by living out of a backpack and traveling around SE Asia. You would still need a huge return to live off that $10K indefinitely, right? It's somewhere around 120% on an annual basis. That's extraordinarily high, so you have to take really big risks to try and get a return like that; and while very highly unlikely, theoretically it is possible.

Let's play devil's advocate and say that your strategy doesn't quite work out: you take that $10K and make a few hundred a month in the market while slowly whittling away at that $10K over several months. Then you end up losing your last $4K in a bad trade. What are the ramifications? You have to go home and work a little sooner than you would like.

That sucks for sure, but that's not the same kind of devastating loss that losing $100,000 would be. Even if you are waiting tables, saving $4K might take a matter of weeks or months. Losing $100,000? That's going to set you back a while; that kind of loss will change the course of your life.

So for the Slacker living on the margin, a simple, low-cost lifestyle with a smaller monthly nut means your trading will be affected in the following ways:

- You can trade with a smaller principal amount of cash.
- You can make fewer trades.
- You can take smaller risks.
- If and when you do lose, you aren't going to set yourself back as far in life. At the very worst, you are just going to have to go back to work sooner. Boo-hoo.

Get Educated

Why are people comfortable leveraging the bank's assets to invest in a home, but not interested in leveraging assets to trade in the stock market? Is it because home values seem more straightforward and intuitive? Or because they feel they have a better "gut feeling" for how the housing market will perform in the future? Is it because they think that home values are more predictable? Is a stock or option riskier because it's just some number on a screen, while they can touch a house with their hands? That's ass-backwards.

Housing, as a lot of people learned recently, can actually be a very dangerous investment because houses aren't liquid assets. Stocks, bonds, and derivatives, like options and futures, can be converted to cash with a few mouse clicks. When the market turns, you can sell a stock within seconds. With a home, you may be looking at months or even years to turn that initial investment back into cash. We would have to be 99.99% sure an asset was going to appreciate if we knew it would take that long to convert it back to cash. And we don't know of any asset classes that can guarantee a return with certainty like that.

We think that people don't actively invest in the stock market for three reasons:

1. They don't know the vocabulary and mechanics.

2. They don't really understand risk.
3. They don't want to take responsibility for their own future.

If you are someone who wants to live life to the fullest and learn new tools for self sufficiency and take full and unfettered responsibility for yourself in every way, you can't leave finances out of that paradigm. You owe it to yourself to take charge of your money and make it work for you. We hope that this book gives you some tools and at least some motivation to move in the direction of taking charge of your financial life.

This Book is a First Step

One thing you will learn if and when you begin to trade is that you will never know it all and that none of us have a crystal ball; the future is unknown. There will always be more to learn, new techniques to try, and new horizons to sail to. We hope that you won't stop with this book but that you will move on to learn more and more about the financial world around you. We live in exciting times where opportunity is literally all around us. If this book provides some inspiration for you to start to learn more, we have done our job; but this book is just one of many you will need to become successful.

An Important Warning - DO NOT SKIP!

Trading is legalized gambling. It's not *kind of like* gambling, it absolutely, positively is gambling. The stock market is a game you absolutely can bring skill to, but the game is rigged to favor the biggest players: the market makers, fund managers, investment bankers, company insiders, brokers and brokerage houses, etc. These entities all have a leg up on the individual (retail) investor—and that's you and us. If you forget that, you will lose all of your money.

Professional Advice

One reason we hesitated about writing this book for so long is that we do not want to cheerlead anyone into doing things they shouldn't do. We don't want to encourage you or anyone else to take more risk than you should. Deciding how much risk to take with your finances is a very individual decision—what's right for us is not necessarily right for you. The two of us don't have professional licenses, we aren't financial analysts and we aren't financial advisors or planners—you have to remember that we are journalists first, and retail investors just like you second.

Since we are unqualified to give you broad-based, thorough, and professional investing or trading advice, we think you owe it to yourself to seek out professional advice before you start trading. What you find in this book are our opinions, and you need to make up your own mind about what is appropriate for you.

We have sidestepped questions about asset allocation or, "how much you should trade," because that's not something we can answer for you. If you find you need individual help answering those questions, we suggest that you speak with a financial planner or other investing professional—preferably one who isn't trying to sell you investment products.

In this book, you will find plenty of examples—but remember that we are not endorsing any particular companies, securities, programs, or platforms even though it's possible we have a financial interest in the entities we've written about.

Risky Business

More than anything else, we don't want you to get excited, jump into trading, and lose all of your hard earned money, and that can happen if you follow the strategies in this book. Because market conditions change continually, the successes you read about on these pages might be difficult to replicate. The strategies and tools we describe and espouse in this book are some of the most high-risk available in the market—that's what makes for high potential profits, however the risk of loss is real. Following what we advocate in this book could cost you all of your money.

It is easy to read the paragraphs above and think, *these guys wrote that because they don't want to get sued.* Well, we don't want to get sued, that's for sure. However, we do believe that a book like this is never going to give you all of the information and knowledge you need in order to trade successfully. You need to go further and learn more from the vast resources available to you—and there are plenty. Keep learning!

Errors, Omissions, and Opinions

Here are the reasons you need to take what is written in this book and then apply your own judgement and seek outside advice:

- There are mistakes in this book.
- There are incomplete or inaccurate concepts in this book.
- Our opinions are exactly that—ours, and they may differ from those of the professionals.

This book is based on our own limited experience and we aren't experts. We are a couple of slacker bums who have traded for many years, and continue to do so in order to maintain our lifestyles. We aren't being funny or sarcastic here—sometimes we win and sometimes we lose, and that's just how it works. If you decide to try to do what we do, you will win and you will lose too. We believe that you can win more often, but we certainly can't guarantee that.

Only Risk what You Can Afford to Lose

Our parting piece of advice as you set off to read the rest of this book, is that you should never risk any asset that you aren't 100% ready to lose. And if that does happen, don't come crying to us about it. You have been warned.

Now, read, learn, question, research, and decide for yourself if this is the right path for you to take on your quest for freedom.

About Your Authors

We met by coincidence sometime in 2007. While visiting family in Portland, Oregon, Nick recognized the license plate on a cherry-looking VW bus —"BUMFZLE"—and having read a few months earlier about some crazy circumnavigators on a boat with a similar name (how many Bumfuzzles could there be?), Nick stuck a note on the door asking if the bus owners had by any chance sailed around the world. Even though Pat and Ali were worried they had a stalker, an email confirmed that indeed the bus belonged to the one and only Bums; and a quick meeting confirmed that Nick and Megan were just about as abnormal as Pat and Ali.

It turns out that our mothers live about eight blocks apart; and as happens with travelers and gypsies, it was a chance meeting. Nick and his wife Megan had just driven into town in their RV with plans to settle in Portland for a year or so, while Pat and Ali were setting off on a trip across the Americas and beyond in their '58 VW bus. Our paths crossed several times over the next few years—in between and during our travels on ocean and land—and as happens frequently these days with "digital-nomads," real friendships blossomed from virtual ones.

Nick

I've always been fascinated with tomorrow. What's going to happen? Then what? What will it be like? Then what? Because it was all around me and readily accessible, that relentless focus on the future turned into a passion for weather forecasting. I could stare at satellite loops and forecast models for hours, and knew something that everyone else didn't: what was coming next in the skies above. I must have been the most annoying nephew at family functions.

After clawing my way through graduate school (where I won the National Collegiate Forecasting Competition—yes, there is one) and limping along on $20K a year in my first broadcast meteorology job in Madison, Wisconsin, I thought I'd hit the jackpot with a gig as the morning weatherman at the NBC affiliate in the San Francisco Bay Area. I more than doubled my salary to $45,000 per year and was on my way to the big time! Sweet!

Actually, not so sweet. This was 1998, and the new television studio happened to be located in the heart of Silicon Valley at the height of the dot-com bubble. Tech stocks were soaring, and every other day an IPO made neighbors our age incredibly wealthy. My wife Megan got a job at a little internet company called Netscape (post-IPO unfortunately), and it seemed like everyone we met, even those with the most menial jobs owned stock or stock options that theoretically made them millionaires. We were so happy for their good fortune.

What a lie. It sucked. We secretly hated those tech snobs and all that their new wealth could buy. The resulting Silicon Valley housing bubble made my relatively comfortable salary feel like poverty. Even worse than our reduced buying power, the conversation around every BBQ centered on the NASDAQ, the darling IPO of the day, or so-and-so's startup. We would nod and smile and act interested, but mostly we felt left out. The ship was sailing, and we weren't on it.

So, we hopped on board and did what everyone else was doing: we got into the "stock market." We scraped together our savings accounts, decreased payments on my student loans, cashed out a couple of small IRAs, and sold my sailboard. With a grand sum of just over $14,000 we opened an E-Trade account and I got started trading in December 1998. We were finally in the game and had a better time at cocktail parties.

I had no training and no background in finance, so I really had no trading strategy other than watching the news. I mostly bought tech companies like Dell and Intel and Microsoft because I had heard of them, but I also bought dot-coms like Webvan and Pets.com that the financial press was talking about. My positions were all very small, making the percentage paid in commission on each trade laughably high. I clearly remember at one point purchasing ten or so shares of a company (that I can't even remember now) at around $4/share with a trade commission of $19.95. If this stock went up 100% I could sell it at break-even. I obviously had no idea what I was doing.

Eight months later, by the summer of 1999, I hadn't realized any losses (I did have a few losers if you accounted for the cost of the trades) and had nearly doubled my money. Not bad—this trading thing is pretty darn easy—you just buy the stocks everyone is saying good things about, watch the news, and then they mostly just go up. If the news says something bad about them, you sell. Not terribly difficult!

Late in the summer of 1999, I got a big promotion and a fat new contract making decent six-figures. At the same time, I also got a little bored with trading. It seemed like all of the hype and excitement about tech IPOs had peaked a few months earlier and the kids around the BBQs weren't talking quite as much about their startups either—in fact, more than a few were out looking for the next big thing. The tide hadn't really turned against the dot-com flood, but the fever was starting to break.

By that fall, I was really busy with my new gig at NBC; and instead of actively trading, I let it all ride and mostly forgot about my E-Trade account and the positions I still had open. At the end of that year, we decided to buy a house; so I sold all of my stock for a hair over $20K, with a net gain of about 43%. Not bad for twelve months of doing little more than watching TV and making a few trades here and there, and with really only eight or so months of active engagement.

In 2000, instead of watching the little graphs in my E-Trade account, I was spending every dollar we had on our crappy little new-to-us home just south of San Francisco. It seemed that everyone else in our neighborhood was doing the exact same thing. Our working class neighborhood was looking good! Houses didn't stay on the market very long; and instead of talking about the stock market at the BBQ, everyone was talking real estate. Yep, kind of the same way that everyone was talking tech IPO's a year or two before.

One day in 2002, I looked around our newly-remodeled house and realized it was home-improved as much as it could be home-improved. We were done. Not long after, someone literally knocked on our door and made us an offer on the house; we couldn't refuse.

Now what? Well, I guess it's time for a new adventure.

While our friends were just starting to lay their proverbial eggs, we decided to sell the nest and fly the coop. Offshore sailing had been a lifelong dream of mine; so once I conned my wife into it, everything happened very quickly. We bought a big boat and sailed under the Golden Gate Bridge for a life of adventure on the high seas (there's a much bigger story here, but you'll have to read my first book, *Get Her On Board,* for all the juicy details). Leaving our careers wasn't an easy decision, but one that changed our lives forever.

We made a few of the classic first-time adventurer mistakes: we overspent on the startup costs (boat), we overprepared and loaded it with every gadget and accessory (SCUBA compressor, genset, washing machine, two refrigerators, etc., etc., etc.), and we were on a schedule that was way too strict.

We also did a lot of things right and saw firsthand that retiring young (and temporarily) was much smarter than waiting a lifetime for that "dream cruise." On that first cruise, yes the beaches were nice, and yes it was cool to have time away from the grind and freedom to do *what* we wanted *when* we wanted—all of those promises delivered. More importantly though, for the first time in our lives, we were forced to take 100% responsibility for ourselves in ways we had never expected.

For example, we couldn't get by on *who* we *were* anymore. Once we were traveling in Mexico, I wasn't a local celebrity; my wife was no longer rubbing elbows with geniuses in Silicon Valley. "What do you do for a living?" became completely meaningless, and we had been unknowingly using that status as a crutch. It was incredibly healthy to let that go. It sounds super cheesy, but we found or rediscovered the real us—and it had absolutely nothing to do with job titles or name recognition.

Personal responsibility takes on a whole new meaning when you head across oceans in your own boat. I will never forget the night we sailed south from

San Diego into Mexican waters for the first time. The ever-present U.S. Coast Guard radio chatter faded to complete silence, and all of a sudden we realized: *if something happens out here, there is no one to call for help.* No safety net, no rescue squad waiting in the wings to save us from danger. We got ourselves in and out of "trouble" plenty of times and have more than just great stories to show for it—those experiences were transformational. We learned to trust ourselves and our resourcefulness in ways we didn't know was possible.

That first cruising experience was a turning point; it was indeed life changing. When we got back, I had a new sense of personal empowerment. Life wasn't happening to me anymore and what "everyone else" was doing didn't mean what it used to either. I started pointing my bow where I wanted to go, ready to put it all on the line to make my vision happen. I've done it time and again, and even though my plans and schemes rarely work out exactly as I expect, most of the time things turn out better than I could've predicted.

After that first trip, risk wasn't something to avoid; instead it meant opportunity. If others thought something was too hard or too long a shot, I knew the payoff for success would be bigger. We came back to the U.S. to ride the last gasp of housing bubble (which we recognized was happening) and to do a little more work in television. We weren't back to make another home for ourselves; we were there to buy assets going up in value very quickly. We bought and sold two houses for a nearly 70% annualized return. Incredible.

Working in television again was fun; but I felt the urge to satisfy my entrepreneurial drive, so I left my job to invent a product and start a small company. Land-locked in Denver, we bought an RV and had all sorts of great adventures crossing the U.S. When I sold the business two years later, we bought another boat and cruised the Pacific NW and west coast of the U.S. while I wrote my first book. When we returned to land-life for another stretch, I started another business helping entrepreneurs and product developers spread their message.

My wife and I have taken several "mini-retirements" over the last ten years, and will continue to do so for the foreseeable future. We don't consider ourselves expatriates—we love the United States, and prefer to enjoy the contrasts of living both inside and outside of the country. For us, adventuring isn't all or nothing, but rather just a continuous part of our diverse lives.

When we are not off traveling, I "work" on a lot of different things, but not simply for money—in fact I think doing anything strictly for the money is a quick road to unhappiness. I continue to work in television, but only on projects that I love and am fascinated by and only with people who meet that same standard. I tell you all of this because what you read in this book about being a Slacker or living the Slacker Lifestyle does NOT necessarily have to be an all-or-nothing choice. Life is a rainbow, and all the colors are beautiful.

Trading for me over the last several years has mostly been a supplement to other income sources; but when my wife and I are out adventuring (and not working at all) for months at a time, we are able to extend the burn and not dip as far (if at all) into our savings. When we are out traveling, we are indeed *living on the margin*.

My hope for this book is that we are able to give you some tools and inspiration to help you follow the same path as we have, and by that I don't mean following in our footsteps. Rather, I hope we can show you a few strategies to help you assume control of your life and point that bow where you want to go.

Pat

My philosophy is that when life puts a fork in the road the riskier choice is most often the most rewarding. To reach where you want to be in life, it's highly unlikely that a series of simple risk-free choices will lead you where you want to go.

I've always wanted to be a trader. Seeing those guys on the nightly news in their colorful jackets yelling and running while the day's settlement prices flashed on the screen just drew me in. I was going to wow them on Wall Street.

My pursuit of trading led me to college degrees in Finance and Economics—and an outing with the Economics Association led me to my promised land. Well, not Wall Street per se, but to the Minneapolis Grain Exchange (MGE) and eventually to the pits of the Chicago Board of Trade—close enough!

Before that visit to the MGE I had no idea an exchange like it even existed—a small, open-outcry exchange trading mainly Spring Wheat Futures. On that first visit, I didn't know what Spring Wheat was; but standing on that observation balcony watching the twenty or so traders yell out their bids and offers, laugh, joke, and make a million dollars a day, I knew where I was going after graduation.

Shortly after completing my degrees I applied for a job as a pit reporter—as entry-level as there is. Never mind that the job paid next to nothing and was only part time—I could still work construction in the evenings and on weekends. Plus, I was married now and my wife had a job and was paying her bills just fine before I put a ring on her finger. With the job offer I had my foot in the door. In my mind I was nearly on Wall Street.

After a few months of standing in the pits reporting trades over a headset to another grunt who would punch them into a computer, I was approached by a broker whom I had come to regard as "the man" in the pit. He had singled me out as the only pit reporter who cared and who didn't make mistakes. For that, he offered me a job.

I turned in my MGE badge, walked back upstairs, got a Frontier Futures badge, and immediately went to work—on the other side of the pit. I was a big leaguer.

I was now the firm's head clerk. And for this awesome opportunity I was being paid the princely sum of eight dollars an hour. Let me tell you, these were heady times for a college grad with two degrees.

Being hired on by these guys would change my life. My boss became a mentor. Immediately upon being hired, I was handed a copy of Sheldon Natenberg's *Options Pricing and Volatility*; and from that day forth I was both taught and quizzed on every aspect of the markets.

"What is a 450 strangle? What does it mean if you bought it? What do you want the market to do?"

"What does it mean when you see the Prudential clerk acting like a nervous twit as he's taking an order over the phone?"

"What is going to happen to the market on Monday if northern Iowa doesn't get at least two inches of rain in that storm this weekend?"
At first I answered maybe one in five questions correctly. But soon the constant quizzing started to pay off and even the traders who had been around forever began to ask my opinion and seem at least moderately interested in my answers.

After two years I felt ready. I had two reasonably competent clerks working under me, meaning I could begin spending more time away from the desk and in the options pit. My wife and I sold one of our cars, took the five thousand dollars, and deposited it in my trading account with the tacit agreement that this would be my one shot. After this it would no longer be OK to earn ten bucks an hour.

My clearing firm was cool about letting me trade and run a pretty healthy margin account balance, knowing that they could always keep my paycheck if I went negative. Fortunately that didn't happen. From day one my account grew—trading options seemed natural to me.

After a year or so trading Spring Wheat Options and neglecting my work on the desk, I started to harbor thoughts of a bigger future. So, one night over a pitcher of beer before a Twins game I asked my wife, Ali, "What do you think about moving to Chicago?"—where the big boys play this game.

"Why not?" she answered with a shrug, and within weeks we were on our way. I didn't know a soul in Chicago and those first few days would test my mettle.

I showed up at the Chicago Board of Trade Soybean Options pit without ever having traded a bean option in my life. I stood outside that pit looking in at eighty locals (traders) and brokers and could hardly see an opening big enough for another person to stand—real-estate is a precious commodity inside a trading pit. There was nothing to be done but to bull my way in, stand my ground, and make a big first trade.

I opened my mouth to yell my first quote afraid that nothing was going to come out. But before long I had quoted the highest bid to a broker. He took one look at me and yelled, "Fifty!" while shoving an open palm off his forehead to make the number doubly clear. The guys all looked at me to see what I would do. If I didn't take the full fifty contracts they'd know I wasn't a serious threat to them and that I probably wouldn't be around a week later. I took the fifty lot and never looked back.

My first year in Chicago, I made some money. Not a lot, but a decent working man's wage. Ali was working as a secretary at the top of the Sears Tower and was able to pay all of our bills thanks to our flash-free midwestern ways. I paid myself $2,000 a month. We had a small 800 sq. ft. condo just a couple blocks away from work and we were happy as clams.

During my second year, things really got rolling. I found my groove and discovered that I was an excellent short volatility trader—something that pretty much requires ice in the veins. I took a lot of risk home each night. We didn't have anything to lose—it was just the two of us, we were twenty-seven, debt-free, and had no real "wants." Looking back, I guess we were always living sort of a simple life compared to what we could have been doing.

It was during year number three, another beauty for the bottom line, that Ali and I had our fateful conversation. Over way too many beers at our favorite pizza joint, Lou Malnati's on Wells, we had the talk. What should we do with our lives?

Our friends were moving to the suburbs, buying big houses, and having kids. This seemed like the most obvious answer. It was certainly what was expected of us.

But fate had already stepped in and put a fork in our road. Being a commodities trader my hours ended at 1:15 every day. With a lot of down time I discovered travel blogs. Nothing exciting at first, but then I stumbled upon the site of a guy sailing around the world and another of a couple cruising around in the Caribbean.

Five pitchers into the night, I asked Ali if she wanted to do it, to sail around the world. In typical fashion, the girl who had been up for anything I'd ever thrown at her said, "Why not?"

Over the next few months, we sold everything we owned, I wound down my trading account without arousing the suspicions of any of the other traders, and we flew down to Florida and bought a boat in a day.

For the next four years, we sailed around the world on a thirty-five foot catamaran. It was everything that an adventure of that magnitude should be. And what it did was complete our transformation; while we had never been too into keeping up with the Joneses we now had zero appetite for it.

What was supposed to be a four-year "mini-retirement," had turned into a lifestyle. We left assuming we would go back to Chicago and resume our lives there, but now that was out of the question. Why go back to that when we could continue to explore the world?

We completed the circumnavigation, sold the boat, and bought a 1958 VW bus in which to travel from Alaska to Argentina and beyond. We were trying to "hippify" ourselves. Live simply and in the moment.

But with this simplicity also came the realization that the almost total disregard I'd shown to my investments during the past four years had resulted in some pretty poor performance. I was going to have to take a more active role in my finances again.

This realization came at the perfect time actually. A year later, the market would implode in spectacular fashion when the financial crisis hit. By paying attention to what was going on, I was able to not only avoid the crash but to profit from the rock-bottom stock prices that followed.

We sold our VW in England after traveling in it for more than two years and sixty thousand miles. We were finally going to have a baby; and while we were not going to be raising her in a North Side McMansion, we also weren't going to raise her in a VW bus. We weren't *that* hippy—we were from Minnesota after all.

We moved to Mexico, had our baby girl, bought an old beat up boat back north in San Francisco, sailed it back to Mexico, had a baby boy, and I continued to follow the markets and trade off and on between travels. I also wrote a book about our sail around the world, and I continued blogging and writing articles to earn a more "normal" income. But at the end of the day it's the trading—no matter how part-time it may be—that pays our bills and keeps us living the life we want to live. Even with two kids, we still feel unencumbered and free to do whatever it is that we want to do with our one life.

The longer we're out here and the more I write, the more we receive e-mails from others around the world asking how we do it, how did we start out, how do we continue year after year, and so on. Now, as my first retirement stretches into its ninth year, I'm here to answer those questions.

The New American Dream – Passive Income

"Oh, this plan is brilliant—this is the one, we could buy big boats and never look back."

"Holy cow man, who needs a boat? We could buy islands with the money we'll make."

"All right, let's get started—first thing we need to do is buy that domain name..."

"Cool man, let's do it..."

Wantrepreneurs

It's probably obvious since you haven't seen the two of us on CNBC or Shark Tank that our subscription-based online community MomsJunkAppraisal.com, like the rest of our brilliant business ideas went exactly nowhere. The two of us count ourselves among the very brightest people we know with several real-life successes under our belts, but the list of product ideas and business ventures we've batted around over the years is truly embarrassing. We know we aren't alone.

Technology has democratized entrepreneurship. There is literally nothing keeping someone with a "great idea" from turning it into millions of dollars—well, nothing except the great idea part.

After all, who doesn't need a dog girdle, gluten-free bagel, diamond-studded welding goggles, edible business cards, or pizza-flavored dental floss? Every random busboy, doctor, and surfer has an idea for a reality show, a book, screenplay, product, or service that promises to set them up with a nice stream of income so that they don't have to actually WORK for a living ever again.

And what then—after they make that cool 10 million? Go off and do what they really want to do in the first place, like travel around the world, or raise wire-haired fainting goats in the Andes Mountains?

Of course that's not how it works out, right? 99% are *wantrepreneurs,* not entrepreneurs and very few actually start the business.

Worth the Risk?

Why don't they take that chance and make the leap? It doesn't matter how good the idea is—creating something new, disruptive, novel, innovative or brilliant is difficult: it's risky, it's stressful, it's time consuming, it's expensive, sometimes it's boring, and it doesn't pay off most of the time. Most decide it just isn't worth it.

Of those who do muster the courage to try, only a very tiny fraction actually succeed in creating something of enduring value which produces passive income. Even then, a life of leisure comes only after years or sometimes decades of 80–100 hour weeks. Let's face it: it's a long shot and there are no overnight successes.

Nick can tell you from firsthand experience that starting his first company (which he eventually sold) was only marginally worth it financially, and in no way did it ever come close to "passive income." He gave 100% for over two years, and while it was a great experience, he could've made about the same amount of money by staying at his job in television.

Even with the chance for success and a life of passive income pegged somewhere near absolute zero for most people, why do the *wantrepreneurs* continue to dream of making it big with fingerless surgical gloves or some other brilliant idea? Because working for a living just plain sucks to some extent—maybe not all the time and certainly not for everyone, but at the very least it sucks sometimes. It just does: unreasonable bosses or customers, short vacations, long hours, being underpaid and overworked—it can feel like indentured servitude. Not for everyone, but for a lot of people.

Slacker!

In a culture of go, go, go, and earn, earn, earn, you might feel a little ashamed you'd rather be teaching paragliding at Torrey Pines, or fly fishing in Patagonia, or building schools in northern India, or counting Tasmanian Devils in their native habitat. Not your bag?—well we bet you have an idea of what you'd do if money didn't restrict you to the job and the house and the commute and the rest of it. If you won the lottery and money were no longer a barrier, you, like a lot of people would retire right away and go off and do what you really want to do. We think that a lot of people (even those who claim they are passionate about their jobs) would quit if they had:

- enough money to live on, and
- something else fun to do.

Is that you? If it is, you just might be a closet Slacker.

When did you get so disenchanted? Your parents taught you about the rewards of hard work, didn't they? If you leave your career for a life of leisure and adventure, won't you miss that sense of accomplishment you get from your job? Won't you be putting your future at risk?

The American Dream

For our grandparents, the vision of a better life was essential for survival. It kept them going while the rest of their lives were pretty hard. We are talking about people who survived famines, wars, genocides, dust bowls and depressions. They needed hope, and for *some* of them, all that hard work paid off. They built big families, businesses and successful careers; and at the end of a storied career, they punched the proverbial clock for the last time and moved to Boca Raton to live out their Golden Years.

So these tough-as-nails forefathers (and foremothers, if that's a word) of ours taught us that being good citizens (ethical, hard working, productive, etc.) would deliver a life of happiness, health, and wealth—and a fair shot at the golden ticket of retirement. No one really knew what retirement should be, but at least you were no longer held hostage to do things you didn't feel like doing. Retirement meant freedom at the end of the long path to the "American Dream."

This American Dream thing that we all hold so sacred is really just a culturally-shared marketing message—that conformity and diligent effort will bring the mileposts of success and acquisition. And once you have all the right stuff, i.e. the house with the white picket fence, lots of cool toys to enjoy, and enough assets stashed away to ensure you'll have enough money for the rest of your life, you will have happiness and security—you can then, and only then, retire to do what you want, and most importantly, *everything will be all right*.

Sadly for a lot of people, this ideal scenario has become unrealistic for three fundamental reasons: debt, wage instability, and lack of value creation.

High Debt to Equity

Unfortunately, that comfortable single-family home, trimmed lawn and new car in the driveway hide a truth that a lot of people feel really uncomfortable confronting—too much of it is borrowed. When you owe money to someone, whether a bank, corporation, or an individual, they own you and the rights to the fruits of your labor (your production) until that debt is repaid.

If you're in that small minority who owns their house outright, doesn't carry any debt and has cash in the bank—we know what you're saying to yourself right now: *I don't owe anything to anyone, so I'm free*. Sure you are. What about income tax? Sales tax? Property tax? You will still owe those, no matter what. If you choose not to pay the IRS for long enough, they'll take that house and haul you off to jail.

There is also inflation to consider. The Federal Reserve puts more and more money into circulation every year, making your cash worth less and less all the time. That means that unless your assets appreciate faster than the rate of inflation, they are worth less and less all the time, too.

So you can see that no matter what your net worth is and no matter how little debt you have, you are continually swimming upstream as debt, tax obligation, and inflation eat away at your assets.

For decades our grandparents told our parents, who told us, that debt and obligation and compliance are not a bad bargain for the American Dream. You get to be part of a system that ensures economic stability for everyone, and quality of life ends up being high for most of us for most of the time. Life is good as a contributing member of your community as long as you work hard at whatever it is that you do so that you will be paid a wage that allows you to service your debts and grow your assets for eventual retirement. You may be a caged animal, but you are a happily caged animal. Not a bad deal right?

Wage Instability

Wrong. It doesn't work that way anymore. The second reason why the American Dream is harder than ever to attain is wage stagnation, or more properly wage *instability*. See, the problem for the worker in a free market economy is that the increasingly specialized skills that make you good at one job will frequently make you less able to do another job.

If you are an auto worker in Detroit, you understand this better than anyone: if you install car window handles and they get rid of handles in favor of electric switches, you may be out of a job or at the very least your current skill set becomes less valuable to the company. And because there's a good supply of workers at any time, wages remain flat or stagnant or become unstable. That's exactly what has happened in the last 30 years across a lot of industries, especially ones that have been undercut by foreign competition.

In the U.S., workers at every level live in constant fear of lost wages when market conditions change, and that fear is the same for the CEO as it is for the assembly-line guy. The American Dream promises stability, but the global economy simply cannot deliver stability while at the same time growing and innovating.

Value Creation

The most important and pervasive reason the American Dream has become more dream and less reality is a fundamental lack of real value creation. Particularly in the U.S. recently, the economy has grown largely on appreciation instead of value creation, which makes asset values more and more dependent on market demand than production capability. (Yes, this book is going to show you exactly how to take advantage of appreciation, but the seeds of that pursuit are exactly the reason why the American Dream is no longer tenable.)

Here is how it works: let's say that you build a house for your family. You take a loan, hire contractors, etc.—the details aren't important. What you have done is assemble components to create something of value: a shelter. Let's say that the raw materials have a value of $50 and the value of the labor to assemble the house is $40. Let's be generous and say that you should get $10 for taking the risk in building the house. The day that the house is complete, that shelter has a real intrinsic value of $100.

A week goes by. Then someone else comes along and says, "Hey, I want to live here, but I don't want to build a house. I will give you $200 for your house." So the house is sold for $200, but there is no real value creation—only appreciation. The house would still only cost $100 to build on a similar nearby lot, but now the house is worth twice that in the free market. This is an example of appreciation. Not a bad thing for the seller—he just doubled his money.

For the American Dream however, this is another nail in the coffin. Appreciation without wage increases has to increase debt, and that's exactly what has happened.

Don't get us wrong, if you own your house, your cars, and your lawnmower outright, love what you do for a living, and can be guaranteed sustained wages or have cash in the bank that will last the rest of your life, then you are indeed living the American Dream of security and freedom. This is the case for hundreds of thousands of people in the U.S. If that's the case for you, you probably don't need this book.

If that isn't you, and you want to leave the working world to pursue your dreams and have adventures either temporarily or permanently, the question becomes:

What to Do?

We think that a lot of people realize the points we make above and are shifting their personal financial ideal to something different than the white picket fence and retirement in Boca at age 65. The "New" American Dream of Passive Income (NADPI) is your pathway to a life of independence and freedom. So the question becomes how to go about making that happen. We've talked a bit about entrepreneurship, but what are some other options for generating the cash you want to live the life you dream of?

Real Estate

Both of us own real estate; however we have not realized much passive income to date. In the turbulent real estate market following the housing bubble, there certainly are opportunities here and there to buy property at a discount with potential positive cash flow; but if you are financing that property with a small equity position, your margins are going to be very slim. If you are trying to live off passive income, the only question that matters is: is there any margin—can you profit?

As a world traveler, you will need to hire a management company to handle your tenants, and those costs will eat into your profits. Management fees will vary market to market and by use, but for residential leasing, you are looking at about 10% of gross rents, plus capital improvements. Short-term rental management such as for vacation properties can fetch 30–40% of gross rents. Also remember that if you aren't working, depreciating those assets to offset income tax is going to make less sense.

The main problem with real estate these days is that it ties up your capital. Gone are the days of putting 0%, 5% or even 10% down to score a smoking interest rate for a non-owner-occupied (rental) property. Today, you'll need a steady job and the best rates require a 20% down payment. If you have $20K to put into a $100,000 property, we think you can make higher returns elsewhere. That may change in the future, but as of this writing, that's the situation as we see it.

If after all of the calculations, you can maintain a 10% annual profit without relying on depreciation, real estate can be a great passive income source; however these opportunities are harder and harder to find these days.

Sell Big Macs

We don't really consider them in the same class as other entrepreneurial ventures, but franchises can be an excellent road to passive income. Major brands like Starbucks, McDonald's, Subway, Dunkin' Donuts, Little Caesars, Baskin Robbins, etc., have proven products, proven business structures, proven markets, proven marketing, proven territories, proven, proven, proven—you just can't argue with the success of these business models. While they may not be very exciting for the budding inventor, they do produce cash and managing from a distance is possible if the right hires are made.

Nick has taken a close look at several franchise opportunities, and aside from having no experience in food service, the other major deal-killer he found time and again was required up-front capital. Starbucks for example requires that an owner have at least two (and sometimes three) locations. After franchise fees and location buildout, we are easily talking between $500K to $1M. Other franchises such as Subway or Dunkin' Donuts might require less up front money, but cash flow can end up low if the owner can't take an active management role.

McDonald's is a virtual cash cow, but the upfront costs are very high. In fact you need a minimum of $250K in hand to even talk to the corporation about a franchise, and by the time you build the restaurant, you could easily be looking at more than $1M. But once you're in the Big Mac business, you are more or less set for life. Many McDonald's franchise owners earn so much that they end up rolling profits into, you guessed it, another McDonald's location.

Clean Dirty Things

It's not glamorous, but cleaning things can be very profitable and a clear path to passive income. If you can make it a coin-op business, this can be completely hands-off. Laundry (coin-op, not dry cleaning), car washes (self-serve, not full service), janitorial, and lawn care are all excellent businesses that can, after you train someone else to do the work, make you money while you are doing something else.

A coin-op laundry is probably the most boring business you could imagine, but it's extraordinarily easy to set up and manage. On top of that, every component can be leased or hired out: space rented, equipment leased, repair outsourced, coin collection service hired, utilities paid remotely, etc.

Nick knows a couple who now own an island in Tonga who ran a janitorial service in the SF Bay Area. They were young, hip, fun, and cool, and they ran a company that cleaned bathrooms. No, not glamorous, but profitable. Nick met another guy who owns a company that leases and services porta-potties. Yeah, it's crappy work, but his hands don't get dirty; employees do the actual work, and he's got a really nice boat.

Is there a downside to owning a business that cleans dirty things? If there is one, it's that it never really becomes completely passive income. Because of the nature of the work, there can be a good deal of employee turnover which will keep you involved in the business.

Innovative? No. Disruptive? Probably not. Sexy? Depends, we suppose; but absolutely a viable road to NADPI.

Blog to Millions

When we say millions, we do mean millions—and there is nothing passive about that. There are people making livable advertising dollars on the internet by writing about things they are passionate about, but frequently those passions are about subjects that used to employ professional journalists for professional coverage. So not only will you be competing with professional writers, you better be ready to work your tail off producing *good* content.

If your blog is more or less documenting your travels and adventures, you may be able to make some money at it, but enough to live on? Get ready for a lot of rice and beans and camping under bridges. Blogging in and of itself, for 999 out of 1000 of us, will not provide enough passive income to live outside of a cardboard box. The same thing can be said of producing video or audio podcast content.

Pat has been blogging about his life since he and his wife first set off in their boat to sail around the world nearly a decade ago. He's gathered a pretty large following and yet despite trying Google Ads a couple of times, he has found the money earned from that to be rather disappointing.

Pat has turned away from the advertising model and has written a book about his travels instead as a way to turn his writing into Benjamins. He's also found a way to write for a magazine's online arm and make a little money from that. And while he enjoys putting down WRITER as his occupation when paying taxes, the truth is that the money he lives off of day in and day out comes from being a trader.

Bubble Boy (and Girl)

Finally, we will mention people who invest quite successfully in the "it" thing of the day or those who ride the bubbles. Who are the bubble riders? At one time, fortunes were made in the Netherlands on tulip bulbs, or tea from India, or salt from Africa, or whatever.

More recently, the it thing was real estate. Then it was precious metals. There will always be an it thing to invest in, and many a slacker dream has been funded by riding these bubbles to prosperity. For all intents and purposes though, this book will not talk much about investing in the it thing of the moment, but we do acknowledge that doing so is a viable path to NADPI.

What's Left

If you are committed to living the New American Dream of Passive Income, there are really only two options left: investment income like interest and dividends, and/or actively trading in the markets.

If you are able to live on your dividend income right now and will be able to do so forever, drop this book, and mail us a check for $500 for giving you that advice and saving you several hours of your life. You don't need to read what we've got to say here.

If that isn't you, please read on…

Slackers and Slacking

"Mom, dad, I've decided to quit my job and go sailing for a few years."

"So what are you going to do for work?"

"Uh, nothing much."

"But you have put so much time and energy into your career at XYZ, why would you jeopardize your future?"

"The ROI is a little too low."

"What do you mean, kiddo?"

"Well, I'm not seeing a very high return for all of my hard work."

"So your solution is to work less?"

"Uhhhh, yeah…"

"Well OK then, we'll keep the spare bedroom free for when you move back home…"

After your parents spent so many years trying to instill a deep work ethic, now you want to live out of a VW bus and travel around the world? If your parents' generation said things like, dude or WTF. Your parents would be saying, "Dude, WTF?"

This new lifestyle of yours isn't what your parents thought your college education would buy. In their worldview of *nose-to-the-grindstone until you retire*, you sound really naïve and shortsighted. If you don't work, you aren't going to have a future. It's just that simple. They're genuinely worried about you, and not because of pirates and pickpockets. They are concerned because it sounds an awful lot like you are turning into their worst fear: a "Slacker."

Your grandparents warned your parents about being an irresponsible bum, and now here you are ready to quit a (perhaps) high-paying job and leave a (perhaps) stable career to go live in a tent or bob around on a small boat for an indeterminate period of time. They may not speak to their friends about you anymore. In their minds you are, "Living in a van, down by the river." What a disappointment you are.

What's a Slacker?

Call one 30-something a "Slacker" and you get a high-five or nod of respect. Say the same thing to someone twenty years older and you might get a boot to the head. Just what exactly is a "Slacker" and what is the Slacker Lifestyle? Why is it that a life of leisurely adventure is both what most people aspire to and at the same time loathed as a symbol of laziness, waste, and lack of effort?

Slacker History

The term "Slacker," depending on what research you believe, originated in England in either 1790 or 1884 to refer to striking laborers. It was first popularized in the United States during WWI and WWII to refer to anyone who wasn't supporting the war effort. Finally sometime in the 1950s, when (outside of Korea) there were no big wars, the meaning of Slacker was generalized to describe those who actively avoided work. To be a Slacker meant not just that you didn't work, but that you didn't *want* to work.

By the 1960s, the "squares" bestowed "slacker" on the hippies. In the 70s and 80s the term belonged to the surfers, then the skaters. By the 90s, "Generation X" (whatever that means) inherited it and all of a sudden flannel became synonymous with comfort before effort. Those were probably slacking's darkest days.

Today, the term is much more nebulous, and it's harder than ever to spot a real slacker from the posers. If you've spent any time in Silicon Valley, you'll see people you're sure are slacking through life, until they walk their dirty sneakers and ripped jeans over to a $300K Lamborghini, and drive off to their next VC meeting. Go to any wealthy beach town like La Jolla, Laguna, or Newport Beach, and you'll find wealthy 50-somethings wearing flip-flops to a power lunch.

These days, slackers are cool.

Slacker Heroes

Originally scorned (and still looked down upon by some older generations), slackers have a long history of being revered and celebrated in movies and on TV. Charlie Chaplin's Tramp, Jeff Spicoli, Beavis and Butthead, and Scooby Doo, Bill and Ted, The Dude, Ferris Bueller, Harold and Kumar; and if you stretch the cultural definition of "slacker" a bit, you could probably include Han Solo and Jack Sparrow as well in a long line of characters less intent on fitting in than just doing whatever they want to do.

The fictional slacker isn't the fool; nope, he's the hero! What do all of these characters have in common? They devalue or even despise conformity, and wouldn't be caught doing "real" work. Instead they're committed to working as little as possible (if at all), have hobbies with little commercial value, and spend as much time as possible *having adventures.*

When we were kids, we wanted to be Han Solo, not Luke Skywalker. Skywalker was a farmer. Solo was a renegade with a badass ship and as far as we could tell, his job was having adventures.

Celebri-Slackers

Real-life Slackers have invaded popular culture—they are everywhere today. From Paris Hilton to The Kardashians to whoever it is on the *Jersey Shore* (which neither of us have seen, BTW), today we as a culture love to see people with an F-U attitude and the apparent F-U money to live however they want.

Not that long ago, we worshiped sports stars for their superhuman physical abilities and athletic feats. We celebrated successful business people for their wealth and foresight. We looked up to politicians for their power and ability to shape society through government. We wanted to be like famous actors and singers for their artistic talents and charisma. Michael Jordan because he could defy gravity like a superhero. Robert Redford for his good looks and because he dated the hottest starlets. As a nation and as a culture, we envied these people for their special-ness, for their unique talents and exceptional abilities. They were role models. Ideals.

Today, talent and ability aren't nearly as important as celebrity itself and the lifestyle that fame appears to provide—the Slacker Lifestyle. We see the freedom and opportunity that being well-known and well connected affords —the ability to call your own shots, not answer to anyone, and the freedom to do whatever you want, whenever you want, even if that means behaving badly.

You don't have to be able to hit a ball a long way to be loved and envied in popular culture. All you need is the right handbag and a catchphrase nobody can forget like, "That's hot."

Consider the more traditional celebrities like the actors and athletes—who gets the most attention these days? The ones with the most talent? Sometimes, but more often than not we are attracted to the rebels—the ones with the F-U attitude, the ones who don't give a sh*t what is said about them, and the ones who generally do whatever they want.

Who gets more press and attention: R.L. Stine or Lindsay Lohan? Lindsay Lohan is a mediocre screen talent with drug and alcohol problems. R.L. Stine is arguably the most prolific children's author of all time. Stine has sold literally tens of millions of books that have reached and entertained more people (in an intimate and important time in their lives) than Lohan ever could. R.L. who? Yes, that's exactly our point—everybody knows Lindsay.

Why do we celebrate the Slacker? We all secretly want to be Slackers; that's who and what we idolize now—but that doesn't mean you have to be a celebrity to be a Slacker.

Values are Changing

Just about every generation, it seems, looks down on the next and says something to the effect of, "You have it easy, kid...back in my day, we had to blankety, blank, blank..." Fill in the blanks: walk to school in the snow five miles both ways, milk the cows for breakfast, copy our term papers out of the Encyclopedia by hand, put coins in a phone to call someone, connect our computers to the internet with a cord, etc., etc. You get the idea; "back in our day, we didn't have all these newfangled gadgets and conveniences that make life so easy."

Why do we look down at the next generation and tell them their life is so much easier? Well, because in most (granted, not all) areas, life really IS physically getting easier and easier. The transfer of goods, services, energy, and money is almost frictionless today. Less labor is needed across all scales of production for nearly any product in any market and most commerce can take place anywhere there is a computer and access to the Internet.

Today, we produce food with comparatively little physical labor; our transportation systems can move anything, anywhere, very quickly; and the electronic connections to coordinate all of it require relatively little administration and are very inexpensive. All of this is done at higher relative quality and reliability and at lower relative prices than has ever been possible before.

Hit "pay" on a web page and your dog's vibrating massage bed will be in your hands from across the country or around the world the next day. Heck, we are collaborating on this book in real time on Google Docs (for free) when thousands of miles separate us physically—that's pretty incredible, and this was barely possible even a decade ago!

Compare the tools we have now to those of ten years ago, or ten years before that, or fifty years ago. The world (of commerce especially) we live in today bears almost no resemblance to the world our grandparents lived in. It's almost a completely new way of life from the moment the alarm goes off in the morning to the moment your head hits the pillow. Modern life doesn't look like the Jetsons, but it sure doesn't resemble what it looked like even a few years back.

Easy Life, Less Time

Given how many time and labor-saving tools have emerged over the last century, you would think that we would all be living a life of leisure while robots deliver genetically engineered superfoods to us poolside. If all these technological efficiencies benefited the average person, we should only have to work an hour or two a day at most, or maybe a day or two every week. But somehow that's not how it has worked out, right?

Instead, a lot of us are working longer hours than our parents did, then come home from a longer commute than they had, and work on the phone or tablet while watching TV in bed—and that's only when we're not flying to see three customers a week in yada-yada, Nebraska. A life of leisure? No way. How is it possible that while technology has evolved to save labor, most individuals have less time for leisure activities than previous generations had?

Labor Harder

The really sad reason that new technological efficiencies don't translate to an easier life for Mr. Worker, is really twofold:

- No matter what the trade or business, the worker is a component in a system or process that produces a product or service for a *profit*.

- A free market economy demands efficiency, and the system produces profits for the business owner first and for the laborer second, if at all.

It doesn't matter what trade or industry we are talking about—a doctor or a garbage man or a barista—the effort the worker puts into their job is ***labor***, and the compensation is only sometimes directly tied to the output of that labor. If a doctor becomes more efficient by seeing more patients at his hospital, he may see an increase in income, but it will not be commensurate with the increased income he is generating for the hospital and for the insurance company. Instead, his personal increase in revenue will be a percentage of the hospital's increased profit, not the hospital's increased revenue. The doctor makes a percentage of the marginal profit, not a percentage of the profit itself.

The needs of the corporation; the need for corporate profit will always supersede the need of the human worker. This isn't an ethical or philosophical question; this is simple economics—and the market demands it.

The laborer/worker will always have to work as hard as the market demands, forever. If an innovation creates a new efficiency—that is, if a technology or efficiency makes a job easier—then the worker will have to do more of what they do or do it faster. If they can't, won't, or don't—the competition in the market will and the company's profit and/or market share will decrease.

It's simple market economics.

Two Types of People

It is really easy to turn this into an argument against, "the man," or the "richest 1%" who own and run the company. While we agree that (from an ethical standpoint) the laborer should perhaps profit more than the owner for the fruits of his labors, that doesn't reflect reality. You can march in the street or camp out in your town's square in protest, but that won't change human nature and it won't change free market economics.

It doesn't matter what type of government we are talking about, whatever its laws or economic policies are, there are two types of people in the economy:

owners and laborers. Most of us are both; but the majority of the population makes very little from assets owned in comparison to the compensation received for labor. Most of us are laborers first, and owners second, if at all.

The modern Slacker isn't lazy or making a political statement when he decides not to work for The Man...no, he or she has simply realized that as all systems of production become more efficient, he/she would rather profit directly from those efficiencies. The modern Slacker would rather be an *owner* than be a *laborer*.

What Changed?

There was a time not so long ago when we worked our tails off for 40 years and then retired to Florida to wait for the end. For 99% of the population, that pretty much summed up the (ideal) overall life plan; but today, we (well, at least some of us, and we are betting that if you are reading this book, you are included in this group) value our time and freedom a lot more than we do our possessions. Our values have changed for two reasons:

- Fewer of us have anything to do with the production of things.
- Material things aren't as precious to us as they once were.

Our parents and their parents produced things. They built houses, or car doors, or fabric or whatever. They lived in a world of tangible goods where they took two or more ingredients and combined them to make a new thing of value. Then they sold that thing or traded that thing for another thing or fixed things or sold insurance for things.

You get the idea. It was a thing-based world, and commerce revolved around objects. Hardly anyone was in the non-thing economy in the 1950s, except intellectuals like teachers, writers, and politicians.

The best measure of your success 50 years ago? The number and size of your things. Small, unimportant people had few or small things. Big, important people had lots of things—big things. As people came to possess more and more things, the things got bigger: houses, garages, cars, cruise ships, stores, burgers, fries, etc. Throughout the 20th century, just about everything got bigger, except airline seats. Those got smaller so that the airlines' owners could reap more profits in order to buy...more things.

We Don't Produce

As the United States and other developed countries became "post-industrial" in the second half of the 20th century, we started making fewer things—or more accurately, fewer and fewer of us were directly involved in the making, trading, and servicing of things. Instead, we sell information or entertainment; we are in financial services or the medical field; we teach or manage or captain or do any number of things that have absolutely no direct association with the production of *things*. This is the information-age, baby!

While grandpa grew wheat, and dad baked bread, today grandson designs interactive store displays that help consumers choose what kind of bread to buy. The cognitive distance between producing and consuming is getting bigger and bigger. 100 years ago, people knew where their meat came from; in fact they probably knew their butcher's kids. Today, most people who eat beef have never seen a cow killed. (Amazingly, many have never even seen a live cow.)

In grandpa's day, owning nice things was a sign that you had accomplished something. He could look at that armoire or grandfather clock or new car and say with pride, "Those are the fruits of my labor." Today things like cars or furniture or electronics have been so thoroughly commoditized that owning them means little more than you were able to find the time to shop for them and you have the credit to buy them. Sure, they are still status symbols, but a genuine measure of accomplishment?

The Real Cost

That new car—a source of deep, genuine pride and symbol of accomplishment? Let's see if you feel that way when it's ten years old, or even five years old. How are you feeling about that 45-inch TV in a few years when the newest one has twice as many pixels and renders in 3D? Value these *things* as a source of pride and symbol of accomplishment? A lot of people are embarrassed when their stuff isn't the newest and best. Another trip to the big-box store can solve that problem.

THE NEW SLACKER

If you have been feeling that trading all of your time for things doesn't seem to be a good bargain anymore, there's no reason to be ashamed of yourself! Shed the stigma! Slackers aren't lazy bums—in fact a lot of us are extremely successful—we just don't center our entire lives around our job and career or stuff and things. We aren't necessarily rebels, we're just independent thinkers; we make up our own minds and cut our own paths. We are our own heroes.

New Slacker Values

It's pretty simple really, we choose:

- time over money and acquisition
- friends and family over career status
- financial freedom over debt
- intrinsic motivation over group thinking

Talk is Cheap

It's really easy to say that you are not as materialistic as your neighbors, but it's a much different thing to live a minimalist lifestyle—one with few possessions. You can say that your family is more important than your job, but actually sacrificing work opportunities to raise your children full-time is a whole different thing. People will tell you that they don't believe in living with debt, but those same folks carry car payments or credit card debt. And anyone can tell you that they follow their heart, but then live the exact same lifestyle that their family and friends do. The proof is in action, not talk.

SLACKER LIFESTYLE AND SLACKER VALUES

Hippies and gypsies are probably our closest modern ancestors, but flowers in our hair, political protests, and free love? Not quite. Wait, what was that last one?

Digital-Nomads

Internet cafes were a great first step, but now with WiFi or a data card, we can make money from anywhere. It's kind of crazy really: palm fronds clattering in the trees overhead, a papaya half eaten next to your cup of coffee, and you just placed a buy order for 10 options contracts that will make you $450 before your afternoon siesta. It almost feels like it should be illegal.

Here you are—thousands of miles away from the physical stock exchange—pressing a few buttons on a laptop and moving thousands of real dollars around. It is pretty surreal. Where's the catch? There is no catch. This is real life now:

You can live literally anywhere you have an Internet connection.

With that connection, you have everything you could ever need to manage all of life's administrative tasks from paying bills to maintaining relationships to even (as we will see) making money. Even if you aren't trading, the fact that you can oversee all of your communication, finances, and commerce from a small screen located literally almost anywhere on the planet is still mind-blowing to us.

Living a digital-nomad lifestyle doesn't have to be nonstop travel. You can just as easily pitch a (figurative or actual) tent someplace you enjoy but where it costs less to live. If and when you do feel like moving on to some other place, there isn't much to it; you just pack your bags and go.

Pat lives with his family on his sailboat in Mexico; but summers in Mexico are no time to be living on a boat. It's sweaty hot. So during the hottest days of summer he rents a condo in Puerto Vallarta; a gorgeous place three blocks off the water up a hill overlooking the ocean on one side, the mountains on another, the town's beautiful cathedral a block away out still another window. There's a pool on the rooftop of the six-unit building—all of which are empty—because best of all, it's low season. Prices are one third of what they are during the rest of the year, and there is air-conditioning to return to after a day out at the boat replacing the water pump!

Nick and his wife take mini-retirements and maintain a home base in Portland, Oregon. When they aren't home, they simply rent their property out to cover costs, and hit the road (or ocean) for a dose of adventure that could last anywhere from a few months to a couple years. Instantly, their monthly costs (their burn rate as we'll talk about later) are less than a third of what they are at home. Being a digital-nomad is dirt cheap.

Aside from perhaps living someplace where the weather is to your liking, the other primary benefit to living the digital-nomad lifestyle is of course this reduced cost. Living just about anywhere besides Europe, the United States, or Canada, is much, much less expensive. If it costs less to live, you spend less time making money and more time doing...whatever you want to do.

Improvise!

We talk a lot about freedom in this book—about doing what you want to do, when you want to do it. If you live by a strict schedule and firm plan, you aren't free anymore—you start answering to, "the plan." If you can't learn to make it up as you go along, you've just traded your job and your mortgage for a new set of self-imposed obligations. That's not freedom.

We'll talk more about this in the *Design a Perfect Life* chapter, but one of the basic Slacker tenets is *going with the flow*. It's not that we don't like to plan—it's just that we don't have the future mapped out in a step-by-step structure of: *first this, then that, then we'll do this other thing next by such-and-such date*. We prefer to improvise, and make things up as we go along.

We think this is a better way to live because: (1) things hardly ever work out exactly to plan, (2) making distant-future decisions dependent on intermediate-future decisions leaves little room to adjust to changed circumstances, and (3) living so far in the future makes it a lot harder to savor what's happening right now.

When I (Nick) was doing weather, I never read off the teleprompter. Instead, I always made it up as I went along—100% ad-lib. Did that mean I made everything up off the top of my head? No, I made my own forecast and knew it inside and out. When the little red light on the camera went on and I knew that tens or hundreds of thousands of people were ready to hear what I thought would happen tomorrow, I just started telling the weather story the same way I'd tell friends around the dinner table.

After a few months on the air in Madison, Wisconsin, I was invited to my first ever large speaking event at a customer appreciation banquet for Chevron's Ortho division. Farmers from all over the midwest had been invited to eat free food and hear about how Chevron's fertilizers or pesticides or whatever could increase crop production. I was there to talk about the El Nino event of that year. I was psyched—Chevron was paying me as an expert—I had better know my stuff.

I wrote a carefully worded three page outline of my speech. We are talking small fonts and no double-spacing. I was going to wow them with all sorts of details, statistics, and science. I had everything organized into major topics and subtopics, and had even written in some jokes to break it up. I was ready!

When I got to the event hall, I got nervous. This wasn't a small dinner—this was a big group, probably near 700–800 people. Most of them were taking advantage of the open bar and having a great time. I could see it was going to be a tough crowd. And as it turned out, I was the opening act—they had hired a professional comedian to entertain during dinner.

When the organizer gave me the rundown, I asked, "Where is the podium?" I needed something to put my notes on and lecture from. "There is no podium," she said, "we thought you could just give us 20 minutes and take some questions."

Oh, crap.

When I was introduced, I left my notes at my table, and ad-libbed my way through ten minutes of the most disorganized blather I had ever produced. I was confused about which points to hit, in which order, and I completely forgot all the funny little jokes I had written so carefully. It wasn't good and I knew it—I probably wasn't horrible (we're all our own worst critics), but I am sure I looked really nervous.

When it got time to take questions from the audience, I was golden. Reacting on-the-spot, I was witty and could address the specifics without having to search through my notes.

I resolved that day that I would never try to stick to a specific plan again. And I never have.

The same sort of go-with-the-flow attitude becomes a requirement when you head out for an adventure. We can't tell you how many times we've been on our way to a destination and changed our minds. Mechanical issues, a chance encounter with friends, weather too bad, weather too good, a local tip on a can't-miss opportunity—we're ready to change course on a moment's notice. That's freedom!

Being On-purpose

One of the biggest misconceptions about Slackers is that we are purposeless. Nothing could be further from the truth. And like any individual, every Slacker is going to have their own purpose: to lead, to explore, to teach, to inspire, etc. For us, pursuit of money and pursuit of purpose don't have anything to do with each other. In fact, we think that pursuit of the almighty dollar can really cloud a person's sense of purpose.

When it comes to trading to *live on the margin*, there is no confusion for us at all—the only purpose is making money. We like that kind of purity of thought. Is trading our purpose in life? No way—it's just a means to an end. Trading is just how we pay the bills—we don't even think of ourselves as, "traders." In fact on tax forms we list our occupation as, "writer." (Yes, we do report trading income!)

What *is* our true purpose in life? It's probably somewhere along the lines of having adventures and sharing them with you—or teaching or something like that. We're still figuring that out, and that's just fine with us. What's the hurry?

We don't want to make it sound like we have all the answers, but let us wax philosophical for a moment about the human condition and the meaning of life, if you will. We don't think it's as complicated a question as people make it out to be; because in our opinion, all human beings want pretty much the same things:

- love and friendship
- enjoyable experiences
- health
- prosperity and security
- a sense of purpose day-to-day

Leaving out how much money is in the bank or how secure our circumstances are—our health and all that—can we agree that doing something meaningful with our lives, being happy while we do it, and having people to share our experiences with is just about all anyone could ever ask for? To live that kind of life would be just about perfect, don't you think?

If those are the basic tenets of a good life, why do we spend so much time and energy as a society armoring ourselves against each other in big cars and behind tall gates, toiling away at jobs we don't like so that we can buy things we don't have time to enjoy—grinding away at our physical and mental health the whole time?

We think a lot of this is accidental, but many people just give up on finding a real purpose in their lives.

Too many people don't work hard to fulfill a particular purpose, but rather to escape a sense of purposelessness—the working and consuming itself becomes the purpose.

We were taught that our sense of self-worth and purpose had to be tied directly to our career or job, and oh by the way, you have to figure it out by the time you declare your major in college. That just isn't realistic for most people—what do you really know about the world or yourself when you're 18–20 years old?

Finding your true purpose in life might be a little easier if you take the pressure off, and get to know yourself a little better. A mini-retirement is good for that.

The Sweet Unknown

The earth (aside from the deep oceans) has been pretty well surveyed by now. No matter how remote you go, or how far off the path you get, it's likely you aren't the first human to show up on the scene. We slacker-adventurers might not be true pioneers, but a little naiveté can make the whole adventure a lot sweeter.

We make special efforts to *not* follow the herd. Hell, we don't even like to read guidebooks and prefer to pretend we were the first to find that excellent little taco cart just two blocks off the central square. And we may or may not share that info with you. Like surfers protecting a sacred break, it just isn't as much fun when everyone else shows up.

I (Pat) sailed into Nuku Hiva in the Marquesas Islands, excited to be entering this amazing natural harbor in this far-off land. I wasn't fooling myself into believing that I was the first to arrive on these shores, but when Ali and I dinghied in and were met on the wharf by a gray-bearded sailor who immediately launched into a well-rehearsed spiel about where every possible thing a person wanted to find on the island could be found. "Go here to eat this, there to fill up propane, over there for internet, here for laundry, there for fresh fruit..."

Thanks man! This well-meaning guy had no idea, but he had pretty much ruined Nuku Hiva for me with his burst of "helpfulness."

There were plenty of places on my sail around the world where I felt as if I was the first foreigner to step-foot: I had coffee made for me in the bombed out home of an Eritrean widow, I helped kill baby birds that would become dinner on a remote South Pacific Island, I sang national anthems with a drunken Russian General and a room full of whores in Yemen, and had countless other adventures in distant lands—but that stop in Nuku Hiva never left my mind—and is probably what drove me further and further off the beaten path.

We've personally never taken part, but you'll find organized RV caravans and sailboat cruising rallies that help people get their adventures moving. A group gives first-timers a sense of security, and it's a good way to meet others with shared values and goals—which is just fine—just not for us. We've never heard anything but good things about events like the Baja Ha-Ha (sailing rally), but being on a schedule and knowing exactly what's coming next definitely takes away from the sense of adventure. The best reason to join an organized event? Setting a firm date for departure. When that clock ticks down to zero, you gotta go.

Real adventure is much deeper and more fulfilling when you get there under your own steam and everything is new and unknown. Seeing and discovering things for the first time makes you a pioneer, no matter how many people have come before you.

Intrinsically Motivated

Extrinsic motivation is what comes from the outside. These are your company's sales goals or bonuses, your boss's praise or expectations, or doing what your parents or friends or the Joneses think you should be doing. We are all trained from an early age that rewards come from the outside and doing what other people want will lead to what we want.

Intrinsic motivation on the other hand means following your own internal compass and rewarding yourself. Slacker-adventurers are intrinsically motivated, and a lot has been written already about the opportunities for self development and growth when you start listening to yourself instead of everyone else. It isn't as simple as better self-confidence.

When we (Nick and his wife) set out on our first cruise, we had no idea that we had been so dependent on the approval of others for our sense of accomplishment. I was a TV weatherman in a large market—I wasn't a real celebrity, but people I didn't know would say hi and give me compliments in the grocery store, movie theater, etc. My wife worked with tech geniuses in the Silicon Valley where being with such-and-such startup was a badge of respect. We were unknowingly motivated largely by the outside respect we got from our jobs.

When we took off sailing, all of that was gone. The ocean didn't care what we used to do for a living, and neither did the locals. Problems with the diesel filter out in the middle of nowhere without any wind? The engine didn't care. Too much sail up? The wind didn't care. No one was going to get us out of trouble but ourselves.

Solving problems, being resourceful, making it to the destination all take a voice from within that gives you the right answers time and again. When you get the engine going again with duct tape and bailing wire or make a three week passage or spear a snapper along a reef wall, you won't hear any applause. In fact the outside world you've been trying to please and impress all these years won't really even care when you tell the story later. This adventure is for you.

Intrinsic motivation tends to be self-reinforcing. The more you learn to trust yourself, the more often you make it to where you want to go without help and support from the outside world, the more you will listen to that voice within. In fact, that voice in your head becomes so loud that you can't help but listen. These are your instincts—and you will rely on them so often that you start to believe them without reservation.

This is invaluable as a trader. Profiting means buying low and selling high; it means buying when everyone else is selling or selling when everyone else is buying. You have to believe in what you think is happening with a company and its stock in order to see when everyone else is wrong.

Minimalists at Heart

It's hard to be free when you are hauling hundreds, if not thousands of pounds of stuff around with you. Slackers do whatever they can to minimize the amount of personal property needed to maintain their lifestyle. It's all really nice to have, but cameras, computers, clothing, boats, vans, surfboards

—anything you view as "yours" is going to occupy time and resources to manage. Slackers do whatever they can to keep the stuff to a minimum.

Still, it's never easy—and it's not because we are in consumer-accumulation mode, either. The challenge is that it's so easy to acquire "tools" in the name of having adventures! We are victims ourselves. RVs, boats, cameras, bikes, and gear of all sorts is constantly complicating our lives and filling our day-to-day with logistical concerns.

Take our particular choice in vehicles right now: sailboats. We spend an incredible amount of not only money, but more importantly time managing these things. Even the simplest repairs or installations can take days or (usually) weeks to accomplish. Everything is much more complicated logistically, and even finding the right screw for the job might take a half-day.

How are we going to get X fixed when we get to a marina? Which marina should we go to? How much does it cost to stay for a few days? Managing the boat is a constant pain in the ass. If there were any other way to get across oceans at the pace we like to travel, we'd gladly trade in the boat. Until that's possible, we are going to be stuck with those responsibilities.

What Do You Do?

In a lot of cultures asking, "What do you do?" is considered rude. With the answer, people tend to formulate all sorts of assumptions: intelligence, ethics, prosperity, security, etc. It's a lot like asking: *Am I better off than you? Am I smarter than you are? Which one of us is ahead in life?*

We think asking that question is a poor way to get to know someone, and our answer might not be what you're looking for. "Let's see, I breathe, travel, shower, read, write, take my kids swimming, build sandcastles, read books about talking pigs, ride bikes, sing songs I make up on the fly like an OG rapper, and sleep whenever the opportunity presents itself." In other words, "I do what I want," says the Slacker to Mr. Newsurfshorts, "that's what I do."

We're not offended by the "What do you do?" question. We just wish that people would ask instead, "What do you like to do?" The way we see it, that seems like a better way to get to know someone; and a better recipe for friendship.

Deeper Friendships

The non-work relationships we Slackers have tend to be more solid and long-lasting than work friends. Professional colleagues number in the hundreds for both of us, but in our collective working careers, the two of us have made just a handful of truly lifelong friends (Facebook friends don't count) that we originally met at work. That's a drop in the bucket compared to the lifelong connections we have made while traveling. The longer we've traveled the more this holds true. Why is that?

Sharing an anchorage at a remote atoll, watching the other's back for sharks while spearfishing along a reef-wall, helping fix a serious mechanical issue in the middle of nowhere—that's where real friendships form. Those bonds are much tighter, the experiences so much more sweet and shared.

We keep in touch with friends made over a weekend eight years ago. The fact that we sailed thousands of miles to reach that destination might have had something to do with the tightness of those friendships—there just wasn't any room in those relationships for egos, and we got to see firsthand the content of the other's character. That's the basis for real friendship.

FINANCIAL TRAPS

You set off from school and the world was your oyster—catch the right breaks and work really hard, and you'll get what you want. And that's exactly what you did. So how is it possible that five, ten, or twenty years down the professional road, you are living for Sunday afternoon football and little else? Why in the world does it feel so hard to get ahead in life financially?

Working Hard to Support a Working Lifestyle

Do you know how much money you spend making money? Pour over your financial statements. If you work for someone else, you'll be surprised by how much it costs to work. The numbers don't lie.

Transportation

The car you drive to work, depending on the make, model, and value, costs on average between $.62 and $1.30 per mile to drive. For someone commuting 20 miles each way to their job, that comes out to between $496 and $1,048 per month of net income. You can "gross up," that cost by 25–35% (depending on income and tax rate) to find the gross income required to support that expenditure. That means that you are spending between $620 and $1,415 of your gross income, just to drive your car to the place where you make money. If you make $100,000 per year, that's between 7.5% and 17% of your income spent just on getting to and from work.

You Gotta Talk

How about communications? Hard to do business these days if you can't be reached 24/7. Options abound from cheap throwaway phones to mini-computers capable of making a call. The iPhone? $100 per month plus the initial equipment cost spread out over 24 months is about $120 per month. Grossed up that's an easy $160. Do the same thing with your computer, your iPad and other digital services. Those all cost real dollars, and it adds up. If your job requires that you be up on your water-cooler gossip, you better have cable television too so that you can talk smack about the latest winner of *Dancing with the Stars*.

Be Smart

How about your education? You can't make money as a doctor or lawyer without a degree. How are you going to pay for that degree? Student loans—just about everyone we know has or had student loans that eat up a significant portion of their net income. Routinely those payments are over $400–$500 a month. Gross those payments up, and we are talking about $500–$650 in gross income. One friend amassed over $200,000 for a non-professional degree from Harvard. Even as a consultant making low six-figures, those loan payments are going to hurt for a very long time.

Show Me Some ID

Most technical and professional trades require special licensing or certification with the state and/or federal government as well as periodic continuing education courses. There are also professional organizations or societies that you will need to be a part of and maybe even some social organizations that everyone in your trade is a part of. Some will have annual or quarterly conventions and gatherings in distant cities. Those things aren't free; and a lot of the time it comes out of your pocket, not your employers' pockets.

Physical Maintenance

How about your health and well-being? Sit in an office all day and you aren't going to stay at your college weight. So add in the costs of sports equipment, gym memberships, and a masseuse every once in a while to loosen that stiff neck. Blood pressure running high? Better think about making sure your insurance is good, and that costs money too. If you have dependents and significant liabilities, you had better make sure you have a life insurance policy in place to protect your loved ones from the burden of your debts should something unexpected take you out of the income picture.

You Need Coverage!

Health and life insurance aren't the only insurance policies you need to consider when you are working hard to support a working lifestyle. If you are a licensed professional of any sort, you will also need to carry either a bond or malpractice insurance or both. Even if someone sues you and loses, it will be an expensive process that may damage both your bank account and your future earning potential.

It All Adds Up

Unless you pack your lunch every day or work at Google, chances are that you have personal consumption directly tied to your job. Professional clothing, a uniform, lunches, and even that daily (or twice-daily) Starbucks are all costs that you only have because you work for a living.

Yes, working is indeed expensive. By some estimates, the average American worker spends 25%–40% of their post-tax earnings on costs directly related to earning the income in the first place. So did that $100,000 job of yours really set you up nicely? That's $60K after taxes. After uncompensated work-related expenses, you have $36,000 to $45,000 to spend on food, housing, entertainment, and miscellaneous. You've got $3,000–$3,750 to work with every month. Rent or mortgage is going to take a big piece of that, and what's left goes for food and entertainment and everything else.

Wow, you are really killing it with that six-figure income. No wonder our savings rate is so low and our debt so high!

Debt

You personally may not carry a lot of debt, but someone you know sure does. The average "unsecured" (credit card) household debt in the U.S. is $12,000. That's a weighted average, which includes everyone who doesn't carry any debt at all. If you look at households who do carry unsecured debt, the average in the U.S. is close to $18,000. At 10–30% interest, that debt costs a lot to hold, and you have to remember that unsecured debt is paid with post-tax, net income. Minimum payments on $18K of debt is almost $500 per month of pre-taxed income.

Unfortunately, instead of using credit as leverage to buy an appreciating asset, most people use debt to finance depreciating assets like cars, boats, vacations to Hawaii, school clothes, or whatever. Financing depreciating assets is accepted as the norm these days, even though it makes no sense:

"Sir, these shoes are available in black or brown for $120 cash...however if you would like to put them on your credit card, they are available in brown or black for $210. Either way, they are worth $10 after you wear them for a day or two...and worth approximately $0 in a week."

Another reason that carrying debt makes no sense at all is because (if you have net worth in an account of any sort with a lending institution) you are borrowing your own money and paying for the privilege to do so. You are in essence saying, "Here bank, please hold onto this money of mine in a checking account." "Oh wow, you are going to give me 0.03% interest on my balance?—gee, thanks."

Go back to the very same bank that you have your checking account and ask for a loan to buy a car. Think they are going to give you a loan at 0.03% interest? Think again. They are in the profit game, the same as anyone else; and they are going to charge you to borrow your own freaking money! Slackers don't borrow money from themselves.

Retirement

Is the "classic" definition of retirement at 60-65 years old a financial trap? Maybe—maybe not—it really depends on your individual financial lot in life. But perhaps more important are future government policy and taxation decisions, as well as total economic growth—none of which can be predicted (by us at least). We don't have a solid answer to the question posed above, but we don't like investing in things so far out of our control. Slackers like us seek personal responsibility now and in the future.

Classic retirement could become a financial trap if social safety nets can't keep up with a growing, aging population, as well as inflation—and that's a distinct possibility—some even say likelihood. If you are dead-set on calling it quits for good at 65, you've got to work hard and save like mad to stash away that cash—and as you do, it's possible your cash will be worth less and less.

And if you are investing in IRAs and your 401K (both of which are a good idea if you are going to work for someone else—it's tax-free money!), you can't use those savings before age 58.5 without incurring penalties. We don't like the idea of someone else controlling our money and penalizing us for using it somewhere else.

Taxation
We hate to be so negative—have we thoroughly convinced you that you will work until the day you die for pennies and scraps? Well, beware—the situation is actually worse, because the government will take those pennies and scraps right out of your hand.

Hey we gotta have taxes. We get it: we as a society need an economic framework for funding things that the society needs to function. Police? Yep, gotta have them. Road work? Yeah, that would be nice. Firemen? Yep, probably should pay those people. Teachers? Should be paid more than congressmen in our opinion. Park Rangers? We suppose so.

Taxation is a huge mess in the United States and in most developed countries, but it's especially bad for those who earn a living through their labors—that's *if* you work. As it stands right now, the tax structure on a percentage-paid basis overwhelmingly favors the wealthy—there is no way to argue about that. At the same time, people who "earn" income pay much higher rates and are often double taxed, while those who receive investment income are taxed at a much lower rate.

Let's take your average multi millionaire c-level executive working for a large corporation. Ever looked at their compensation packages? Often they make a lot more on their stock or stock options than they do in salary. In fact a lot of famous CEOs draw laughably small salaries—some only a dollar. Ever wondered why?

Well, if he or she were paid even $200,000 per year, they would be taxed at a 35% effective tax rate. So aside from any deductions (and we realize we are making some gross assumptions), their federal income tax would come to $70,000.

Now let's say that the very same CEO was instead paid a salary of $1 per year, but was given stock options (which they exercise let's say a year later) in the amount of $200,000 per year. The capital gains tax on the stock is 15%, so the total tax bill would only be $30,000. So, same compensation, but $30K in taxes vs. $70K? Easy choice—if you were that CEO, why would you ever want to "earn" income when you could be paid in equity instead?

Slackers, if they make money in the markets, pay taxes like the CEO does via capital gains, not via earned income.

Why Not Slack for a While?

So, given all of these systemic problems which are completely out of your control, why swim upstream? Why not learn to play with money like the big kids do. Work less, play more, and enjoy your life instead of toiling away for security that the system may not be able to give you. The rest of this book is dedicated to introducing some of the tools you can use to do just that.

The Slacker - Trader

If you have what it takes to Slack, you may have what it takes to trade. We think that the attitude and psychology necessary to step outside of the nine-to-five workaday world for a life of adventure lends itself well to making money in the markets. We've already established that when we are talking about Slackers, we're not talking about alcoholic beach-bums, so if you can take full responsibility for yourself and understand risk outside of what everyone else says it is, you may have what it takes to be successful trading in the markets.

Trading Mythos

Just about every conversation we've ever had about how we make money goes something like this:

"So what do you do for a living?

"Uh...I'm kind of retired in a way, but I am still working a bit from time to time."

"Drug dealer?"

"Yep, my own cartel."

"Seriously?"

"No, I trade in the stock market a few days a month and that seems to do the trick..."

"So you are a day trader?"

"Sometimes, I guess, but I use other strategies too."

"So what exactly do you do?"

What follows, if they seem genuinely interested, is a flurry of questions and not very well executed explanations where charts, and frankly a book like this would be more effective. Understandably, this is too much too soon; the wannabe early retiree/slacker's eyes glaze over and robotic nodding ensues. They aren't necessarily lost but you can see from the look in their glassy eyes:

This is too complicated,
Too dangerous,
Too uncertain,
I could lose my home,
I might die,
I could be financially ruined,
Someone could take all my belongings,
I could lose my retirement,
It's dangerous,
My friends and family won't respect me,
I'm not being productive,
I might die,
I could never do this,
While I would love to live that kind of life, this isn't for me...

The interesting thing is that this list of objections could just as easily be applied to a backpacking trip across South America or sailing around the world as it could be to trading. People seem to be really intrigued with the idea of living a more interesting life, but when they realize that they can't do it from the safety and comfort of their easy-chair or office suite, they put the whole idea out of reach for themselves; they convince themselves that it isn't possible.

Faux Complexity

A lot of things aren't nearly as complicated as they appear at first glance—in reality they are very simple with a ton of little nuances and details. Those details and nuances are probably never-ending and you can spend a lifetime perfecting your technique and building that knowledge base. But the basics? That might be just about all you need to get rolling!

Take sailing around the world—you think, *that must be hard; there must be a lot to learn,* right? Well, Pat and his wife did it despite never having been on a sailboat before. How can that be?

It turns out sailing a boat isn't all that difficult or complicated. You pull a couple of lines, up goes the sail, the wind blows across it, and the boat moves forward. Everything beyond that is just tweaking—fine tuning. The same applies to trading; you study a stock, follow its price movements, and buy when you think it's a good deal. As you get more comfortable you begin to tweak—you look at charts, follow different indicators, try short-selling, use options—you are always fine tuning.

Faux complexity happens for a couple of reasons. First of all, the person doing the teaching wants to look competent, so he or she uses a lot of jargon or over-explanation. Doctors do this, lawyers do this, engineers certainly do this—it's their way of flaunting their own capabilities; of demonstrating superior intellect or capability. It's part of the value creation dance.

Ask a motor-head about the difference between a two-stroke and a four-stroke engine. He will go on and on and on about stroke and ignition and carburetion, etc. In reality—in the practical day-to-day operation of an engine, the only real difference you and I will notice between a two-stroke and a four-stroke is that the two-stroke needs oil mixed with the gas, it's lighter weight, and it's noisier.

The second reason things look more complex from the outside than they really are, is in between your two ears. "*Whoa, that _____ is impossibly difficult to understand,*" is just your brain trying to bogue out of learning something new. Your brain, like the rest of your body is a marvel of efficiency. Wasting brainpower to delve into the intricacies of everything it's exposed to would burn limited time and energy, so the brain has evolved to pick and choose what is most important. It waits for your conscious mind to say, "*Hey we have to know this stuff.*"

Trading—in the beginning—looks like an extremely complicated system. Traders use all sorts of unique vocabulary and slang, and in most trading books you will see thousands of concepts and just as many trading strategies. However, at the end of the day, no one involved has a crystal ball to see into the future—no one particular tactic will give you the ability to predict exactly what will happen next. You, like every single other market participant, are simply trying to guess whether a particular stock is going to go up or go down, and (it would be nice to know) by how much and when. After that, it's all just "buy low and sell high." In the end, it's all very simple.

We think the defining characteristic needed to get over any new endeavor's faux complexity is courage. Courage is often more important than book smarts because brain games are what keep you from taking the necessary steps toward your goals—they keep you from diving in, from learning what you need to learn to succeed for whatever that goal is. But with the courage to move forward comes the realization, in the end, that reaching your goal just wasn't as complicated as you thought it would be.

Secret Sauce

If there is one question we think a lot of would-be adventurers and wannabe traders have kicking around in the back of their minds is something along the lines of: is there any sort of fundamental talent or attribute that makes one person more capable than another? Is there a secret sauce; and is this teachable? We're not totally sure, to be honest with you, but we will say this:

There is no set of attributes that make one person a more adventurous adventurer or a better traveler or a more successful trader than another. As far as we know, there is no special sauce, but there is a paradigm that all doers share: the willingness and the need to take 100% responsibility for their own lives and their own destiny all the time, no matter what they are involved in. That means that it's never someone else's fault, and there is never an external influence that truly limits what is possible.

Heading off across the ocean in a small boat or putting your entire liquid net worth on the line for a single trade takes courage, confidence, and determination. Those who are willing to take ownership of the outcome whether good or bad—those people are the doers. Those who live in the shade of the doers and blame others for bad results are the talkers. And those who look to others to lead the way (and there is a difference between seeking leaders and seeking knowledge) are the dreamers—those are the guys and gals who live with regret and instead of blaming others, they blame themselves.

Dreamers look to leaders.
Talkers blame the leaders.
Doers are the leaders.

Our point in this chapter is to convince you that if you have what it takes to head off for a grand adventure, you may have what it takes to make money in the stock market.

Middle-Class is Easy

One popular misconception about cruising sailboats or being a vagabond in an RV or living out of a backpack on a tropical island is that it's all sun, sand, surf, and cold beers at the end of the day—one long vacation! The easy life! Slacking is all about relaxation in comfortable climates! Right?

Nothing could be further from the truth. We can tell you from firsthand experience, both inside and outside the corporate world and inside and outside the white picket fence that it's much *easier* physically and emotionally to work at a middle-class job for a middle-class wage to afford a middle-class lifestyle than it is to head off for a full-time life of adventure, even if it's just temporary. The *American Dream,* or at least the pursuit of the *American Dream,* is much, much easier than living the Slacker life.

What you don't see in the pretty pictures of the white sand beneath the palm trees are the biting sand flies, jejenes and the bobos. There is nothing comfortable about riding in a dugout canoe through a rainforest, or shortening sail at night in a building wind thousands of miles from land, or finding a transmission mechanic in a high mountain village when you don't speak the local language. What's the opposite of easy? Yeah, this stuff is kinda hard and kinda uncomfortable sometimes.

Wah, wah, wah, you say. And you are right. We don't mean to say that this is a life of nonstop drama and danger while courageously overcoming tremendous tests of wit and strength and annoying bugs, but we are saying that riding the L-train to an air-conditioned office, then meeting for dinner and drinks after work before settling back into a pillow-topped California King to watch late-night TV is a very easy life in comparison. If you feel that an easy life is the "good life"—why would you ever choose to give that up? If the goal of life is to last as long as possible in as much comfort and safety as possible, then why are you even reading a book like this?

For the Reward

The fact that you picked up or downloaded this book should tell you something about yourself. Perhaps, you don't want the easy life. If and when you move past the dreaming and the talking and into the doing, you will find that there is always a more direct journey and a more predictable outcome than the one you are choosing.

Why drive a '58 VW bus at 50 mph when a plane will get you there in 2% of the time for 20% of the cost? The idea makes absolutely no logical sense. Traveling the world on a sailboat? Bobbing around atop miles of deep water to cross an ocean at a walking pace? Huh, are you kidding me? That's ridiculous—you know there are better ways to get there, right? There are direct flights to Tahiti, you know. Are you irrational? Irresponsible? Stupid?

The fact that you are dreaming those dreams and reading a book like this should tell you that somewhere in your heart you know that there is a reward waiting out there for those who want to be their own man (or woman) and get from point A to point B, whether financially or physically, under their own steam. You just might be the type of person who is able to set aside all the very logical reasons to go in the pre-defined and seemingly secure direction—to instead cut your own path and leave your own wake.

Live Like That

There is a great scene in the documentary, *Comedian* where a young comic by the name of Orny Adams is complaining to uber-successful Jerry Seinfeld about his slow rise through the ranks and his worries about all of his friends who have bought the big house and the big car and have families and security and all the rest. The young comic says he feels like *real life* is passing him by. Seinfeld just laughs with some pity and tells Orny this story:

The Glenn Miller Orchestra (1950s) is traveling to a gig in the Midwest in the middle of winter. It's snowing and sleeting and their bus breaks down a few miles outside of a small town. The band is stranded with nothing but their dress clothes and instruments. They shiver off into the cold night to try to find a hotel. They come upon a house, windows lit up with the glow of a fire. Inside is the perfect family scene: the archetypal family is gathered around the warm glow of the hearth with books and hot cocoa in hand. Shivering outside in the cold, one band member says to another:

"How do people live like that?"

Completely by chance, Nick and his wife came across the (now not so young) comedian in 2012, sitting on a corner in Del Mar, California with his luggage next to him. He was on a cell phone, complaining to someone about how he didn't like the accommodations he had down in La Jolla. A full twelve years after Seinfeld told him this story, and he was still sitting on street corners waiting for a ride. I guess he took Seinfeld's story to heart. He lives like that because that's his art—not just telling jokes on stage, but living the life that comes with it. This is his art—he has to live like that.

Artistry

Inarguably comedians, musicians, painters, etc., are artists. They have something inside of them that wants to get out; something they need to express. There is a yearning to create—they can't *not* do their art. They forsake the established path to take the road less traveled or cut a new path altogether. Some artists actually do do their art for the promise of riches or fame, but very few of them continue along in obscurity if the dollars don't roll in. The rest do their art because they *have* to.

For adventurers, it's the same thing; experiencing things that others won't, that's our art. That's why we do irrational things like sail across oceans at a walking pace or drive old VWs across continents at the speed of an underpowered scooter. It's not always easy, but the reward is a life lived artfully. That's the only way we know how to live.

Sure, it's more likely that your house will sink if you live on a boat; and it's a lot easier to drive your car from your suburban McMansion to the nearby mini-mall to pick up your stuffed-crust pizza than it is to take a dinghy ride to a surf landing then wander up to the cobble road to catch a chicken bus to a mercado where they don't sell any of the foods you grew up with.

We are riding busses without windows and eating $.30 tacos not because we can't afford real transport and real food, but because there is real artistic expression in living this lifestyle. This is our art.

Trading as Art

The same can be said when it comes to trading. Trading is riskier than earning money from a job. A fry cook at McDonald's has more guarantees and stability than a trader ever will. Trading is a lonely endeavor—no one to hold your hand and tell you what to do. Like the comedian standing on stage, or the painter in front of the easel, or the singer or poet or guitar player—this in an activity where the outcome is 100% up to you. If you kill or you bomb, there is only one person responsible—and that is you.

When you are trading, the choice of what to buy, what to sell, how much, and when are completely in your hands. When you make the right decisions, you make money. When you make the wrong ones, you lose. It's very Darwinian in the same way that the great painting sells and appreciates in value while the bad painting ends up on the scrap heap. Good songs, good books, good movies all find an audience. Bad ones don't. Trading is art, and a trader is an artist. It just happens to be an art form where there are real winners and real losers.

No Net

Personal responsibility has gone missing from our lives in the last 50 years. Social safety nets ensure that no matter what dumb things you do, you won't be entirely responsible. Smoke cigarettes for 40 years and get lung cancer? Someone will end up treating you. Lose your job? Government will cut you a check. Can't make your house payments? Let the bank foreclose—you aren't on the hook. Burn the roof of your mouth on hot pizza? Sue the pie-maker.

We think this lack of ownership and personal responsibility is why people feel that something is missing from their lives. Their art is gone, and it really isn't a surprise. The art just isn't art anymore when the painting can't fail and every song is a hit on the radio. When you live a life in which all contingencies are covered and the question of success (or at least no real failure) has been answered before you even start, there is no real expression. It is just a series of predefined steps.

If we imposed the social safety nets on our painting analogy, it would go something like this:

- buy canvas, paint, and brush
- dip brush in paint
- apply paint to canvas
- allow to dry
- sell at auction

That isn't going to make for very good art, is it? But that's exactly how a lot of people look at their lives: step one, meet my mate, then we marry, then we buy a house, then we have children, work and save, put kids through college, retire, die. Insert yourself into whatever life-stage you are in now and there is always a predefined "next step" you "should" be taking.

The life of the trader is 100% opposite of this pre-defined life; the trader is operating without the usual societal back-ups, and really the same can be said of any true adventurer. When you put yourself or your assets on the line with no *one* and no *thing* to back you up and catch you if you fall, there is real risk and real responsibility. That isn't just a financial perspective, but a life perspective. You could even make the argument that this is how human beings evolved to live—and why we flourished as the most successful species on the planet, aside perhaps from cockroaches.

Trading Mindset and Personality

Traders—especially the really good ones—have the mindset and mentality that allows them to step outside of everyday society's (or the market's) trance and turn their insights into profits. Here are a few traits that a lot of good traders share:

- Inherently skeptical; like to see things with our own eyes. Recognize people's opinions as opinions and only confirm them as fact when we can form our own opinion from firsthand experience.
- Tend to be highly analytical and make calculated, reasoned (even if incorrect) decisions.
- Research everything, and will even research the source of our research.

- Not necessarily "type-A," but usually very confident and self-assured.
- Doers—good traders are decisive and don't get bogged down with regret.

Caution vs. Skepticism

The list above makes us sound very cautious. You might think that we are the nervous Nellies who never take a risk, but that isn't the case. Caution is about seeing and (when necessary) avoiding risk. Skepticism is completely different than caution even though it can make you look really cautious. Skepticism is about asking questions—the right questions—in an attempt to understand an unbiased truth.

Questioning assumptions and opinions is where market opportunities lie. It's like uncovering a little pot of gold that no one else has. Being skeptical allows you to better see where the **real** risks are hidden, and when the "obvious" risks might be overblown, overhyped, or overstated.

Caution is slowing down when the fog descends. Skepticism is questioning whether there is really anything you might hit and asking whether slowing down will make a difference anyway.

Why is this so important for an adventurer or trader? Because with modern media and the ability to gossip in real time from every corner of the globe, we are swimming in a sea of caution and fear. Those who can ignore the hype and overstated risks are the ones who find opportunities; and those who can't find an unbiased, independent perspective end up following the herd.

We can't even remember how many times we've heard something to the effect of: *"You are going to travel/live in Mexico? That's crazy. Don't you know that there are drug killings all over the place?"*

That isn't fact, that's opinion. The murder rates in Mexico are similar to the United States (and in many locations are much lower), and are mostly lower per capita in urban areas. It's just that in the U.S., officials are much better at sweeping up the mess than they are in Mexico. But like the U.S., Mexico has drug violence and it's contained to specific areas and to specific demographics, i.e. drug cartel members. Tourists are almost never harmed.

So where is the real risk in being decapitated while visiting Mexico? Well, if you get involved in the drug trade, the risks are real; and the risk of losing your head may be higher than in the United States. If you are a tourist or hanging out on beaches playing Bocce Ball, the risk of being killed by narco-violence is pretty much zero.

Opinion as Fact

The market is very much the same: opinions are stated as fact, and statistics are often bent and massaged. This isn't necessarily a bad thing—the highest profits are found on the stocks that have the most positive or negative opinions. The more people that have piled on the bandwagon of someone else's opinion, the more that sentiment may be pushing the stock too high or too low. When the market realizes its overreaction to opinion (which itself is always changing), we can profit.

Self-Confidence

We could really go off the rails here and into self-help guru-speak, but we will boil it down:

> *Belief in yourself is absolutely fundamental to success as a trader—there are no exceptions. Coincidentally, self-confidence also happens to be critical to casting off those lines and heading over the horizon for a life of adventure.*

A lot of people never get going because in the beginning there is a paradox: How can you have self-confidence when you don't have any experience? How can you believe you can sail around the world when you don't know how to sail? How can you have confidence wagering thousands of dollars on a predicted stock move when you have never done it before?

Do Do

There is no substitute for doing. In spite of what "experts" might say, there really is no way to completely prepare for an unknown and unknowable future. Ever. It doesn't matter how many seminars you go to or how many books you read—action is what turns self-confidence into self-assurance; which in turn builds even more self-confidence. Winners tend to win because they believe they can and prove themselves right time and again.

We are not telling you to just go off and jump into trading. You have to know what you are doing, but realize that book knowledge is a tool, not a solution. This book, like all the rest, is not a substitute for what you will learn by actually trading. You will learn more about your own trading psychology after you hit that "Buy" button for the first time than this or any other book can ever teach you.

The same goes for your adventures. You will learn more about anchoring your boat by anchoring than by reading about anchoring; you will learn more about tennis by actually playing tennis than from reading a book about it; you will learn more about photography by taking pictures than from reading your camera manual, etc. You can only really gain self-confidence and aptitude by doing.

The interesting thing is that self-confidence is not skill-dependent; self-confidence in one skill tends to lead to increased self-confidence in others. It's no accident that achievers in one field tend to be achievers in other things that they try.

Arrogance vs. Confidence

So to be successful you have to step forth confidently into the unknown; and you have to be very sure of yourself while doing something that you don't have much, if any, experience with. Isn't that a little arrogant?

Yes and no. Arrogance might be what the outsider sees. But what really matters is what you feel on the inside. Self-confidence is good, hubris is bad—being overconfident will cost you a lot of money and could sink your ship both literally and figuratively. Convincing yourself you know and understand something that you really don't will lead to costly decisions every time.

Back when I (Pat) was trading in the pits of Chicago, I lived just three blocks from the trading floor; so I walked to work from home wearing my canary yellow and baby blue trading jacket filled with trading cards and stacks of option pricing sheets. Right down Jackson Boulevard every morning past the guys in their three-piece costumes and shiny penny loafers. I walked among them feeling ten-feet tall and bulletproof. CEOs, law-firm partners? They had nothing on me.

But when I stepped into that trading pit, I was among my peers and knew that any hubris I was feeling was going to do nothing but get me bitch slapped to the floor. When the bell rang opening trading for the day, I knew that trying to be a big-shot in front of the gang would do nothing but lose me money.

Trading takes a total belief in one's self, but that does not mean that you believe you are always right.

As a pit trader, I saw every kind of mistake that could be made in trading.
One day a trader, Tommy, was bidding twelve to a broker who was offering at twelve and a quarter. Twelve! Quarter! Twelve! Quarter! They yelled back and forth for five minutes with one eye on the futures price until another trader, Frank, suddenly came out of nowhere and bid twelve and a quarter. SOLD!

Tommy was pissed. He felt twelve and a quarter was too much to pay and that he had just been "cut."

"Nice trade bitch," Tommy grumbled.

"Fuck you," Frank replied.

Frank then turned to hedge his options trade by selling futures at a slightly higher price than they were currently trading at. If he got the higher futures price it would make the option trade look like a better deal. But in that moment the futures price dropped and Frank missed the price he thought he was going to get for the hedge. The trade was quickly moving from marginal to definite loser.

Tommy smirked and goaded Frank. Frank meanwhile tried to act like it was no big deal. He was going to show he was right, and he waited to make the futures trade, hoping the price would pop back up. It didn't. But he still stood there acting defiant and proud.

Tommy, in his most condescending voice offered to take the options off Frank's hands for eleven, which would've represented a $6,250 loss to Frank. Frank politely told him to fuck off and then walked out of the pit. Everyone knew he was finally going to go and tell the futures broker to make the trade and get himself hedged, essentially locking in his now large loss.

Frank let Tommy get under his skin. He let an OK trade turn into a huge loser simply because he wanted to show Tommy up. He wasn't going to let that little punk Tommy be right. I learned right then that it's more important to believe in yourself and what you are doing than to worry about proving it to anybody else.

Traders with something to prove, lose, while traders with *nothing* to prove, win. Quietly.

Decisiveness and Commitment

If we boiled down the difference between those who dream of taking off on a grand trip and those who actually do it, or those who make money in the market and those who lose it, we'd have to say that it comes down to firmly committing. Simple–yes, but profoundly true and psychologically challenging as we will talk about later.

People will tell you that "untying the dock lines" was the hardest part of sailing away, but they are unknowingly lying to your face. Leaving isn't the hardest part. Deciding to leave is the hardest part. Once you have really decided, the rest is just putting one foot in front of the other. Untying the dock lines is then just the step you take before putting the engine in gear.

The confusion comes when people think that buying the boat is making the decision to leave, or that moving on board is making the decision to leave, or that upgrading to a new radar is making the decision to leave. Those might be steps in the process of getting ready to decide to leave, but setting an actual date or week of departure—that's deciding to go; that's committing.

After you untie those dock lines, you learn very quickly that the ocean is in control, not you. At that point, your only power is in deciding and reacting to its mood. The plan—which countries to visit and how long to stay—that will change along the way, but the commitment to go and to continue on as weather and ocean dictate—that can't change. The path changes, but the *destination* shouldn't.

The market behaves like the ocean. Sometimes it's smooth, sometimes it's turbulent, and sometimes it's confused. As a trader, you have zero ability to affect the market—all you can do is react to its behavior. Being decisive means taking action when and where it needs to be taken, no more and no less. As a trader, decisiveness is really your only power. This makes decisiveness perhaps the most important quality to try to cultivate.

The Iceman

I could go on and on talking about how trading in the pits made me (Pat) a better trader, and how I learned it was all about decisiveness. When I first started out in Chicago I was twenty-five years old. I had been trading for about a year and it was still very easy to second guess myself.

In pit trading, a broker, standing on the top step of the pit, receives an order from a customer. "Sep sixes eight bid!" he shouts, red faced with his arms stretched out, left hand holding a crinkled order and right showing pinky, ring, and middle finger extended, palm in. He wants to buy the September $6.00 calls for eight cents.

Within two seconds, a dozen of us traders would scream back, "Quarter!"—we would sell at eight and a quarter. Eight and a quarter would be a winning trade.

Now I'd have about one second, literally, to decide if I thought selling at eight was a good deal too, because if it was then somebody else was going to make the trade. In that one second, fifty other traders were scanning their pricing sheets—trying to make the same decision while rattling off a dozen calculations in their head. Now, maybe eight wasn't a good price and everyone would agree that eight and a quarter was actually the right price; but if it turned out that eight was a good deal, then that order was about to get taken out.

This is why being decisive can be the difference between a good trader and something less. Hemming and hawing over this trade wasn't going to make you any money. Being decisive was. In other words, deciding if eight was a profitable price to sell at or not—and deciding very quickly. If it was a good price but you hesitated, somebody else was going to get it, and you would've missed an opportunity to make some money.

"SOLD!" The trade was made at eight. It took three seconds for the trade to happen from start to finish. It was a good deal. Did you get it or did you hesitate—unable to decide? That one second was the difference in the pits.

Early Birds and the Echo Traders

In my (Pat) second year trading soybean options in the pits of Chicago a new market opportunity called serial months opened up. We were already trading options with expiration dates due on six months of the year, and these serial months would simply fill in the gaps. There was nothing unknown or surprising about these options—they were the same thing we were all standing in the pit trading every day of the week.

Orders for these new options didn't come in right away, but soon brokers started asking for quotes. They'd receive an order from their customer and then yell out looking for a bid and ask price on the option. The day these serial options began trading I had printed off pricing sheets for them so I'd be ready—and I assumed everybody else would too. I was wrong.

When the orders came in I was the only one giving a market to the brokers. Because there was so little liquidity I gave markets with a wider bid/ask than the more highly traded options. This gave me higher profit potential in exchange for the slight risk that I'd get into a position that I couldn't get out of.

After a while brokers didn't even ask the pit for quotes, they looked straight to me. For about two months (before the crowd realized these were the very same thing we all traded for a living) I—a 26 year-old kid—was the sole provider of liquidity for an entire market as all the other pit traders ignored what was happening right in front of their faces simply because it was new—it was an unknown to them. I was cleaning up, and I wasn't having to fight a soul for it. Seeing the opportunity, calculating the risk, and stepping forward was all it took.

There was a handful of traders in the pit—guys that were well liked only because they could tell a good story, or they always offered to buy lunch—who would invariably be one second late on every trade. When that order came in the pit and I yelled out, "Quarter!" I would hear them over my shoulder like an echo—quarter. When I yelled, "Sold!" I'd hear it again—sold.

In the pits there was a rule, whoever was first got as much of the order as he wanted. If I said "sold" first the entire order was mine, be it one contract or one hundred. If I took the full one hundred the "echo traders" would beg for ten, for five, for anything. Sometimes traders would throw these guys a bone, other times they were ignored. The echo traders lived like this day in and day out, and they probably still do; I don't really know—my decisiveness in the pits led me out of the pits and across oceans—their indecisiveness led them nowhere.

Pat's trading style these days is rarely as time sensitive, but the same need to be decisive still exists. Deciding on an entry point for a trade is often the easy part. Actually pulling the trigger and making that trade at that point is the hard part. It's all too easy to think, "Maybe it's going a little lower and I could buy it there instead." But if you believe it's a good deal at the current price you need to make it. Be decisive dammit, quit waffling!

Second-Guessing

Second-guessing things is probably human nature, but most people go too far. When the second-guesser in your head wins every argument, you are going to spin in circles wasting time and money. And that's why people buy big boats or RVs then never actually take the "big trip." The little voice inside says, "One more year of saving," or, "When Jimmy goes off to school," or, "When housing prices rebound." Those people never go. They sell the boat or the RV for a loss just a few years later. Sadly, they continue through life with unfulfilled dreams.

Even after you have left the dock or arrived at the surf spot in Costa Rica, you may (probably will) think about whether leaving your career was a good idea, or whether your savings will hold out. At best, these little negative voices telling you to turn the ship back to port are annoying, but at worst they can spoil the entire journey. It happens more than you might think. There are tons of boats for sale all over the world where the owners abandoned their dream when they realized that "Cruising isn't for them," or, "They aren't ready to retire."

One of the problems with dreams is that we tend to over-glamorize them and build up a vision for the future that can never measure up. During the dreaming stage we envision nothing but good times—white sandy beaches and crystal clear blue water with a gentle breeze and a cold drink in our hand. What we fail to realize in the dreaming stage is that the reality of living the dream can be challenging, uncomfortable, frustrating, etc.—it's not all unicorns, fairy dust, and Mai Tais. When reality hits and things aren't as awesome as we'd imagined they would be, sometimes we second guess ourselves too quickly, we bail out without having given the dream a fair shot.

Second Guessing Trades

Second guessing your trades can be a disaster and cost you a ton of money. As an example, let's say (keeping it simple at this point) that you decide to buy a stock that has been declining recently. It's a company you believe in, selling products you know and understand, in a market that you have watched closely for some time. You believe that this stock is oversold and that buyers will come back into the market and the trend will reverse. Let's say that you buy the stock at $10 on Monday, and at *some point* later you think it will get up to $15.

Instead of rallying, the downward trend continues; you watch that stock continue to decline. $9 on Tuesday, $8 on Wednesday, $7 on Thursday, $6 on Friday... How do you feel about that decision to buy the stock at $10? Absolutely terrible of course—every cell in your body is screaming, "Sell, sell, sell, SELL!!!!! You made a mistake!!!! Cut your losses!!!!" So you sell at $6 for a huge loss.

Then what happens? On the following Monday, the stock shoots up to $15. If you had held on just one more day, you would have seen the profit you'd been expecting. It turns out that the rally wasn't a matter of if, but when. If you had been able to ignore the second-guesser in your head, you would've won. Instead you lost.

In reality, if you truly believed in your trade at $10, you should've been eager to purchase even more stock when it got to $6. *Unless* a fundamental change occurred in the company that would hamper future profitability during that week, your initial decision was the right one. Sticking with it until the profit is realized was the right thing to do. Easy to say that in retrospect, of course.

Being decisive, taking responsibility for your decisions, and moving onto solving the problem or answering the question at hand is the most productive way to live and trade.

Design a Perfect Life

We aren't here to judge you, but if you are reading a book like this, it's because you want something new in your life—you want to *do* something you aren't yet doing. You may be totally satisfied with life as it is and want something different, or perhaps you are sick of what you are doing and want something better. Either way, you are at point A and you want to get to point B. So the big questions are, of course, where is B, and how are you going to get there?

We know what you want: a plan that will cut the distance between A and B to get there the fastest.

Most people set a goal, jump right into planning their route, and skip over the design process altogether. We think this is a mistake. If you start with a design, the plan is going to evolve without a lot of hassle—all of those little decisions are going to turn into obvious choices. The plan is going to take care of itself, so let's start with a design.

Designing vs. Planning

Have you ever worked with an architect on a new kitchen or with a professional website designer? If they are worth a lick, the first question they have for you isn't, "Where do you want the fridge to go?" or, "Do you want red fonts or yellow?" Instead, if they know what they are doing, they ask questions like: "Do you entertain frequently?" or, "Do your kids eat breakfast at the dining room table or in front of the TV?" or, "Will your website visitors interact with you directly, or are they just there to buy your crazy cat t-shirts?" Designers are concerned with function first and foremost, turning choices based on need into solutions that fit that need.

That's not how most people live their lives; instead of designing, they plan: first I'll do this, then I'll do that. I'll get my degree from this University, then (hopefully) I'll get a job in that industry, then I'll marry someone who is like this, then we'll go to this place for this long, then go to that place for that long, then, then, then, then... Come on, does it ever work out that way anyway? It never does.

And while life is happening to you, it tends to shape you; you end up getting designed by life rather than the other way around. Did you mean to get that beer gut and spare tire? How about the high blood pressure? Of course not—life just designed your body for you. How about all that credit card debt you've been carrying? Of course you didn't want that—it resulted from habits and small decisions that all added up. Did you plan on having a job that infuriates you on a daily basis? No way was it something that you planned for your life. It just happened.

Designing your life is about figuring out how you want your life to *function.* What do we mean by "function?" Well, how do you want your life to work or operate? We are not talking about what you want to accomplish or how to get to some goal, we are talking about what you want to actually be doing on a day-to-day, hour-to-hour basis.

Once you have the function figured out, the design evolves and everything becomes obvious. "The plan" isn't as necessary anymore—the path just lays itself out in front of you very naturally. The best part is that you don't need to think ten steps ahead—two or three will do.

If you ask a true Slacker what their "plan" is they'll (as they hold back a smirk) say something to the effect of, "We think we may do X, but that may change," or, "Our plans are written in sand at low tide..."

We slackers know that with our lives designed the way we want them to be, future decisions become obvious choices. In fact everything becomes so obvious that you stop stressing about decisions as much because you aren't compromising anymore; you are just doing what naturally comes next.

When You Grow Up

Why do people plan incessantly but forget to design? We think it's because they are so hung up on what they are going to ***be*** when they grow up (or be next year or whatever) that they forget that what they ***do*** is way more important to quality of life and satisfaction.

There is a vast, vast difference between being and doing. Being is for your ego. Doing is what your life actually is on a day-to-day, hour-to-hour basis. Being is a story you tell other people or a fiction you tell yourself about yourself, and doing is the actual reality you are living.

"You are a fireman!" That's great—you have become a symbol of respect in your community, as close to a real hero as they come (we aren't being sarcastic here; mad props to firemen—they are some of society's true heroes). *Being* a fireman is a super duper cool story to tell yourself and your neighbors. Being a fireman sounds awesome—the problem for us is that we don't want to *do* what a fireman has to *do*.

What does a fireman actually do? A lot of the time, a fireman hangs out at the firehouse with other firemen. Then an alarm goes off in the middle of the night and a bunch of stress ensues. It's hot, dirty, dangerous work, and most of the time the good deeds and heroic efforts don't appear on the local news. Then you go back to the firehouse and clean smelly soot and water off of all the equipment and load it back up on the trucks, and then you sit around (figuratively, not literally) with other firemen until the alarm goes off again.

Being a pilot is cool too (Nick is a licensed pilot); you are in command of a machine that flies through the air much faster than anyone can drive on the highway. The view from the cockpit is incredible, and for the professionals, the uniform is pretty spiffy. But what does a pilot actually do? He or she sits around in a cramped space breathing dry, recycled air, hoping nothing really exciting happens. The plane can fly itself better than the pilot can by hand, so the pilots manage the autopilot and flight director (computers), waiting to get to the destination just like everyone else in the passenger cabin.

Ask a commercial pilot what life is like day-to-day, hour-to-hour, and a lot of them will tell you it's pretty boring: waiting in security lines, eating fast food, sleeping in hotel rooms, and jet lag. What a pilot does isn't nearly as glamorous as "being" a pilot. The same goes for a lot of things.

Being *it* is much different than doing *it*. If you find yourself unhappy with what you are doing, it might just be because you've been too focused on being, and not focused enough on doing. Time to change that.

Design!

If you buy into our argument that designing means figuring out what you want to actually do in your life instead of what you want to be (in your head), then the questions actually get a lot more difficult; you have to ask yourself what you want to actually *do* on a daily basis. Do you want to surf? Build a company? Play with your kids? Hang out with office mates? Wear shorts? Wear fancy suits? Work in an office? Work at home? Sail a boat? Live where it's warm? Live where the seasons change? Eat out? Eat in? Live in a place where you are very unique? Live in a place where you can fade into anonymity? Interact with people? Keep to yourself? Hike? Make things? Play baseball? Those are the questions of doing, and they are tough questions to answer.

Think long and hard about what you want to do and less about what you want to be. When you do that, a lot of design questions answer themselves. Sit down with a pad and pen and write down what you want to do, and every time you see that it's actually something you want to be, cross it out.

Doing Nothing

People think that the point of the financial game of life is to reach a situation where you can do nothing. We've tried doing nothing and can say with authority that doing nothing sucks. Thinking you want to do nothing is a big mistake—ever seen the depression rates among retirees? The point of being a Slacker is that you want to control your own destiny and do more of what you want to do—not to do nothing all day.

Redefine Retirement

Since this is a book about taking some time for ourselves and *living on the margin*, we really have to change the definition of what retirement is. Retirement does not need to begin at age 65 and it does not need to be forever. This outmoded paradigm of saving up $X so that when we turn 65-years-old we can simply continue to live the exact same life we've always lived neglects the reality of what most of us will face.

When you do retire, whether now for a little while or later for good, you are going to change what you do on a daily basis in a radical way. Whether now or in 25 years, you aren't going to be working in the office every day. You aren't going to be attending professional conferences. You aren't going to be taking a two-week vacation here and a long weekend there so that you can focus on doing nothing. Everything about your life is going to change whether you like it or not, so why not redefine retirement itself?

Why not retire for a few years in your twenties, work full time for a bit in your thirties, retire again before forty, work some more, and retire for good in your late fifties? Or maybe if you like what you do, you can just keep on doing it until you can't anymore. Sound good? You can do that you know—you're steering this ship you call life.

Left in the Dust

The big argument people have against what we like to call *mini-retirements,* is that they worry that they'll be left behind. Technology will continue to race forward and their specialty will no longer be relevant. Or if they leave their job they'll have to start all over from the bottom.

How do we address those concerns? Well first, the truth is, you may/probably will be left behind in your career or trade, but you need to remember that just because you are out slacking doesn't mean you are stagnant; that you aren't learning and growing. With your newfound free time you're going to pursue new hobbies, develop new skills, and perhaps most important of all, meet new people outside your current inner circle.

The new people that you meet are going to be more interesting, more innovative, and more successful than you'd have ever thought slackers could be. You'd be amazed at all of the entrepreneurs, inventors, and professionals of all types who end up anchored next door off that beautiful Caribbean beach or down a long dusty road in Baja. And that's when you'll learn that just because you were once an accountant does not mean you must always be an accountant.

Let the future take care of itself! When we left our (inarguably successful) careers to head out on our first adventures almost ten years ago, there is no way we could've known that someday we would end up writing popular blogs and books, invent products, start and sell companies, *or even meet each other and write this book.*

These opportunities just sort of popped up and became obvious choices, and they were all things we decided we wanted to do, not things we wanted to be. We had no ambition to become bloggers, writers, inventors, company owners, etc. We simply saw something we wanted to do, did them, and moved onto the next thing that seemed interesting. By the time you read these words, we may be partners in a llama farm. Who knows?

Missed Opportunities

We started taking our first retirements when we were in our late 20s. Pat was twenty-nine and had a couple of very good years in the soybean options pit when they decided to take off. Could he have made a lot of money during the years he was away sailing? Probably. Does he ever sit around wishing he'd stayed to make that money instead of sailing off on what has to be described as one of life's greatest adventures? Absolutely not. Nick left a great job in a top television market at twenty-nine to head south on his own boat. Does he ever wish that he had hung around and socked away a bit more cash? No.

The fact of the matter is this: *you can always make more money, but you can't make more time.*

Spearfishing at 90

If there is one thing we can guarantee, it's that you will age and croak one day. According to the Social Security Administration, about seventy-five percent of us will live to age 65. According to the actuarial tables: if you do make it to 65, you can expect to live 15 more years—19 if you're a woman.

Do you want to sit in a recliner with a slow drip of painkillers at age 75 or would you rather be spearfishing at age 90? Pretty easy decision for us—give us an active lifestyle until the day we drop dead. Convalescence while we pitter away the last of our savings? Wow, nothing sounds worse.

But that's the classic model. So, 15 years of "retirement," huh? Yippee flipping doo dah. Just think of all the fun you're going to have between 65 and 80. After you've worn your body down by stagnation, stress, and lack of stimulation, you are bound to find the last few years pretty lifeless and bleak. Take a minute—imagine it.

Wouldn't you prefer to be doing what you *like* to do all the way to the end?

It boggles the mind to think that the majority of Americans aim for the magic age of 65 to begin their retirement—that they structure their entire life around that singular goal. And only three out of four of us make it to 65! A seventy-five percent chance of even making it to retirement? Those odds suck. They'd be good odds on a trade. You could make a lot of money if you could lock up seventy-five percent winners. But when you're gambling on your life? You wouldn't play Russian roulette with those odds.

Not Getting Younger

In our travels, we are the youngins in every anchorage. Just about everyone else is 60+ years old. They're mostly having fun—no one is saying they aren't, but it had taken forty years of hard work and a lucky roll of the dice on the mortality tables to get them there. The trip itself was undeniably more difficult for these older folks than it was for us "kids."

This cruising stuff isn't always backbreaking work, but raising sails, bashing across the ocean in storms with little sleep for days on end, diving under the boat to cut a fishing net loose—the list goes on and on. Not much in life gets easier as you get older, and adventuring is the same.

We certainly aren't ageist or think that as we age we become less capable—we don't believe that at all, but if we had a dollar for every time one of these older cruising couples said to us, "You guys are doing it right. We wish we had done this at your age," we would be eating a lot more steak and a lot less hamburger. Let's listen to our elders—if they say go when you are young, then let's believe them!

THE DREAM

Now with all of that nonsense about working until you are too old to do anything fun out of the way, let's start thinking about what you want to do with your first mini-retirement. This is the fun part—identifying what you would do if money were no longer a barrier or if your free time were no longer limited.

Everyone has a dream—that idea that came to you in the coffee shop one day over a vanilla latte, or hit you out of nowhere in the shower so many years ago, or perhaps something you have been carrying around in the back of your mind since childhood. If you don't have a dream, you don't have anything, so start here.

Slacking as we have defined it isn't about sitting around watching TV or sipping cervezas under a palapa and watching the world go by. You will need a motivation to trade profitably—you have to want it. You may have been using that ephemeral, "retire at age 65," thing to get you up and out the door every morning, but now you need to find something else.

Dream big, but keep it real—too often people put their goals so far out of reach that they give themselves excuses for why reaching them is not possible. So if you're working at 7–11 and you dream of buying a 120-foot yacht to cruise around the world with a supermodel on your arm next year—you are either going to have to revise your departure date or maybe consider lowering your standards a little bit.

The key to realistic dreaming is to merge ultimate dream with current reality. If you can attain your ultimate dream, but not for forty more years, you are slipping back into thinking about the long-term "someday," which never actually comes. Why not live in the reality of today and have an equally awesome, though scaled down version of that dream right away? So instead of the 120-foot yacht and the supermodel, scale it down to a 40-footer and any cool girl (or guy, as the case may be) you can convince to come along.

Today

We aren't self-help gurus—we aren't going to tell you to "live in the now" or be more "present," but we are going to tell you to get your head out of the really long-term nebulous future that you can't comprehend or predict anyway. That way of thinking just isn't productive, and living that way is letting life pass you by. That may be what you've been doing up to this point, so let's start by looking around your life right now to see where you are.

If it takes some Buddhist meditation to wake you up to what is happening in your life right now—today, then go for it, but we don't think it's necessary. Stand back and take a look at your life as it is at this very moment, as you are reading this book, and ask yourself with all seriousness: what is possible?

What's possible today? Not next year, not in five years, but TODAY. What could you do now if you were diagnosed with cancer and were told you had 18 months to live? What's your current reality dream? Hike the Appalachian Trail? RV across Europe? Ride an enduro bike across Africa? All right, now we're talking—these are all very doable. And it's doable at a young age if that's where you are in life. If you don't think waking up on your own boat anchored off a white sand beach, swimming to shore for a fresh caught grilled fish lunch and a noontime cerveza is a good dream—a dream worth shooting for—then we need to talk. Or you need to talk to a psychiatrist.

Grab a legal pad and do some writing—you've heard it before—but get that dream solid in your mind and put pen to paper. Do it now.

First Questions

The first big questions that will pop into your mind as you visualize this dream of yours are inevitably going to be: "How much money do I need?" and, "How long can I afford to go for?" Both of which are answered by your *burn rate.*

The burn rate is a crucial number that will determine how this mini-retirement of yours is going to work out. It's going to affect everything from how long you can be a slacker, to how often you have to trade, to how much you risk per trade. It's a very important number, and not one that you want to underestimate. We'll go into more detail on burn rate below, but to start—let's step back into the reality of today and spend a little time looking at your spending now.

Where is my Money?

In economics, "margin" is the minimum an enterprise can earn and still pay for itself, i.e. turn a profit. When we say *live on the margin*, what we're advocating is that you support your life and lifestyle on your personal profit margin. What is that? Well a company's profit margin equals revenue minus expenses.

But wait, you say—*my life and lifestyle <u>are</u> my expenses*. Well don't be offended, but that's how *workers* look at personal finance. Workers work to attain assets (money) that they then use for themselves and their lifestyle. If their revenues equal their expenses, they live paycheck to paycheck. If their revenues exceed their expenses, they save or invest. Then one day, they (hopefully) retire, and (hopefully) live off of their assets, which (hopefully) last until they die. That line of thinking requires a lot of finger crossing and a rabbit's foot in your pocket.

Owners on the other hand treat their personal finances like a business; like an enterprise. They have assets that work for them—their assets produce revenue—and using these assets to produce revenue has associated costs. So for the owner, revenue minus costs of producing that revenue equals profit, or margin. To protect their assets so that they can continue to produce revenue, the owner lives off of the margin, not off of the assets themselves.

If you want to live on the margin, you need to change your mindset from that of a worker—from spending it all to keep up with the Joneses (*where did all my money go?*)—to being an owner, raising revenue while cutting costs.

The worker lives off the assets his/her labor produces. The owner ***lives off the margin*** *that his/her assets produce.*

How Much

If you have an idea of what you'd do if money weren't a concern and you are ambitious enough to think your dream adventure is at least possible sometime down the road, you are probably looking around at your assets and thinking about what you might need to set off on that journey.

Whether you have a crappy old car and $100 in the bank or you have $1 million in a diversified portfolio with luxury cars in the three-car garage, the questions are always the same: How much will this dream adventure of mine cost? How far will this set me back in my life plan? How long could I go if I threw caution to the wind and set off on this adventure? You're probably thinking something on the order of:

"I've got $100K, and I could probably live my dream on $25K a year, so with a small cushion, I could take three years off from work to go live my dream. But...it took me five years to save that $100K, so taking three years off will set me back a total of eight years in my retirement plan."

Well, that line of thinking is not a bad start at all, but if that's as far as you go, you are still thinking like a laborer—like someone who works for a living. Why not think like an owner would from the very beginning? Think of this endeavor as a business, with assets that can produce revenue. All of a sudden, that $100,000 could go much further and you could stay out a lot longer.

Or even better, maybe you don't need $100,000—how about $10,000? Maybe the key for you isn't a fat bankroll. Maybe it's an understanding of and commitment to lowering the expense side of the equation. You can't know without taking an honest look.

Pay Attention TODAY

If money is the first concern, then start down that road today by understanding your finances right now. Tracking your expenses is simple and can actually be sort of fun, in a nerdy accountant sort of way. Get out a yellow legal pad, or open up a simple spreadsheet on your laptop, name a few columns like food, car, insurance, entertainment, rent, utilities, whatever. The more specific the better, but for many first time budgeters simple is often easier to handle. Just shove receipts in your pocket all day and when you get home at night take a quick second to punch them in.

At the end of the month you'll be surprised—we guarantee it. "I spent how much at the pub?" "How did I spend that much on food and not gain twenty pounds?" "Four-hundred dollars just on lunch?" "Six-hundred on gas?" Track this for a couple of months and you'll be armed with some solid information that can help lead you to your eventual slacker burn rate.

Compare Budgets

Make another column in your table that itemizes your forecasted expenditures while off on this grand adventure you have in mind. Do a little googling, read some blogs, and use the same categories if you want to.

Compare your current expenditures to those you expect on your trip. These don't have to be perfect estimates; this is only to give you an understanding of just how much drastically lower your monthly expenses can be compared to a typical U.S. suburban existence.

	Laborer in Suburbahell, IN	Slacker in Spanish Virgin Islands
Rent/Mooring	1200	150
Utilities	150	0
Cable	100	0
Cell phone/Internet	100	50
Car/Taxi	375	100
Gas	150	50
All Insurance	350	0
Food	900	500
Entertainment	600	300
Miscellaneous	200	200
Total Burn Rate	$4,125	$1,350

[fig 6.1]

What you see on the right-hand side of the table above are realistic numbers for someone to cruise on a relatively simple boat and live at anchor in the islands. We know because we've lived on boats with our wives for a combined ten years, and now Pat and his wife do it with two kids. While our budgets tend to exceed this number sometimes, it's well under that at others.

When we spend more, it's by choice and not by necessity.

Every person is going to have a different burn rate, even on the same adventure. The key then is to determine yours as best you can. After a few months living the dream, your budget will evolve and your burn rate will change; you'll find new things to cut and new things you can't live without. That's okay.

FUNDING

Okay, so you've determined a reasonable burn rate for driving your vintage VW hippie bus around the world. You've included a cushion for repair costs, border crossing fees, and eating every meal out. Now let's talk about how you're going to fund that three year (or whatever) mini-retirement.

Some would-be adventurers think that they are going to be able to head off on their trip and take breaks from their travels to make money along the way. This can and does, "work," for some people. We've met a few travelers who've stopped along their journey to fill their accounts by working in IT, or running charter boats, or working in hospitality. But that isn't slacking, it's working in foreign countries. We aren't into that.

Unless you are already sitting on significant assets, to make this dream come to life, the first thing you are going to do is go into savings overdrive. This step is what separates those truly committed to going, from those that will remain dreamers. This is where the rubber meets the road—it starts right now, not the day of departure. At first, this is going to cause some pain. The pain will be short lived though. Trust us—you will learn to live without *Dancing with the Stars* in HD.

The Cut

You are armed with a budget—we've already figured out your current Suburbahell burn rate and broken it down into categories. Hopefully you are suitably appalled by how much money you are spending to live a life that's nothing like the life you really want to be living, and you are now ready to make some changes. The cut might feel a little painful at first, but we guarantee this feeling will pass, and the future-you (post adventure) is going to laugh at your old ways.

The truth of the matter is that living your dream is going to scramble your priorities and going to completely re-focus you on what is truly important to well-being and happiness. Nearly every adventurer we know has come to the realization at some point that the life they were living previous to setting out was one filled with waste—wasted time and wasted money. When they return, all of a sudden a two bedroom condo with full-time electricity and endless water from the tap seems luxurious, and the McMansion they left just a few years ago now looks laughably unnecessary.

Unplug

It's time to take responsibility for our own entertainment and stimulation. First thing on the chopping block really should be the cable bill. Slacking is not about being entertained by a glowing box that does all your thinking for you. It's about freeing up your time and your lifestyle to be able to take advantage of new opportunities, as well as explore and pursue the things that have always interested you—items on the "bucket list," if you will. If you find yourself bored once the cable is gone, then start channelling that energy into something else. Learn to play the accordion—not enough people play the accordion—you'll be the hit of every party.

Hey, TV can be a great source of learning, information, and keeping your kids occupied, but if your priorities are shifting and you want to grow out of your current life and into a new one, it's a time burglar—stealing hours and days and even years of your life when you could be making monumental, life-changing progress. According to A.C. Nielsen Co., the average 65-year-old will have spent nine years glued to the television! *Years* of precious, irrecoverable time parked in front of a television? That's like three full years watching thirty-second advertisements.

That's time you could use for something else. If you have an idea for a product that can unclog any toilet in just five seconds, but never found the time to pursue how to go about actually making that product or selling it? The answer is not going to come to you while staring blankly at the Kardashian sisters. Wait, bad example, maybe staring at the Kardashians would get a new toilet product on the market.

Cutting cable—at $125 bucks a month, $1,500 in just one year, equals one full month of living the good life. The life you really wish you were living. The Kardashians won't miss you, and you won't miss them.

Cuppa Joe and His Little Friends

You have the current budget in front of you, and you can see the fat all over the place now—time to go on a diet! Cut that $5 morning latte at Starbucks, cut that $12 lunch, cut out the latest smartphone and its two-year contract. You don't need that tenth pair of shoes unless they are flip-flops!

There's an endless list of these small steps you can take to save you thousands of dollars per year. Cutting out the small, unnecessary expenditures isn't rocket science; and we aren't writing anything that hasn't been said and written about a million times before. You can buy yet another book at the bookstore to point this stuff out to you, or you can use common sense. Take a look at your daily life and the budget you've prepared, and think about where you would rather be a year from now. Focus on how badly you want to be there, and make the cuts today.

Some Biggies

Don't stop with the small stuff—there are other major steps you can take, and these are the ones that are going to save you big money. These are the steps that will save you enough money to buy that sailboat in just a couple of years, or to fund a full five year bicycle trip around the world. These are the steps to take when you are really committed to setting yourself on a new path.

Get Out of Your Car

There is nothing so draining on the pocketbook as a car. It's sometimes hard to see this; but the fact of the matter is that cars cost an average of fifty-eight cents per mile according to AAA; and if you have a nicer, newer car with poor mileage, it could be costing you more like $1.30 per mile. That money goes fast—just think, it takes less than one minute to drive a mile on the highway —$50 per hour to drive the Interstate? Ouch.

When you get rid of that car, you get rid of the car payment, the car insurance, and of course, the gas. Meanwhile you also get rid of a depreciating asset. That car you spent $20,000 on isn't going to be worth a quarter of that in just a few short years. Get rid of that car, and you are going to put $3,000 to $10,000 of post-tax earnings back in your pocket.

So what are you going to do without a car? "I have to get to work." Okay, obviously, first choice is to carpool with a coworker, or take a bus. Or you could really step up to the plate and ride a bike. Of course sometimes there are no buses where you live and you can't ride a bike fifty miles right? So what does one do then? See if you can work from home and skip the commute altogether.

It may not even make sense to keep the job! When they were getting ready for their first cruise, Nick's wife Megan quit her job in order to save the commute, sell the car, and take a part-time job at West Marine to get a healthy discount on boat parts (BTW, the markup on everything at West Marine is extremely high!). With the car savings and the discount, she was working half a day per week instead of five and she was breaking even!

Move

Radical, we know, but this is HUGE! A basic tenet of the Slacker lifestyle is to downsize your life. There is no better way to downsize for most of us than to change where we live. Think about it. Why do you need so much space? Why do you spend thirty percent (at least thirty, but often more) of your take home pay on a house that requires not only a big chunk of your money but a big chunk of your time to maintain as well? Does your happiness depend on how many rooms you have or how much square footage? Of course not. You are not your house.

Now think rationally and economically about your housing situation. Most likely your slacker dream doesn't include the home you are currently sleeping in anyway. Most dreams take place in a new city, a new state, or a new country. There's something about new places and better weather that attracts all of us. So if your dream doesn't include this home, then why not start today?

You live in an eighteen hundred square foot space with rent of $1,800 a month, plus utilities, plus a thirty minute commute to work. Meanwhile, there is an eight hundred square foot place a fifteen-minute walk from work for $1,150 a month utilities included. You save $650 a month on rent, and better yet, $600 a month on your car payment, gas, and insurance, because you sold your car. That's well over $1,000 a month that could be saved by downsizing and simplifying your life.

These are big steps, no doubt, and most people will instinctively say they can't do it for this reason or that reason. But if you sit down and analyze the numbers on your present housing budget, and then go rental shopping, many of you will realize that this is something you can't afford not to do. Downsizing your life now is the biggest step you can take towards living the life that you truly want.

The Rest is Easy

Start with the small steps, and you'll be amazed at how the bigger steps don't feel quite as intimidating. Lose the cable TV and the daily Starbucks latte, and you'll start questioning other purchases as well. *Do I really need that new pair of shoes? Can I get by with a monthly massage instead of a weekly massage? Do I need to get a massage at all?* You tend to build up a bit of momentum and the decisions get easier. So start small and the rest follow easily.

Once you decide to move into a smaller space; you need less things to fill it with. You won't be as tempted to buy a new piece of art or furniture when you know it's just one more thing you'll have to move into storage. You'll find the question shifts from *how much do I want this*, to *how badly do I need it*? Most people find that their true needs are tiny compared to their wants. Wanting only what you need will eventually become the litmus test for all purchases.

FINANCING YOUR DREAM

Don't borrow from anyone—we are going to pound this dead horse into the ground until you throw this book down in disgust (do not try with e-book readers). DO NOT head off for your adventure with a pocket full of credit cards and a plan to pay them off when you get back. That might work for the college kid who plans to come back and wait tables for a couple years while living in the parent's basement, but that plan has absolutely no place in this book.

Our strategies simply do not work if you are trading with borrowed money, so don't even go there. Erase that thought from your mind. You need cash—your own cash. So that leads us to an important section of this book. Time for some crystal clarity.

What Are You Worth?

Financially we mean—the hard numbers (we know you are a good person). Today—at this moment—how much cash could you come up with to finance your Slackerdom?

Figuring out your total assets is fairly straightforward. Your liquid assets are your bank accounts, investment accounts, and the cash in your wallet. You have non-liquid assets as well. You might have some equity in your house (not nearly as much as you think, we're willing to bet), you've probably got a car that's worth a few bucks, a lawnmower if you've been really unfortunate, and countless other things lying about that are worth something to someone. Could be a buck, could be a hundred bucks, but it all adds up.

There's a market for just about everything you own—it may be just a fraction of what you paid, but almost all of it can be sold. These days with eBay and Craigslist you can find a buyer for anything. When we started preparing for our first adventures, we were in our late 20s and hadn't really accumulated all that much stuff, but we still found an abundance of things to get rid of.

While selling everything you own can be fun, it's also time consuming—so much so that Pat's wife even quit her job a month early just to handle the unloading of all of their junk. This is where you need to make a decision. Is the time you are investing in selling this stuff worth what you are pocketing in return. In retrospect it would've been a smarter financial decision for his wife to keep working and for them to set all of their junk out by the curb for the alley trollers to pick up for free.

Dream Budget

So far, we've talked about trying to forecast a realistic burn rate and figured out how much you are worth. Now let's roll that into an overall budget. That budget should be made up of three things: startup costs, return fund, and burn rate. Neglect any of these and you are back to living in the dream world of "someday." Undoubtedly, these numbers will evolve over time, but you need to have a starting place.

Startup Costs

Whatever you have in mind, there are going to be initial capital expenditures —stuff you need to do or buy to blast off into your adventure. Startup costs will vary depending on what you want to do of course, so there is no way we can tailor this section to any adventure in particular. But you have to know this—it's an extremely important number and unfortunately, is one that everyone—ourselves included—tend to underestimate.

Let's say you are going to buy a boat and sail off to the Caribbean. You've found the boat in Florida, made the offer, and you are now the proud owner of a twenty-year-old piece of plastic with a pole and some fabric designed to carry you across the water. Great! But that's just the beginning.

You live in New Jersey, remember? You've got to consider transportation costs for you and your belongings. The airlines aren't going to fly your surfboard down there for free, they're going to want a hundred bucks for it. Once you get to the boat, you are no doubt going to be spending a couple of months getting it ready. This is going to include too many trips to the ship chandlery to remember. And now that you own the boat, you are going to be paying that slip fee at the marina as well. So time is money. Boat adventurers are notorious for underestimating what it's going to cost to get underway.

What if you aren't going sailing but are going to hike the Appalachian Trail? With this sort of adventure, you can be a little more exacting in your startup estimates. You are hiking after all, there is only so much stuff you can carry, but there are still going to be plane or bus tickets, guidebooks, inoculations for Lyme disease and maybe a tetanus shot, too. It all counts, and it all adds up. If you aren't miserly now, you are in for a shock when the paycheck from work stops showing up in your account. Start now.

Anyway, this startup number is important for us to have a rather firm grip on so that we can determine just how much money you are going to have to invest and to trade with. So again, be honest with yourself, and overestimate as much as you think you need to in order to not come up short on this.

Underprepare

You've decided that this next austral winter includes an unsupported LandCruiser trip across the Australian outback. Awesome—now let's start shopping for the perfect vehicle and all the right camping gear. Wrong!

Don't overprepare. A lot of people love planning the adventure more than the adventure itself. There are thousands of boats sitting at docks all over the States that are more than ready to sail around the world. Instead, though, they just float at the dock chafing through their dock lines while the owner continues to put in sixty hours a week at work to fill the "cruising kitty" as it's known in the obnoxious world of yachties. This guy would've had more than enough money to go cruising for a year or more if he had simply chosen to forgo a few of the amenities and gadgets that he felt he needed on his boat.

If sailing the islands, or even around the world, is your slacker dream of choice, you can do it sooner rather than later by not over preparing. That sounds counterintuitive for an odyssey as epic as sailing around the world, but you need to keep in mind that you aren't leaving one day and sailing around the world nonstop from that point. Chances are you will spend a while cruising within a couple hundred miles of where you start out.

That means you have plenty of time to cruise that new-to-you boat and figure out, based on actual experience, what you truly need aboard the boat to keep going. We'll make a bet right now that you'll spend thousands of dollars less this way—money in your pocket instead of spent on useless crap you'll never use—money that will be used to keep you out slacking longer.

Same thing goes for an RV trip across America. People tend to want the experience to be just perfect, so they buy their dream RV and then take it to a shop to have every bearing greased, every rusty hose clamp replaced, every mirror replaced with super extender mirrors, and on and on. But you're in the States for crying out loud. You are never more than a phone call away from the nearest mechanic. Roll the dice a little, set out and drive; and if you break down, consider it part of the adventure.

And for that person who wants to go live in Bali to surf and practice meditation. What does one really need in order to live in Bali? A couple pairs of shorts, shirts, and... Nope, that's it. You could move to Bali with nothing more than a backpack; and within the week be living two blocks from the beach and wondering why you ever thought you would need three t-shirts.

Don't over prepare. The money you save will go to one of two things. Hopefully it will go towards extending the burn; but worse case—if that RV does break down because you failed to replace that old alternator, you'll spend the money then to fix it.

Be Careful at Costco

A common argument people use to over prepare themselves is, "We won't be able to find this stuff in Colombia, so we better stock up and bring three along." Remember that people have been getting by just fine for years without a Walmart a mile away.

Whatever your dream, wherever it may take you, somebody has been there before; and they didn't need to import their current life and drop it right in the middle of their new life. You don't need two years worth of AA batteries just because it seemed like a great deal at Costco. You can buy new batteries anywhere when yours run dead.

FedEx is Cheap

Need part # 3KH-405-231 to fix your PX6405-D93 camcorder? Well, sit back, chillax with the locals, and wait for FedEx. You'll probably meet some new friends, have a couple unexpected adventures, and end up with a few new stories to tell.

And on that note—most people around the world and especially away from the United States are unbelievably helpful and generous with a stranger in need. Outside of government officials (and there are exceptions there as well), most local people are sympathetic and helpful when a traveler is broken down. Between locals and FedEx, there is no need to prepare for every contingency. Save that money for now—you never know what it could buy you later.

Return Fund

Another number that's nice to know from the start is what your return fund looks like. In other words, what is the minimum amount of cash you think you need to have in your pocket when you finally decide this particular mini-retirement has come to an end. Hopefully, you won't need this fund, but if for nothing else, it's good to have peace of mind because most of us do come back, whether by choice or not. Very few just head off into the sunset and never return. The return fund is insurance against living in your mother-in-law's garage when you get back.

Often—when first thinking about a return fund, people think of it in terms of how they are currently living. But what you need to remember is that on your adventure, you are going to drastically change the way you live. You will downsize your possessions, consume less, and (probably) live in a smaller space. At the end of this journey of yours, you will be a different person from the one you are today, and almost certainly you will require less to live happily than you do as you sit there reading this tonight.

Burn Rate Risk

Okay, so we've got our assets, we subtract our startup cost and we subtract our return fund and we come up with X. X is the dollar amount that we've got left for A) our burn rate, B) our investments, and C) our trading account.

The grand and central idea in this book is that we want our trading profits to equal or outpace our burn rate, A, while our investments continue to grow. If we do that, then we don't have to live off the money in B or C, our investments or trading account. If we can do that, we can keep on living the dream without setting ourselves back financially.

At this point you should be able to see that as you change your lifestyle and consumption habits you also change the amount of money you need to risk as well as the level of risk you need to take in order to maintain that lifestyle—the less you need to live happily, the less you need to risk the money you've got to support that happiness. We will say it again:

The less money you need to live happily during your adventure, the less you need to risk in the market to Live on the Margin.

Let's make this point clear: if you've got $50,000 to trade with and a burn rate of $2,500 a month you are going to need to earn a five percent return on your money each and every month to cover the burn. Cut that burn rate to $1,500 and you only need three percent. You trade smaller numbers because you need smaller numbers to cover your burn. Your risk is slashed.

The Burn is the Key

You may not have a lot of control over how much is in your bank account today, and even if you make the cuts we suggest, your forecasted total net worth on departure day is not something you can magically inflate. It is what it is. But you *can* control your burn rate—and the higher the burn rate, the higher the financial return required to continue living on the margin.

The larger the principal you have to invest and trade with, the lower the return you will need at any burn rate to sustain the burn. So how much time and risk you are going to need to take while trading depends entirely on two things—first, and most importantly, your burn rate—and second, your assets available to trade with.

If you've got a million dollars in the bank and a burn rate of $100 a day, you aren't going to need to trade much in order to cover that burn. If you have $100K to play with you are going to need to risk more—more often—in order to keep on surfing. We put together a couple fictional examples below to help ram the idea home.

Bart the Peon

Bart is a twenty-something-year-old on his third job out of college, bored to tears, who daydreams of spending his days surfing Costa Rica's best waves while living in a tiny bungalow across the dirt road from the beach. Right now, he's renting a small apartment, got $20,000 in his Fidelity trading account, a car worth a few thousand bucks, and no debt; so he's free to walk away whenever he wants.

He's figured out a burn rate of $1,200 a month and he's happy to come back to the States with nothing but the clothes on his back and a flash card full of pictures. If he does nothing but surf and eat grilled ahi, he's got enough money to mini-retire for a year and a half. Not bad at all.

On the other hand—if he is going to extend the burn, he is going to have to do some serious trading. Trading is going to be a part of his adventure—but tracking stocks, reading the news, and doing a little charting won't feel so bad when it's eighty degrees, sunny, and he knows that after a couple of hours he is going to be paddling out on smooth head-high waves.

Again, though, trading is going to take some commitment; and with a $20,000 stake and a $1,200 burn, it's going to take time. Bart needs to earn a six percent return every month in order to live this life indefinitely. Earning six percent per month is a challenge—not going to happen without a hell of a big commitment, and not without taking substantial risk.

By sitting down and trading for a few hours a month, Bart can stretch that sixteen months into two years, three years, or even more. Say he's able to earn four hundred dollars a month making just a few trades. Every three months, he's essentially bought himself another month. That little bit of extra money can help keep him in Costa Rica, on the waves, for two full years.

Bart's not going to retire for good—he's in his twenties for crying out loud—he can do this now, again in his thirties, again in his forties, and again in his fifties. Trading is not going to stretch that twenty grand out for the rest of his life, but it's going to stretch it out well beyond the sixteen months that doing nothing but surfing would.

Kelly the Exec

Now let's look at a woman who has quite a bit more money. It doesn't matter how she earned it, but Kelly is in her thirties and has $400,000 in the bank. She's got a high-paying job and coworkers that she likes, but sailing around the Caribbean for a few years has always been on her bucket list.

Kelly doesn't want to come back broke. She wants at least half of that money waiting for her in a few years so she can jump back into the fold. So, first thing first, she puts $200K into her investment account, buys a few stocks that she likes, a handful of index funds, and calls it good. Barring a total market collapse, her money should still be there, more or less, in a few years.

Next, Kelly buys a sailboat in Florida for $75,000 and puts another $25,000 of improvements into it. She deposits the $100K she has left into her trading account and sets sail. She's calculated a very generous $2,500 per month burn rate—giving herself forty months of cruising ahead.

Using the $100K to trade with Kelly is going to need to earn a 2.5% monthly return to cover her burn rate and extend her mini-retirement indefinitely. This is still going to mean she needs to make a couple of successful trades a month. It's a challenge to make a return like that in any kind of market, but it's absolutely doable.

Shoestringers

What if you don't really have any money at all? Well we hate to tell you this, but it takes money to make money in the stock market, so you are pretty much out of the *living on the margin* game. Shoestringers can't fund their adventures off of trading profits, but we don't want to end it there by saying you just plain can't live your dream.

We do know of several people who set off for an endless trip with a few hundred dollars in their pocket and as of this writing are still out traveling with a few hundred to their name. How do they do it? Some work along the way, some set down roots somewhere for a couple years at a time, some come back home for a few months each year to work. Could you do that? Probably.

Could we do that? No. We aren't the type. We like to rent cars and explore new roads when we get someplace. We like to eat out. We like to take breaks from our travels to spend time with friends and family. We got our fill of the rice, beans, and Cap'n Crunch diet back in college.

We aren't designing our entire lives around retiring at 65, but we also aren't interested in scraping by either. We like to trade to keep fuel in the tank, because who knows what we will want to do in a year or two or ten? That's just us.

Who Are You?

So you are not Bart or Kelly or Mr. and Mrs. Shoestring—but you are somewhere in between—or you are going to be somewhere in between by next season. Everyone's situation is unique, so it's time to sit down with your spreadsheets or maybe just a yellow legal pad. Write it all down—get some real numbers together. Knowing where you are is the first step in figuring out where you want to go.

- assets
- startup
- burn rate
- return fund

Figure it out. Do it now.

Basic Investing Strategies

Investing, stripped of all the bells and whistles, is simply using assets to make more assets. Hopefully you are already doing that: investing in stocks and bonds, investing in precious metals, investing in real estate, investing in your uncle's cupcake restaurant, etc. Let's take some time to analyze those investments; and instead of thinking about what is right or wrong and traditional or nontraditional about our portfolio, let's think of these things simply in terms of performance and whether they fit into our lifestyle.

Cash is King

Something we all have is cash—hopefully more than just what is in your wallet. Cash includes checking accounts, savings accounts, and trading accounts, too. You probably don't think of cash as an investment, but it is: its value can go up or down. Unfortunately due to inflation, mostly it just goes down in value; you can think of cash investment performance as stable, but slightly negative.

Yet we love being in cash! Cash is wonderful—as of this writing, it's the most liquid of all assets. The real value in cash is in the opportunities it presents. Cash allows you to trade, which of course we are going to spend a good deal of the rest of this book talking about.

We tend to think of the cash portion of our portfolio as the fuel in the tank. Without it, we can't do things. So while some people think that a cash position is wasting its ability to appreciate, we believe it's like a full tank of gas, ready to take us places, whether with trades or with travels.

Without cash or the ability to convert to cash easily, you won't be able to trade when that stock you love drops three percent on a rumor that the CEO is really a robot. You'll be certain he is actually human and that the market will eventually realize this and bounce back—but without cash you'll just be a bystander. There is a reason every backpacker has a $50 bill tucked in their bra or underwear, and why every sailboat has at least a few hundred bucks stashed behind some removable wall panel—without cash you can't move, you can't take advantage of unexpected opportunities.

Real Estate

For years we were told that buying a home was an excellent investment, but things went wrong when too many people used their house as a big passbook savings account or ATM that they could climb inside and expected to return oodles of money forever and ever. Obviously, that doesn't really work.

Here is how the investment performance of a mortgaged property really works: if home appreciation (annualized) plus any positive cash flow (neglecting depreciation) is greater than the mortgage interest rate, then it's a good investment. If it's less, it's a bad investment. If it equals interest rate, it's a bad investment. Simple, right?

The only problem with this line of reasoning is that a) you don't really know the appreciation until you sell at the market price, and b) the structures themselves are actually depreciating assets (maintenance, capital improvements, etc.), and c) they are perhaps the most illiquid of all assets and particularly sensitive to broader economic cycles.

If you do own property, an argument could be made that leveraging (mortgaging) that property at a low interest rate and using that cash for other investment purposes is a good idea, however be aware that it really depends on the performance of those other investment instruments. For example, the five year S&P return at the moment stands at 1.3%, while home prices continue to struggle to recover from the blasting they have taken during this time. So if you took money out of your home to invest in an indexed fund that matched the market, you wouldn't have made any money at all—in fact you would've lost.

Both of us own real estate (residential and commercial), so don't think that we are against it. Interest rates as of this writing are at historic lows, and holding that debt could theoretically protect us from inflation, but appreciation and positive cash flow? Not happening right now for us—performance-wise these have not been great investments.

No matter our thoughts on the subject of real estate as an investment, for the slacker looking to live on the margin, we are looking for assets that are either very liquid, or producing positive cash flow, and as of this writing, we think those opportunities in real estate are few and far between.

REITs

Real estate investment trusts are securities that sell like a stock on the major exchanges. The trust itself invests in real estate, either through owning and leasing or by holding mortgages. Equity REITs own and rent properties, while mortgage REITs hold mortgages or mortgage-backed securities. Hybrid REITS do a combination of the two.

If you really want to invest in real estate, REITs are a great way to go because they are liquid; you can trade in and out of them like stocks or options. You do want to do your research, of course, because some perform better than others.

"Retirement" Accounts

Retirement accounts today are your 401ks, IRAs, and brokerage accounts. About 40–50 years ago, when corporations and unions started realizing how vulnerable pensions were to looting during a sale or takeover, they started looking for ways to protect their workers' retirement accounts, while at the same time paying less for pension programs for a workforce that was becoming more and more mobile. Pensions became smaller and fewer, while "matching funds" programs allowed vestiture and promoted employment stability.

With the inevitable slowing savings rate, the government saw a threat to Social Security and enacted laws that allowed tax advantages for 401K and Individual Retirement Accounts (IRAs). This was a win-win for everyone looking forward to 45 years of employment followed by retirement at age 65. More responsibility was put on the shoulders of the individual worker—it was up to you to save for your future—not the corporation or government.

These really are great programs for the individual investor working for a company—you are getting free, tax-exempt money. The one downside to 401Ks and IRAs comes with penalties for taking your money out before you are 58.5 years old.

Passively Managed Investments

If you have a 401K or IRA, you are very likely investing in passively managed financial products sold to you by your broker, financial planner, or (not really sold but promoted by your) human resources manager. These are typically mutual funds based on an index. Index funds try to track (perform the same as) a market index such as the S&P 500. Basically the fund owns a basket of stocks that will mimic the return generated by the S&P 500, whether or not it's up ten percent or down ten percent on the year.

The perceived benefits to these index funds is that because they are passively managed—meaning this basket of stocks is purchased and then more or less left alone—there isn't a lot of work involved for the fund manager, and thus he is paid less. Lower management fees mean a higher return for the investor.

The problem with that reasoning is that because you are paying fees in the first place you are guaranteed to underperform the market by that much—wouldn't you just be better off buying the stocks yourself? The other more obvious problem with this approach is that these funds and fund managers are happy whether you make money or whether you lose money, so long as they've done their job and kept you within a point or so of the index they are charged with following.

Why would we ever be happy with losing money? Our goal is and should be to make money in any market, up or down. There is no rule that says we can only profit in a rising market. It may be easier, and trading systems may be skewed that way, but it doesn't have to be.

Actively Managed Investments

Active management funds are, obviously, the opposite of passive management. Active management funds do not try to match the market; they try to outperform it by actively trading in it. Just to be clear, investing in an actively managed fund doesn't mean that you are actively managing it—someone else is. He or she is called the fund manager.

Fund performance is directly dependent on the skills of the manager in charge. Seems obvious that these funds would all have managers fighting tooth and nail for the highest returns, right? They've got millions and billions of investor dollars under their control. But the truth is that many of these managers routinely underperform the market. Additionally, while they are underperforming they are charging the investor higher fees than a passively managed fund would.

Even worse is that a large percentage of these actively managed funds are actually considered "closet indexers." These are funds that market themselves as actively managed but are really doing nothing more than matching the stock index they are benchmarking. Remember, the fund manager gets paid regardless.

So while you may hope and expect that your fund manager is reacting to market conditions on a day-to-day or hour-to-hour basis, in reality he may very well be doing nothing more than playing with ten or twenty percent of the funds' money while the vast majority sits in the account attempting to match the index it's based on. Remember, he doesn't want to lose, so he is going to manage his risk to the minimum sold to you as the customer.

Another obvious downfall of actively managed funds is that as an investor you are now "trading" fund managers as opposed to trading stocks. You are searching for the right manager, the one who will be a winner. And how would you know who is the best? Online rankings? Magazine articles? Will those resources also tell you when the fund manager is a drunk on antidepressants who just had his house foreclosed on? It might be helpful if they did, but that's not going to happen, so you and I will be doing nothing but projecting future performance on past performance. Shaky ground.

ETFs

Exchange-traded funds are really popular these days, because you can trade the actual fund yourself as they have shares and a share price. The ETF holds assets like stocks, commodities, and bonds, which is a lot like a mutual fund; however, ETFs can hold assets that mutual funds cannot—like agricultural commodities and even gold bars.

One of the biggest benefits to ETFs is transparency—you can see pretty easily what they are holding. Most ETFs track an index such as a stock or bond index, so they tend to move with less volatility than any one of their components—that can be really good if you are a conservative trader and want to get some "diversification" without buying little bits and pieces here and there.

Most people don't understand that the ETF shares themselves are actually only bought and sold by "authorized participants" on the open market, and then only in "creation units," which are huge blocks of thousands of ETF shares. So the only parties directly trading an ETF are big institutional investors. If you are the little guy (the retail investor), you can then buy or sell shares of these ETFs from a retail broker on the secondary market, but not from the ETF itself.

All by themselves, ETFs are fine investment vehicles; but for our purposes, they don't make sense. We want to have direct knowledge and understanding about where our money is working, and with an ETF, researching the underlying assets held would be just too time consuming.

"Retail" Investing and Trading

Trading securities is at the heart of all of the strategies in this book, and if you are reading this book, you are most likely a "retail" investor. By trading securities, you are in full control of your investments from purchase to sale, and the responsibility is 100% yours. This is perhaps the best opportunity the individual has to bring his or her own skill to bear in the market to try and maximize profits, and you guessed it: *live on the margin*.

We'll state it here and in several other places in this book that there is a vast difference between investing and trading. Investing generally refers to purchasing a security with a long-term perspective—you are not interested in the day-to-day and month-to-month ups and downs but rather you are interested in the *company's* performance over years.

Trading on the other hand is a proactive strategy focused on profiting from the intermediate ups and downs of a company's stock over days, weeks, and maybe even months. The two of us are both investors and traders—we hold both short and long-term positions. This book really has very little to say about investing. The highest potential profits over the time scales we care about are in trading.

There are many types of securities—such as equities like stocks and bonds—as well as derivatives. Bonds are debt instruments—you are basically lending your money to an entity. Bond trading is something we know very little about, and while investing in bonds can be a useful way of keeping your money "safe," the returns are so incredibly low, that we don't usually bother. That's not to say they don't have a place in your portfolio. Talk to your investment advisor about whether bonds are right for you.

The two of us focus almost all of our investing attention on trading stocks and derivatives; specifically derivatives called options, which we dedicate an entire chapter to in this book.

IPOs

Initial public offerings (IPOs) get a lot of media attention, but we don't play them anymore. Nick used to trade them on their opening days back in the late 90s when it seemed that almost every tech IPO was guaranteed to move up at least a bit in its first couple of sessions. The last time Pat traded an IPO was

Visa back in 2008, which as of this writing is the largest IPO of all time. Even then, he was picking up shares to hold as an investment, not trading in and out on a "pop." He held for a couple of years.

Why don't we play the IPO game anymore? Well, the investment bankers ruined it for us. Investment banks are the entities who bring a private company "public," and they have every reason to make as much money as possible right out of the gate, then trade out as quick as they can—and guess who sets the rules on when they can get out of their positions? Yep. So the investment banks have learned that they want to set the initial stock price as high as possible for the opening day, and many times, these prices are completely unrealistic judging by where the company's earnings or potential earnings are at. So instead of seeing the stock price spike higher, many IPOs in the last couple of years have dropped lower, especially in the tech sector.

Sure we could sell them short if we think they are headed south, but since they are brand new public companies, their performance is going to be unpredictable anyway, so why take an uneducated gamble?

Value vs. Growth

When you hear people talk about "value" or "growth" stocks, what they are really saying is, "This stock is going up slowly, while this other one is going up very quickly." The same goes for "value investors" vs. "growth investors." Value investors buy things that they think will go up rather predictably and may pay dividends, while the growth investor likes stocks with greater volatility.

The strategies outlined in this book focus primarily on stocks that are going up or down more quickly than the "value" stocks. We like volatility; we like growth; we like risk. As you will see later, this really comes to bear on which sectors and which industries we like to trade.

Dividends

When a company is making money and has a stable business model and forecast or wants to reduce their tax liability, often they will pay their shareholders a dividend. This is paid out on a per-share basis and will vary based on how profitable a company has been over the previous period, usually the previous quarter. For example, XYZ might pay $.50 per share to its shareholders. Now if you have a high enough net worth, living off of your dividends can be really nice. But if you need $1,000 per month, you will need to own a lot of shares, which in the case of XYZ, could tie up a lot of capital.

Commodities

Commodities fall mainly into three categories: agriculture, metals, and energy. The agricultural industry is heavily dependent on the weather. During the North American crop growing season, the markets can swing markedly based solely on things as micro as last night's rainfall in the Dubuque, Iowa, area.

Metals are often viewed as "safe haven" investments in times of economic uncertainty, stock market declines, high inflation, and a host of other scary scenarios. Quite frankly, for us, trying to put a value on a hunk of metal is akin to choosing black or red on the roulette table. Over the long term, we may choose correctly fifty percent of the time; but we're slackers, long-term isn't part of our plan.

Meanwhile, energy—mainly oil and gas—experiences price swings based on wide ranging macroeconomic forces. Many of these occur halfway around the world in the middle of the night back here in the Western Hemisphere. A slacker could become sleep deprived tracking this market. These are the types of headlines you'll read trading oil:

Crude-oil futures fell slightly in Asian trading Friday, easing after an overnight rally prompted by gasoline supply disruptions in the U.S. and rising tension in the Middle East.

Crude rallied 4.1% in the U.S. Thursday, erasing losses earlier in the week, as a spike in gasoline prices following a fire at Exxon Mobil Corp.'s massive Baytown refinery in Texas spilled over into the crude market.

If you plan to trade crude oil, you can count on seeing "rising tension in the Middle East" headlines on an almost daily basis. Unless you have the mobile number of our good friend Mahmoud Ahmadinejad over there in Iran, you probably won't know what the hell rising tension means.

Commodities trading does not cross over into our slacker lifestyle very well. We find the markets to be more difficult to keep tabs on than we do equities, because there is less information available. It is also much more macroeconomic than most individual stocks; so that even if there is sufficient data available, it's often so widespread in nature that it's difficult to grasp in a short time period. We find commodities trading to be extremely risky for those not investing considerable time in studying these markets. So while there is no good reason (other than saving yourself time) not to trade commodities, there is no pressing reason to trade them either.

Allocation

With all of these investing choices in front of you the next questions are: What should I do? How should I spread my investments out? How much should I risk and where?

We can't tell you what to risk or where to invest, but we can help you decide how much you need to risk in order to live the lifestyle you want for a year, five years, or whatever your goal is. If you are really feeling like you need to put together an overall life/retirement/financial strategy that integrates your mini-retirement, you should probably look to other resources like books, the web, or a financial advisor.

Nick and his wife worked with a financial planner before their first cruise, and found it incredibly valuable. They made it clear from the very beginning that they were not interested in buying any of his investment products, which changed the conversation from a sales pitch to a goal-setting strategy session.

When it came time to end that first mini-retirement, my wife and I (Nick) were able to step back into "regular" life for a time and participate in the housing bubble. We bought and sold two homes between 2004 and 2007 at significant profit. Without meeting with the advisor before setting out on that first adventure, we probably would have spent even more on the boat and returned to "real life" (temporarily) without enough liquid assets to be able to make high double-digit profits on real estate over the next three years.

If nothing else, a financial advisor can help you figure out what you might want your return fund to be, and that's a very nebulous concept for someone who thinks they are going to take off on a never-ending life of adventure.

"Diversification"

*"Well let's see Frank, you're forty-five—that means you should have forty-five percent of your portfolio in bonds; good ol' government bonds; good as gold Frank. Better even. Then you'll want fifty-five percent in a **diversified** pool of stocks, yes sir. **Diversify**, that way you won't get killed in that there stock market where the gamblers peddle their wares. Nope you'll be covered all the way around. You want to be **all in** Frank, but **diversified,** see, so that even when those fancy website stocks fall you'll still have good ol' General Electric there to pay the light bill."*

The above has been said *ad nauseam* in the asset management business, and if twenty years from now you want to look back and say, "Look there, I made five percent a year—not bad, not bad at all. Better than a stick in the eye," then you go right ahead and follow that advice. Or if you've got a million in the bank and a monthly nut of three grand, then yes, do it, diversify and ignore what the market is doing—have fun with everything else. We're jealous.

But that's not you, and that's not us—for most people, true diversification is a myth.

The Myth

Let us tell you right now, you will never be diversified. If you've got a million dollars or more, you might be able to achieve some level of diversification; but the average Joe with $25,000 in his account would only be diversified by buying one or two shares of everything, thus eating up all his wealth in commissions.

You may think that if you have a 401K and can choose which funds to invest in, you are diversified. "Well, I have 25% in my XYZ International Growth Fund, and 40% in my ABC Domestic Value Fund, and 35% in my QRS Precious Metals Fund, so of course I am diversified." Maybe, but probably not. Your funds probably own the same stocks, or REITs, or Index funds as one another. So what you end up owning are funds that own other funds that own the same assets at the end of the day. Not only are there a lot of management fees eating away at your profits; but if they own the same underlying assets, that isn't diversification at all. That's a shell game!

Building Wealth vs. Living on the Margin

When it comes down to figuring out your own financial goals and laying out your portfolio, you need to take the view from 30,000 feet and know yourself and where your insecurities lie. The strategies we talk about in this book are about trading to create enough income so that you can live off of the money that you do have, or to extend your burn to continue your adventures for a while longer. We are not trying to "build wealth," we are trying to "live on the margin."

Getting Started

We debated whether or not this even needs to be said, but—yes you do need to have steady, reliable internet service when you want to start trading. There is no "set it and forget it," in our trading strategies. If you find the perfect weather window to make that trek to the top of the volcano or dash across the ocean to the next island, you need to close out any trades. Long-term stock investments—those you may be able to let ride while you are offline—but otherwise, you are going to need to be connected to trade. When the connection is gone, you are out of all your trades—no exceptions. So how do you go about this trading thing?

This chapter is going to focus on some of the very basic mechanics involved in making your first trades. We realize that everyone is going to start from a different place; and that if you have some experience trading, what follows is going to be a little boring. We have to address a few of the basic questions we've received over the years or else the rest of the book isn't going to make a lot of sense for some people.

If this is new for you, don't feel dumb—none of it is as complicated as it looks. You just need to get some vocabulary down and you'll be able to navigate the trading world a little easier.

Markets

It seems obvious, but most people don't really know how markets work and those that do tend to take advantage of those who don't. It happens every day.

A market is a place where people buy and sell things, right? Farmers market, corner market, stock market, housing market, etc. You can also be "in the market" for a new car or a new wife or a job. The market can be soft, or it can be a bull market, or a bear market. The market can be up or it can be down, or even moving sideways. There are marketers and there are market makers. The market as most people think about it is kind of a nebulous concept.

> *"The market" is actually many things, however what a market actually DOES, is always the same thing: it finds value and creates a price.*

Market Participants

The stock market works differently than the grocery market with its fixed prices. It's also not like a home purchase where you have an asking price, an offer price, and negotiation to find a price somewhere in the middle. The stock market is a little bit more like an *auction* but with a lot more buyers and sellers involved.

There are basically three different market participants in the stock market:

- Market Makers. These are the people and firms who provide the liquidity in the marketplace, which means that they are required to buy and sell when nobody else will. They "make" the market.

- Electronic communication networks (ECNs) are computerized order placing systems, and just about everyone is using ECNs these days in some respect—even the big guys. ECNs and trading algorithms have revolutionized the market over the last 15 years. The speed of their trade executions has meant that trading firms have actually moved their physical servers closer to the physical market in order to try to get a millisecond or two of advantage.

- Wholesale firms. If you use an online brokerage to trade, it is very likely that they sell their orders to a wholesale firm who actually executes the trade through an ECN.

At a normal auction, the selling price is determined by the highest possible bid from a buyer. Imagine an auction in which you have a whole bunch of sellers standing around selling the same paintings at their highest asking price and a whole bunch of buyers standing around trying to buy one or more of those paintings at the lowest possible price—this is what is happening in the stock market all the time.

Market Orders and Volatility

In the stock market, there are several types of orders (which we will talk more about below) you can place to make a trade: market orders, limit orders, trailing stop orders, etc. We'll just briefly tell you that a limit order is where you tell your broker that you will only buy or sell if the stock price reaches a certain number, i.e. "I will buy XYZ stock if it gets down to $10," for example. A market order on the other hand is where you tell your broker, "I want to buy XYZ stock, just get me the best price you can."

So what ends up happening is that a lot of buyers are simply using market orders—they are saying that they will pay whatever they have to pay to get the stock they want or sell at whatever price they can get. This leads to volatility—meaning that every time someone tells their broker to buy or sell at the best price they can, the price moves up or down, and the transaction gets done without any haggling or negotiation at all.

Market orders are executed at the bid (if selling) or ask (if buying) price, which drives prices up and down with every trade.

Imagine if this applied to home purchases. You would basically be telling your real estate agent, "Buy me that house—pay whatever price they are asking—right now." Alternatively if you were selling your house, you'd tell your agent, "I don't care what you get for the house, just sell it for the best price you can get today." Obviously, if all (or at least some) of the buyers and sellers are doing the same thing (buying or selling at the best price they can right at that moment) all the time, you can see that the final price paid for this house, and ones exactly like it, is going to go up and down every time a sale goes through.

Sounds a little wild, doesn't it? That's the stock market.

Exchanges

Trading a stick of gum for a tic-tac is the same basic idea as trading cash in a trading account for a stock or derivative. There is no need for a formal place where we can meet to trade money for a house or a piece of gum for a tic-tac, but when it comes to trading abstractions of real things like companies, we need to have a formal place with formal rules. We call these places of trading *exchanges*.

So you don't trade stocks in the stock market, you trade stocks on a *stock exchange*. You don't trade futures or options in a futures or options market, you trade them on an *options* or *futures exchange*. You don't trade soy futures in the futures market, you trade them on a *commodities exchange*. You get the idea.

Stock Exchanges

A stock exchange is probably what you are most familiar with: the New York Stock Exchange (NYSE), the NASDAQ, London Stock Exchange, Shanghai Stock Exchange, etc. Stock exchanges trade securities. Securities are financial instruments tied to the public companies listed on the exchange. Securities are one of three things:

- debt, like bonds
- equities, like stocks
- derivatives, like futures or options

So on stock exchanges, you can trade any of the above. Futures and options are traded on options and futures exchanges, but since they are so closely related to their underlying equities, there really isn't a physical difference at the exchanges—it all happens in the same place.

MAKING A TRADE

Up until a couple decades ago, the individual investor/trader (also known as a "retail" investor) didn't have any direct access to the public exchanges. If you wanted to buy or sell a stock or commodity or derivative of some sort, you called your "stockbroker," on the phone. Depending on what level of advice he was giving you (and you were paying for), you either said something on the order of "What do you think about XYZ stock?" or simply,

"Please buy twenty shares of XYZ." Your broker then used the cash you had on account with him to make the purchase.

How did he do that? Well, he would make a phone call to his trading desk (or key it into a terminal), they would make a call to their floor trader and then he (or she) would actually execute the trade and fill the order, which by the way was placed with a "market maker" (which is the entity providing liquidity in the actual trade). Each of these middlemen served a purpose and had to get paid, and the broker had to make a pretty large commission to pay all of the people downstream to actually execute that trade. Even today there are stockbrokers who use this antiquated model and charge $120 per trade, which is absolutely ludicrous.

Today, it works a little differently, and online platforms have taken away the need for so many middlemen which has lowered the cost of a trade substantially. With an online broker (and by the way, all brick and mortar brokerages have online platforms), you keep money in a trading account which you can then access through an online interface. Typically, these user interfaces are very slick—you can see research, charts, news, quotes, option chains, etc., etc., all in one place in an internet browser window. When you decide you want to buy or sell something, it's very straightforward, and is as simple as hitting a "buy" or "sell" button.

Brokerages

If the stock market is a grocery store and the market makers are the checkers, then the brokerages are standing at the checkout making the actual purchases on your behalf. Which brokerage to choose is a personal decision, but there are many great options. We have experience with all of the following:

- Fidelity
- Vanguard
- E-Trade
- TD Ameritrade
- OptionsHouse
- TradeStation

We could try to do a comparison between them, but by the time you read these words, we are sure that their features will change, their trading commissions will change, and their designs will change. It's probably best to do a little googling and decide for yourself—they all offer pretty much the same features.

Requirements

As an individual investing and trading your own money, there are no licenses required. You don't need any degrees or certifications of any kind. All you need is cash in a trading account. How much cash? Most brokerage accounts have minimum balances, but not all. Fidelity requires $2,500 minimum, TD Ameritrade requires none, etc. If you want to trade on margin, your brokerage will probably ask you if you have trading experience, and the minimum balance will likely be a bit higher. If your trading will fit the "pattern day trader" definition of more than four day trades in a five business day period, you will need at least $25,000 in a margin account, but there is no minimum for a cash account.

Trading Accounts

Brokerages offer several different types of trading accounts: cash, margin, option (a type of margin account), and IRA trading accounts.

Cash accounts are pretty straightforward. You transfer some cash from your checking or savings account into a trading account; and you can buy stocks, bonds, mutual funds, ETFs, or other investments. When you hit "buy" on the screen, they will show you how much the trade is going to cost; and when you confirm, that amount will be deducted from your account. When you sell an equity, that sum (minus any commission) is deposited back into your cash account—hopefully at a profit. Most of the online interfaces have really slick accounting to show your positions, whether you are up or down, by how much, a history of your trades, etc., etc., etc.

To trade any leveraged financial instruments like futures or options, you will probably need a *margin account.* Margin accounts are where you can use some of the broker's money to make an individual trade. They are going to lend you a certain percentage more money than you actually keep on account which increases your buying power. If the broker sees that you are overleveraged, they may make a *margin call,* and force you to reconcile your account. Neither of us usually end up trading on margin however, even though we do use margin accounts. While the broker would be happy to allow us to trade $50,000 in a $25,000 account; we don't often need to, so we don't.

Options accounts allow you to trade options. There are generally different levels, the most basic of which allows you to buy *naked* calls and puts. The next level usually allows writing *covered* calls and puts. And further up the chain is an account that will allow you to *write* naked calls and puts. We have a whole chapter dedicated to trading options, so if this vocabulary is foreign to you, be patient, we'll be going through it in detail later on.

IRA (Individual Retirement Account) trading accounts are a good way to trade with money you won't need until you retire for good. You can't usually trade any derivatives like options, but you can trade and profit without realizing any (or at least less) capital gains tax. These accounts aren't appropriate for the strategies in this book—we are talking about trading and living at least partially off that income, not waiting until age 58.5 for access to our money.

Level II Quotes

Most quotes on Bloomberg.com or Yahoo Finance or CNN Money or any of the major news sites are now given in real time, but check the fine print—

some may be on a 20 minute delay. Online brokerages are going to show you everything happening with a stock and its price in real time, as well. In addition you can easily see the bid, ask, last price, as well as trading volume and endless other fundamental and technical tools. With this data, you've got everything you need to place a trade.

For highly technical day traders who want to know a bit more about what is going on second to second, you can subscribe to a substantially more expensive data feed called *Level II Quotes.* These will give you an edge up on other retail investors because you will see more information about *who* is making what bids and offers and in what quantities on individual equities.

If you are trading in and out of positions on the order of minutes or seconds apart and trying to profit on pennies of price change, you need Level II. If not, then you don't. Our strategies don't require Level II. Too stressful and time consuming for slackers.

Types of Trades

We are not talking about trading strategies quite yet here; what we mean is what types of trade orders we can give to our brokerage when we want to buy or sell something. It doesn't matter whether we are talking about calling the broker on the phone or trading online—these are the instructions we are giving when we say, "Buy," or "Sell."

Market order. This is where you are simply buying or selling at whatever the current price is (or the current price is when the trade is actually executed). If you see the stock is trading at $35.80, and you place a sell market order, you are saying that you will accept whatever the price is when it gets into the hands of the seller (market maker). That price may be a little higher or a little lower than $35.80. These are the easiest orders for the broker to fill, so sometimes they are cheaper than others.

Limit order. This is where you are saying, "I will buy X number of ABC shares at $Y price," or, "I will only sell if the price gets up to $Z dollars." If the price never gets down to your buy price, your order won't get executed. If it never gets up to your sell price, it won't get executed. Another thing that can happen is if the stock rises or falls way above or way below your limit price, it will get executed at your limit price.

Sometimes limit orders don't get filled because the broker is obligated to fill them in the order they receive them. So they may fill other orders ahead of you before the price rises or falls beyond your limit. Brokerages can't guarantee a limit order will be filled.

Stop order. In essence, you are saying you want to buy or sell whenever a stock reaches a threshold price. When it does, the stop order becomes a market order, so the actual price can be above or below your stop order price. This is probably the best way to ensure your order gets filled when a stock is quite volatile and you don't want to sit there watching for it.

Stop Limit order. This is the same as a stop order; but instead of converting to a market order when the price is reached, it converts to a limit order. And like a limit order, it may or may not get filled.

Here is how it's different than a simple stop order. Let's say you place a sell stop limit order for $31 on ABC stock with a limit of $30. The stock then proceeds to fall to $31, which converts it to a sell limit order and your order will be filled at the next best available price as long it's above $30. In the case of a sell stop limit order, if the price were to immediately dip down to $29, the sell order will not get executed until it gets back above $30.

Trailing Stop order. This is the best way to put a limit on a maximum possible loss without setting a limit on the maximum possible gain. A sell trailing stop order sets the stop price at a fixed price below the market price with a trailing amount. If the market price rises, the stop price rises by the trailing amount, but if the market price falls, the stop loss price doesn't change. If the stop price is hit, it becomes a market order. A buy trailing stop order is the opposite, and is most useful in a falling market.

How Much to Trade?

When we are getting down to the nitty-gritty about trading, we get this question more than any other: *How much should I trade?* The answer is so individual that it makes any specific answer for any specific person almost completely irrelevant, but we'll tell you a little bit about how we decide how much we are going to actively trade. What is right or wrong for you is going to be different, so you have to make up your own mind here.

You need to think long and hard about your own financial and life situation and remember that while you do hope to win—that your trade is a profitable one—it may not be, and you could lose. So never, ever trade any money that you could not afford to lose. At best, it's too stressful, leading to poor judgment and poor decisions; at worst you will lose money that you would need for more important things, like eating.

Potheads

We employ a "pot" approach to answer the question of how much to trade. What this means is that we have each separately decided that at any one time we are going to limit ourselves to actively trading $X, in total. Pat's $X is probably not the same as Nick's $X whose $X is different than yours. You should never let yourself be influenced by how someone else trades. As we've said many times, how much to risk is a very individual question.

This magical number X is not fixed; it can go up or down depending on our own needs, our total current portfolio value, and most importantly, the current market conditions.

How much should $X be for you? We can't answer that—only you can, but the maximum amount should probably be the maximum amount you can afford to lose without causing permanent financial damage or undue stress.

For one person that $X might be $100 and for another it might be $1,000,000.

Never actively trade money that you can't afford to lose. The risk of loss is real, and risking too much will lead to overly-emotional decisions and bad trades.

How does pot allocation work? Let's say, for example, that you have decided that your pot has $10,000 in it (yes, it would suck to lose $10K, but you would recover). That means that the total cash you are willing to put into all of your active trades is $10K. If you purchase $4,000 of XYZ stock—now you have $6,000 left in the pot to trade with. Let's say you sell half of your XYZ stock for no gain or loss the next day. Well, you now have $8,000 in your pot. Yep, pretty simple; nothing novel to this approach yet.

Now let's say that the next day, XYZ doubles and you sell your remaining position for $4,000. How much do you have in your pot? No, not $12,000—you have still have $10,000 in your pot. Remember $X is the total amount allocated for active trading. Just because you profited from that $10,000 does not necessarily mean that you should then increase your total actively traded assets. $X has nothing to do with profit or loss.

If your entire $10K pot is tied up in one or more trades, but you see an opportunity that can't be missed; you'll be tempted to increase the size of your pot. But should you? This is a much more difficult question to answer, isn't it? Because instead of limiting your risk to the $10K, you are asking yourself whether you want to increase your overall portfolio risk. That is a completely different decision, and one that needs even more scrutiny.

The decision of how much money to put into any one trade should be completely separate from the decision of how much you should risk in active trading at any one time.

We like this simple pot strategy—because limiting your pot to $X means that you are comparing trading opportunities against one another, rather than fighting with yourself about whether or not you are taking too much risk overall. The former is healthy and productive. The latter is a waste of time and energy.

How little can I start with?

We get some form of this question all the time: How little can I start out with? I only have $1,000 to play with, what should I do? Or, I've got $10K to my name; is that enough to trade with? First of all, let us tell you that it doesn't matter what you have in your bank account or what your total net worth is; we ALL have to ask ourselves how much we should be trading with, and the answer changes all the time.

Here is a (hopefully) somewhat more satisfying answer. Money comes and money goes throughout one's life. You may have $1,000 to your name now, but you may have $50K in a year or two or ten. Wouldn't it be smart to "learn" how to trade and profit while playing with $1,000 rather than $50K? Trading is not black magic; it's a skill that can be learned and applied, and the best way to learn is by actually doing.

So if you are toiling away at your dead-end job and have $1,000 in your account, yes, you can trade with it. Many brokerages have $0 account minimums. Will you make much money on your $1,000 trade? No, you won't make much, but will you be learning a new skill that may serve you well when you do eventually have a little more cash? We think so. And you might just turn that $1,000 into $2,000, which makes it easier to make that next thousand.

How many trades?

As a little fish in a big ocean—and especially as a slacker who hopes to minimize the actual time spent trading—we think that it's a bad idea to have more than two or three active positions open at any one time. Four maximum. It is just too hard to keep track of each one. You'll see "professional" traders on TV and in movies with a bank of ten LCD screens with twenty different stocks, but that's all for show. Plus, think of how hard it would be to travel with that many screens anyway.

Limiting your positions is actually easier than you might think; because if you follow the strategies in this book, it's going to be hard to find more than one or two opportunities at any one time anyway.

Paper Trading

There are a lot of tools available for the first-timer to practice trading without using any real money at all. There are trading clubs, computer software, and online teaching tools and most online brokerages allow you to keep a dummy account that uses fake money to practice with. We think that using these before ever using real money is a great idea. Even just knowing what buttons to push to execute a trade and exactly how your online brokerage displays your position and tracks your performance is going to make real trading less stressful. So go ahead and paper trade for a while before you use real funds.

We do, however, have to tell you that trading with "play" money has definite limitations. So much of trading performance is based in personal psychology, and you won't have a chance to really learn about your emotions and reactions until you have real money in a trade. For example, if you start to see a loss on a fake position, you are much more likely to hold on and see if it turns in your favor. However, if you are down a few hundred dollars on a real trade, every cell in your body is going to be screaming, "sell...Sell...SELL... SELLLL!!!!" Same thing happens with winners in fake money accounts. *Let it ride* becomes the motto when the money isn't real. At that point, paper trading just becomes a game.

When Pat first started out as a pit reporter at the Minneapolis Grain Exchange, he would listen as the clueless goofs around him paper traded as if they were standing face-to-face with the guys in the pits. "I would've bought those at 605 from Lee and made a killing. I'd be up $2,000 right now." These pit reporters were simply playing a game—a game that had no relation to reality. Pat wasn't immune to it either. He made money day after day in his head, but not until his hard earned cash was backing real trades did he realize just how difficult cutting off losers and riding winners really was.

As we'll talk about later in our section about selective potential past performance (SPPP), the whole, "I would of made $X if I had done Y," is something all traders are prone to ponder. It's fiction though, and as we'll talk about in the Trading Psychology chapter, it introduces biases.

Trading with real money is going to teach you a lot more about trading than paper ever could.

Paying the Piper

So you've done good and made a bit of money in the markets. Awesome! But your country needs you...to pay taxes! We aren't going to get into a long discussion about how to decide what country to keep your bank account in or strategies for minimizing taxes. What we will tell you is that if you are a United States citizen living abroad but making money in the U.S. markets or otherwise, you will still owe taxes to Uncle Sam. How much? Well, tax law seems to change every year, so it's fruitless trying to reproduce the rules here in this book.

We will tell you this much: we never make trading decisions based on taxes. Holding investments over a year normally changes the rate from short-term to long-term capital gains, but holding XYZ stock for a year and a day just so the rate will fall from 30% to 15% (as an example—these rates depend on several factors)? We've never made a decision based on that. For the trading strategies outlined in this book, we will only be concerned with short-term capital gains.

Accounting

Our online brokerages make accounting very easy. All online trading platforms include sophisticated account management interfaces that allow you to transfer money in and out very easily. You can parse total return into daily, weekly, monthly, and yearly performance. We can export spreadsheets to hand off to our accountant, or in Pat's case, to import into his tax preparation software.

Trading Strategies for a Slacker

So we've established two things: you are or are going to become a Slacker for a while (or maybe forever), and you've figured out just how much this adventure is going to cost you. Your friends back home are going to believe that money is just appearing in your pocket like magic. To them, you are a magician with a bottomless pocket.

So Mr. Magic Slacker, we need to decide what kind of trading you are going to do—what kind of magic you are going to perform. But even before that, we have to lay the foundation. What stocks are you going to trade? How are you going to buy them? How does all this work? What's the trick?

Trading vs. Investing

Investing is buying a stock and keeping it for an extended period of time—at least six months, or more likely, years. Both of us are long-term investors in a few select companies, so we don't completely poo-poo a buy-and-hold strategy. There are companies we believe in so strongly that we are happy to weather the occasional corrections because we believe over years and years and years, these stocks will pay for new boats and college funds. But "buy and hold" as an overall financial strategy? Not enough return for us.

When you **buy and hold** stock in your portfolio, you are bound to have some winners. Over the long-haul, say twenty years, *all* of your trades may even become winners—if for no other reason than inflation has put more money into the market, regardless of economic growth. There's no disputing that after all those years, you likely will have made money. But how much money? Enough to live off of month to month?

Face it, you need a lot of dough invested in a buy-and-hold strategy to be able to simply live off dividends and the proceeds you take whenever you feel the need to infuse your bank account with a bit of cash—there's that word again —if you want to do anything with it, it has to be cash.

"Crock of Shit"

In a 2011 interview, a t-shirt and tennis shoe wearing Mark Cuban (successful entrepreneur and NBA team owner) famously announced to an obviously unsuspecting *Wall Street Journal* interviewer, "Diversification is for idiots." This revelation came almost immediately after stating, "Buy and hold is a crock of shit."

"BUY AND HOLD IS A CROCK OF SHIT."

Exactly! Now, Mark Cuban is our kind of guy. Our reasoning, and his, is that in order to be a successful trader you need to be liquid. When the market is crashing, you don't want to be the guy worrying about how to get out; you want to be the guy trying to figure out the best way to get in.

If you are in cash or can go to cash with a click of a mouse, then you are liquid and can take advantage of opportunities. If you are in managed funds through a 401K, you are three phone calls, two faxed forms, half a day on the internet, and two business days of wire transfers (at best) to get liquid and get out or get in. A lot can happen in that amount of time. Mutual funds aren't very liquid! (We do acknowledge that ETFs are a good alternative to mutual funds because they can be traded on the open market; but beware, ETFs are traded by retail investors on a secondary market.)

However, when you're holding a large chunk of your portfolio in cash you are that guy who gets out when the market is tanking. You can watch the market crater without the psychological baggage. You can sit back and analyze what is happening with a detached calm, watching your favorite stocks and looking to pounce when they've reached attractive levels. It's much easier as a cash-holding trader to be the guy buying low, instead of the guy panic selling at the same low.

Active Trading

We're not saying *never* buy and hold, *never* invest, but we are saying be leery of it as a way to *live on the margin* unless you have a very very large investment portfolio. If that's working for what you want to do in your life, then stick with it. If not, you need to be more proactive. We are going to become traders—our own money managers if you will. And as managers we have to start by picking our roster.

You Are Smart

Our number one trading tenet is that you only invest or trade in companies that you love, understand, and use or interact with on a regular basis. As a Slacker, this is ideal because you do not want to be spending your days analyzing company balance sheets or trying to decipher just what in the hell it is that the company you are trading even does to turn a profit. There are well over 6,000 companies listed on the New York Stock Exchange and NASDAQ. You can't possibly expect to understand more than a tiny handful of those.

You want to find ten companies whose products or services are a regular part of your everyday life. You have to be able to decipher the noise from the market; and 95% of it is noise, just like static on the radio. We need to know that the companies we are investing or trading in are good companies, with good products or services. With this solid basis, you'll be more able to take advantage of short-term price fluctuations and turn your insights and beliefs into successful trades.

Opportunities Are Everywhere

In 2009, Pat and his wife were traveling throughout Europe in their 1958 VW bus. Not just traveling in it, but living in it—full-on Slacker style. At the time they were finding that everywhere they went, companies were still trying to charge an arm and a leg for wireless internet. Everyone but McDonald's that is—apparently the only free WiFi in Europe. So when they needed to get online, or when it was rainy crappy weather, they would pull into Macca's and relax for a while with a soda and a fully-charged laptop.

Their timing coincided with a widespread redesign of Mickey D's restaurants as well as the introduction of coffee drinks. They noticed while they were there that the coffee drinks were really selling and that the food was being served hot and fresh, unlike experiences in the past. In fact, while living in Chicago they had completely written McDonald's off. The restaurants had been so bad so often, that they just stopped eating there completely. But now it felt like the chain as a whole was turning a corner, and they liked what they saw. That's when Pat bought his first shares of McDonald's (MCD).

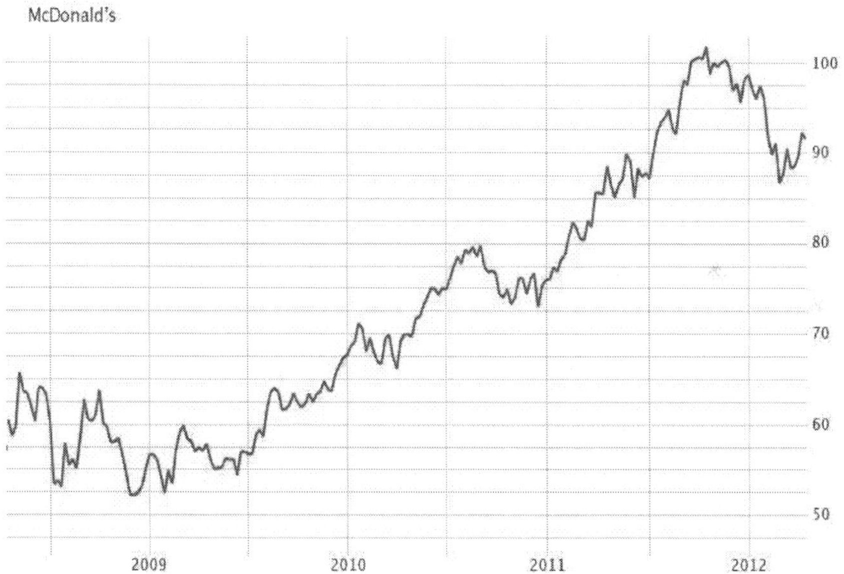

[fig 9.1]

Since then MCD has performed wonderfully, going from about sixty dollars a share in 2009 to a hundred dollars two years later—a tidy return.

What Pat likes best about it is that he still eats there regularly and will be able to discern for himself when he doesn't feel the company is progressing or performing to the same standards as when he first invested.

As of today, Pat still likes the maker of the Big Mac. But this isn't love. If the day comes he'll have no problem breaking up. "It isn't me, it's *you,*" he'll tell Ronald as he clicks the sell button. He has already done it with Burger King. But who knows, maybe one of these days he'll be wowed by a Whopper again. Pat's body is a glutton for punishment—a true wonder of genetics.

Nick, on the other hand prefers a nuts, twigs, and tofu diet (not really), and not only wouldn't be caught dead eating a McMeatsubstitute burger, but would never invest in the company. It's not because of ethical beliefs, he simply doesn't have much experience with the product and isn't able to keep tabs on the company's boots-on-the-ground performance. Investing in MCD would be a mistake for him.

Now if In-N-Out Burgers Inc. ever went public, Nick would sell his entire portfolio to join in the IPO. He loves those burgers, always goes "animal style" and the fries aren't bad either. Sadly, In-N-Out is private, and doesn't seem to have any plans to go public, but if they ever do, Nick will be first in line.

Don't get fancy!

Who do you think you are? Warren Buffett? You don't have a team of a hundred analysts dissecting every company on the planet. You don't have experts (with your best interest at heart) sitting down to explain to you how or what the hell Deutschland Distribution and Finance Development Corporation does to make money or how the new Softwood Lumber Agreement will affect bilateral trade between U.S. and Canadian timber mills. Unless of course you use and understand Pacific Northwest forest products companies. That kind of analysis takes too much horsepower, and you don't have it.

No, we have to be smarter, and to be smart we have to stop trying to *act* smart. We have to stop investing in companies we don't understand.

The real problem for most Americans trying to dip their toes into trading/investing their own money is that they dip them by watching Jim Cramer—a professional with a huge team working under him to find and highlight obscure companies so that he can talk as if he knows everything about their inner workings. You think he knows all about those companies off the top of his head? Now, Jim is a smart guy, but he has producers serving up lobs when they start taking phone calls. He is such a great showman that he makes it look like he's all-knowing and all-seeing, but a lot of that information is fed into his earpiece. Booyah!

So Cramer says Solar Panel Solutions Corp. is a "buy buy buy," and the viewers buy. And at first the stock goes up. But then it levels off and starts trending lower, and the people at home don't know what to do. They don't know anything about solar stocks other than they think solar panels are a neato idea and every house should have some on their roof. They don't know why this particular stock is going down, what other companies to compare it to, and they don't know much about its financials other than the P/E Ratio that pops up when they check the price every day—they don't know anything.

And of course, Cramer has moved on to the "Lightning Round" or whatever he calls the grand finale of his nightly circus performance. He's not actually invested in Solar Panel Solutions because legally he can't be. Instead, his "charitable trust may or may not have holdings" in that company. The SEC has explicit laws against hyping things you may have direct ownership interest in. Cramer's charitable trust may own some of the things he hypes, but he really has no investment in them financially or emotionally. He simply moves on to the next segment.

The only time he might mention the stock again is if it happens to take off. Sure, if a stock goes up thirty percent after he says it's a buy, he'll revisit it to show you what a genius he is, but if that stock languishes, we usually don't hear much about it. It's a perfect example of something we'll talk about later which we call selective potential past performance—or SPPP, and you will see it all over Wall Street and the financial press. Heck, you'll probably do it yourself! Beware of self delusion! It's trickery we tell you! Trickery!

The Starting Line-Up

To be successful, we need to actively use the products and services of the companies we invest in. We Slackers don't have time to scour the news daily to discern whether or not the earthquake in Shandong Province took the Shenhua Energy Company's grid offline and knocked the production of Trengoo Semiconductor Manufacturing Corporation's facility offline as well, leaving our stock with a three month backlog. We have no business trading companies we don't understand.

We need our stocks to be a part of our lives so that we can see them in action constantly, determine firsthand whether or not they are performing to the standards that we as share owners expect. And while this sounds like advice geared towards investing, it's really at the heart of our trading as well.

If we are following a core group of ten stocks in our daily lives, it's much easier to follow that group of stocks on the daily ticker as well. We will immediately notice moves in their prices that seem to bear no relation to reality, and we will be poised to take advantage of those moves. We will, of course, talk much more about that in the following chapters.

How We Pick 'Em

This is so much easier than you'd think. Grab a notebook and carry it around with you for a few days. Here we go!

You wake up in the morning and flick on your coffee maker. You love this coffee maker. You've tried two or three others, but they always burned your coffee. This one, though, oh what a perfect cup it makes every time. And it's heavy, like it was made out of solid materials instead of cheap plastic. It looks nice too, even sitting on the kitchen counter day in and day out. And all for just a few dollars more than those that you replaced. Yep, this is a great coffee maker. Write that down.

It's time to head to work. You climb in your car and you actually look forward to the commute because you get to drive this awesome ride. It's an all-new model that seems to be becoming more and more popular, based on how many you are seeing on the road. It gets better mileage than any car you've owned before. It wasn't the most expensive car, but it filled a niche between the lower-end Hyundai and the BMWs and you think it's a tremendous value. After five thousand miles, you couldn't be happier. Write it down.

At work you need to make some copies. You dread making copies. It never used to be such a hassle; you just laid your piece of paper face down and pushed the button. Now the copier control pad looks like it belongs in a NASA Mars Rover control room, and it never works. You and your co-workers actually have to call IT twice a day to come and perform their magic voodoo on it in order for you to get the simple copies you need. Write that loser down, too.

Back at your desk, you type away at your computer. Amazingly, your computer is the one thing you never have to call the IT guy about. It just works. It does everything you need it to, and it has done so for years—through all of the upgrades and replacements. It's the reason, in fact, that you bought the same brand for your home computer as well as for your tablet. You love your computer and know that that's a rare and wondrous thing. Write it down.

The number of publicly-traded companies that you interact with on a daily basis will surprise you. These are just a few examples. You've still got your favorite fast food restaurant for lunch, your beverage of choice coming out of the vending machine, the trip to the bank, to the pharmacy to pick up your high blood pressure medication—and you'll find dozens more in the course of a week. Jot them all down so you can take a closer look when you are done.

The Research

Now that we have a nice long list of companies, it's time to research them a bit. What do we want to look at? There are a million theories on how to value a company and base your decision on whether to buy or sell. We're going to keep it pretty simple. Because it *is* pretty simple.

We already know whether we are going to be buying or selling the stocks based on our feelings towards these companies in our daily interactions with them. In order to keep this from becoming too confusing we're going to concentrate on companies we want to buy (most people will never "short" a stock). Later on in the book we'll talk about options, and how to trade companies that you think are going down, but for now let's only look at the companies that we like; the ones we think are doing a good job at whatever they do.

Getting Information

Later, we are going to talk a lot about how to analyze companies and how to analyze stocks and options, but how will you find all of this information? Information is everywhere—we are afloat in a sea of information. Finding information isn't the problem. The question is: what information should you pay attention to?

Rule number one—don't pay for information. We can't even imagine ever recommending that you pay for something that's available for free. Yet, you are going to find all sorts of subscription services available on the internet promising to give hot stock tips, price targets, access to untapped analysis, etc. Some of these infoproducts sell for $500 or more per month. Ask yourself this: if these people actually had real inside information or had a strategy that couldn't lose, why would they be telling you or anyone else about it? Wouldn't they be better off keeping it to themselves? If we had that kind of information, we would quickly make ourselves fifty million each and disappear on our yachts, not sell it for $500 a crack. That's right; we think stock newsletters are a scam.

Your trading platform—whether Ameritrade or Vanguard or whatever brokerage you use—is going to supply you with a newswire service that will parse news stories specific to any company you may have on your "watchlist." These platforms also have analysis tools, charts, and just about any metric you could ever want to analyze a company. Beyond that, you'll find all sorts of "news" on the interwebs and TV. Just googling a company is a great start.

Types of News

What should you pay attention to and what should you ignore? You have to consider the source.

Large, legitimate news sources. CNN, MSNBC, USA Today, Yahoo Finance, etc. These are the most trustworthy sources of news. They do fact checking, they vet sources, they get confirmation. Their news is right; but all of this takes time, so these big guys are the LAST TO KNOW. If you learned something about a company from a corporate website or one of these big news outlets, you should consider this "common knowledge," and the effect on the stock price will probably be "priced in."

Market or stock analysts. These people usually have advanced degrees in finance and have passed series 7 and 63 exams which are highly technical. They specialize in analyzing a particular industry or sector. Sometimes their information is published in broad market sources like *The Economist* or *The Wall Street Journal*, and sometimes published to the web by their employers to market whatever their employers are trying to sell.

Analysts are either directly or indirectly employed by banks, brokers, investment firms, and fund managers to help those entities gain an advantage over the rest of us. This is a really important relationship to understand, because while analysts are understood to be independent and provide an unbiased assessment of companies and their stock, they are working for or on behalf of banks and other institutional investors. These entities have a tremendous financial stake in what the analysts say. To say there is a conflict of interest here might be the biggest understatement ever.

Analysts have tremendous power to move markets, and they are more or less employed by people who have a lot to win or lose based on their reports. When an analyst changes their "rating" or "price target" for a stock or company, it might be because someone out there wants the market to react based on that information—and it often does. In fact simple analyst statements can send stocks soaring or plunging in a matter of minutes.

Right, wrong, biased, unbiased—it really doesn't matter—when an analyst speaks, the market usually does listen and react. Analysts hold tremendous power.

You will see analysts statements and reports re-published (ripped off) by bloggers as well as quoted in the mainstream financial press. Because this information has the ability to affect stock prices directly, you need to be aware of when the report was released and whether you are getting it from the original source. If you get the info early, it may not yet be priced into the stock. If it has been a day or two or even a few hours, you probably missed the boat and the effect on share price is reflected already. Websites like seekingalpha.com have quasi and retired analysts who sound like they know what they are talking about, but beware the quality of what you will find.

Bloggers. With the advent of the internet, everyone is a writer/expert these days (including us); and it's really easy to spew baseless opinion about whether ABC stock is headed to $X. If you are finding information on stocktwits.com or motleyfool.com, you may find some lines of reasoning that make some sense, and that may help you form an opinion about a stock or company; but these individual bloggers have almost zero influence on the market. They are guessing and speculating.

There is an exception however. Bloggers blog because they have time to blog. Big time successful traders don't have time, and even if they did, they don't care about sharing tips with cyberspace. Writing is hard, so bloggers tend to copy each other. If you see a rumor repeated over and over and over again on several different blogs, even though there is no factual basis or hard announcement, these blogs in total can influence the market to some degree. Don't write the bloggers off altogether, especially when you see rumors repeated time and again.

Your neighbor Biff. We will say the same thing about your uncle Frank, your coworker Marianne, your buddy Eric, and even the well-dressed guy you sat next to in first-class: a lot of people pretend to know a lot more about investing and especially trading than they actually do. They "like" this or that stock or company; they "think" next quarter will be good or bad for this or that reason. It is all speculation. If someone gives you a stock tip that you hadn't considered, ask yourself first if you know and understand that company; and if you don't, then ask yourself if you even want to. If the answer is no both times, then ignore the speculators.

Insiders. Be wary of "insider" information, and not strictly for the reasons you think. If you have a friend who works at a company you trade and he or she gets a little loose in the lips at the bar after a few drinks, they might tell you a little something that just might hint at that company's next quarterly earnings, or their top secret drug patent, or whatever. Now you are thinking you just might have some info that could make you some money in the markets!

Bad idea. Not just because you might get busted by the feds, but because good insider info is harder to come by than you would think—and how are you going to know the difference ahead of time? You can't.

The information that truly moves markets like earnings or business development announcements is closely guarded by the C-level executives in the organization. They don't share that kind of stuff with mid-level management and certainly not with sales, engineering, or administrative employees. So unless your friend with the loose lips is running the show at XYZ Incorporated, he or she probably doesn't know jack. And if by any chance they do share true "insider" information with you, then it really isn't insider information, because they are probably sharing elsewhere, and those people are likely sharing too.

Your trades will be kept on record for a long long time, and if ever there should be a scandal of some sort, the SEC is going to be looking very carefully for those who might have profited. No need to lose sleep over a single trade. Leave that to the real insiders who can probably afford better lawyers.

Hens in the Henhouse

What do you hear most distinctly in a henhouse? The rooster of course; you can't pick out the sounds of individual hens at all. See, when there are a lot of voices, the loudest ones stand out.

When evaluating news of any sort, it's really important to understand that the most dramatic and drastic opinions often get the lion's share of the attention. When it comes to politics, MSNBC and Fox News are great examples of highly biased and opinionated people getting the most airtime, but it happens everywhere else too. Let's apply this idea to the financial press.

The one thing you will see a lot of in the financial news: predictions. Every talking head and blogger has an opinion about where the market is headed from here; price targets for specific stocks, etc. Each will hedge and say that this or that "could" happen, so that they are covering their tails, but remember that often it's the wildest predictions that get the most attention—those are the ones that stands out.

It's the guys who say Apple is going to $1,000 per share or that Google will cease to exist in five years that get the most hits on their blog. It's the guy who says the presidential election will determine whether we hit DOW 20,000 or sink to DOW 5,000 who ends up on CNBC. It's pretty rare you see someone being interviewed by Maria Bartiromo say, "Uhh well, I doubt the market will do much in the next year. Maybe up a couple percent, maybe down."

Is there an independent body that later checks to see who was right and who was wrong? Nope, but wouldn't it be great if there was? What's worse is that the incorrect predictions are mostly (but not always) ignored. An "expert" might make 100 wildly inaccurate forecasts, then correctly call one big move, and now he is the guy who called the crash before everyone else. Be aware that while the loudest voices in the room aren't necessarily the right ones, they are the ones that the market takes most note of.

Now there are technical forecasters out there making really good forecasts and making a lot of money for themselves and their clients, but if you think they are sharing that information for free on their blog or on TV, you are delusional.

Some Useful Jargon

We could and probably should write a whole book of definitions for the "trader-speak" and other jargon you will see in market news, but we'll just touch on a few and sprinkle it in here and there throughout the book. Who are these "bulls" and "bears" anyway? And why does it matter if they are "long" or "short?"

Bulls, bullish, being bullish on the market, etc., all refer to positive sentiment. When someone is bullish, it's because they think the market or a particular stock is heading higher.

Bears, bearish, bearish market, etc., all refer to negative sentiment about a stock or the market in general; it's a market filled with pessimism about future performance. When someone is bearish on a stock, it's because they believe it will fall. Technically speaking, the market or a particular stock is in "bear territory" after it has fallen ~20% from its highs, but even that's a bit of a loose definition.

Here's a little extra to impress and annoy your friends with: it's said that *bull* and *bear* are used because of how those two animals behave in a fight. The bull points its horns confidently higher, while the bear paws the ground beneath. Who knows if this is right, but it sounds good.

Long and short refer specifically to a trader's position in a trade, but they are also often used interchangeably in casual conversation (and somewhat incorrectly) for bullish and bearish. Being long a stock means that you are holding the stock or call option with the expectation that it's going to go up in value. "I am long XYZ," specifically means that I own stock in XYZ, however many people use it incorrectly to say they think XYZ is going up.

Being "short "can mean a few things, because "shorting" a stock or "short selling," is specifically the practice of selling a security with the intention of buying it back at a lower price—"covering." In casual conversation, people sometimes say they are short XYZ, when they really just believe the stock will fall. You can also be short by using options—buying puts or selling calls is the equivalent of being short (more on this later).

Fundamental Analysis

So you hear that a condo is for sale for $200,000. Is that a good deal or a bad deal? Or that a car is selling for $20,000. Is that a bargain or a ripoff? Depends on whether that condo is in Malibu or Detroit, right? It depends on whether we are talking about a Lamborghini or a Yugo, right? To evaluate the worth of something, you have to know a little something about it. With cars, it's the brand and model; and with the condo, it's the location, size, condition, etc. With companies, we use numbers that you may not have seen before. Don't be frightened off by this. It isn't as complicated as the title of this section makes it sound.

"Fundamental analysis" is basically taking a company's numbers and using them to evaluate its theoretical worth. Fortunately for you and us, the most common numbers are freely available on the internet, leaving you to use them however you wish.

The most basic and probably most useful fundamental analysis method for the beginning trader is to compare companies within the same industry, peer to peer. McDonald's to Burger King, Ford to GM, Apple to Microsoft, etc. From there you can get an idea in your mind if the company you are interested in trading is trading at a bargain basement price, an average price, or a significant premium.

10-K Reports

Once a company goes "public" and sells shares to the public, they don't get to keep as many secrets. A Form 10-K is a yearly report that the SEC requires from public companies that gives a summary of the their performance. The 10-K is not necessarily the same as the "annual report to shareholders" that you may get if you own one or more shares of a company even though they are sometimes released together. They are usually available online.

Most of what you see in a 10-K is unbelievably drab and boring: things like executive compensation, company history, subsidiaries they may own, etc. But the 10-K does include something that can be of interest: audited financial statements. If you don't have any familiarity with these, they are going to look complicated and boring, but if you take a little time, you can learn a lot. Here are some of the things you will find (which are often also available on your online trading software):

Earnings Per Share (EPS) = Net Earnings / Outstanding Shares

Beginners often find themselves considering share price when determining the value of a company.

"Wow, Google is trading for $700, they must be really good."

"Look at Ford, only $9, what a dog."

While these assumptions may or may not be true, they aren't really any indication of a company's value. Not until combined with the number of shares a company has *outstanding*; the number of shares they have sold or given away to its employees or anyone else.

EPS is a very basic number that tells you exactly how much money the company earned for each share of the stock that's outstanding. It can be useful in comparing the company's performance versus companies in the same sector—the other companies doing roughly the same sorts of things. But that's about it. EPS won't give you a very good picture of how the company is valued by the market. Also, over time, EPS can change because companies sometimes buy stock back, reducing the number of outstanding shares and thereby "artificially" boosting EPS.

Net Profit Margin = Net Profit / Revenue

So you can see that earnings by themselves don't tell the whole story. A company with increasing earnings is a good thing; but if costs increase more than revenue, then the profit margin is decreasing and that's not such a good thing. Profit margin is important because it shows how much of each dollar in revenue is kept by the company.

This is the net profit margin, meaning that it takes into account all of a company's expenses. If you take two similar companies and compare their net profit margin you can get a pretty good idea of how things are run. In general, a company with a high profit margin shows that it's in control of its costs. A similar company with a lower profit margin might indicate the company has a bloated payroll or has to pay more to buy materials.

There are many reasons for differing profit margins, but when two similar companies are compared it can be a good indication of which is operating more *efficiently*. The market values efficiency, and so should you.

ROE = Net Income / Shareholder Equity

You are *living on the margin,* right? That means you are living on what you earn by trading, and hopefully not living on the money you use to trade with. If you can do that, you are living off the net profit margin. Think of the money you use to trade with as your equity. If I trade with $100,000 and make $5,000, and you trade with $10,000 and make $5,000, who is the better trader? Our earnings are the same, but clearly you are better at it—your profit margin is way higher.

ROE, or return on equity, is an important measure of how much profit a company earned in relation to the shareholder equity. Shareholder equity is simply total assets minus total liabilities.

A basic example involves two similar companies that each earned $10 million last year. The difference is that Company A has total equity of $100 million, while Company B has $50 million. Which is better?

Company A has a ROE of 10% while Company B's ROE is 20% ($10 million / $50 million), so even though Company B has less equity, they are making a better return for their shareholders. The market values companies that have a high ROE, and so should you.

P/E = Stock Price / EPS

Oh, the darling number of every wannabe investytalker who knows a thing or two about the market. P/E is the "price to earnings" ratio. This is the most widely-used number out there. This is the number that those who don't know very much about trading throw out there to make it seem as if they *do* have a clue. We're not saying that P/E isn't an important and useful number—it is—but it's often an overused and overemphasized number.

P/E is a company's stock price divided by their earnings per share. Let's say Company ABC has a P/E of 20. This indicates that investors are willing to pay $20 for a share for every $1 the company earns.

(Strictly speaking, earnings are revenues minus costs, expenses, and taxes. It's really important to note that costs, expenses, and taxes are subject to all sorts of fancy accounting practices like deferment and amortization. So when you are looking at two companies' P/E ratios, keep in mind that the E part of that equation is going to depend on each company's structure and accounting practices.)

The reason the P/E ratio isn't more important is that it's so subjective. Two investors can see the same number completely differently. A company with a low P/E could be viewed by one person as having low prospects for the future. Why pay more than the actual earnings if the company is going to be earning less and less each year? The other investor however may simply see a low P/E as the company being overlooked—a gem that just hasn't been discovered. People like Warren Buffett have found these companies time and time again. He spots the supermodel when she is still a skinny nerd with thick glasses and a low P/E.

On the flip side a company with a high P/E may be viewed by one investor as overpriced while the other investor might see it as a sign that the company is going to outperform quarter after quarter.

So what is high and what is low? Amazon has a P/E of 297 while Delta Airlines is 8. Too expensive and too cheap right? Well that's the rub, nobody really knows for sure. It's completely up to you and the market to decide. P/E is really just a benchmark to give you an idea if the company you are interested in is reasonably fairly valued compared to other companies doing the same thing. So compare it to competitors and then decide for yourself.

It can also be helpful to look at P/E over time:

For example, if the stock price (P) has been going up and up and up, but earnings (E) haven't changed, then P/E is going up too. That means that people are willing to pay more for a stock that isn't seeing commensurate higher earnings. Start asking questions: what does that tell you about how the market feels about this company? Is this justified? Is the stock becoming overvalued? Is this a company with new and innovative products on the way? Do you think they will capture more of their market? Did they just get a new CEO? If P/E is going up, you need to look to the future and focus on what the market sentiment is for the stock.

On the other hand if earnings (E) have been going up and up and up but the stock price (P) hasn't been going up commensurately, then P/E is going down. That means that the company is earning more money in comparison to what people are willing to pay for the stock. What does that tell you? Is the stock undervalued? Are their revenue forecasts going down? Are their products getting stale? Is the market for their products losing steam?

Whatever the answer to these questions, using these "fundamental analysis" numbers forms a basis to start asking yourself questions about what you think about the company and what others think of the company. And—always, always, always—remember that anytime stock price is involved in a calculation, it's based on expectations for the *future* and not just what is going on with the company right now.

Volatility and Beta

A highly volatile stock will often see moves across a larger range of prices. A low volatility stock has shown itself to not have these large price swings; it moves a lot more slowly and less dramatically.

Here is where we are going to introduce our first piece of truly analytical data: a stock's beta. Beta is a measure of how a company's stock responds to a move in the overall market. A beta of 1 means the stock moves the same percentage as the market, a beta of less than 1 means the stock will be less volatile than the market, and a beta of greater than 1 that the stock price will have greater volatility than the market. This number, like all the others we have talked about is available on any trading platform's stock analysis tools. You don't need to know how to calculate it, you just need to know how to interpret it.

Most likely, our favorite companies are going to fall into both categories; high beta and low beta—some are going to be less volatile than the market and others will be more so. This gives us a hint as to how we may want to trade them.

For example, when a company has a low beta (say .8), meaning that it tends to move less than the market does, but you see it down three percent while the market is unchanged, there is often (unless there is significant news) a prime opportunity for a retracement (a move back up)—assuming again that the news available for the stock's move is benign.

The companies with high beta (say 1.5) can be great opportunities too. These stocks bounce around giving you opportunity after opportunity to make money. When the general market is stagnant these stocks will still swing a couple of percent up and down. The trick with them is to get to know their behavior.

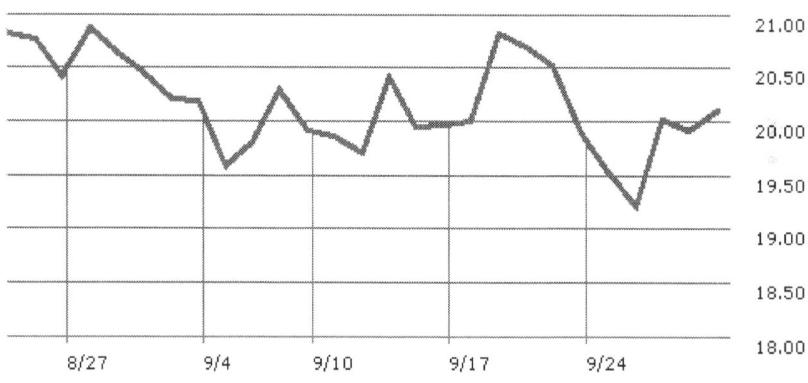

[fig 9.2]

For a while we were into trading IMAX. There was a period of about six months where they traded from about $17 to $24. The great thing about the stock were the repeated pullbacks—they would go up a couple of dollars, then drop a couple of dollars, over and over again. Their beta was around 2 at the time. They never seemed to move 1%—it always seemed to be 4%. This was happening while the overall market was steadily climbing. It was really the perfect slacker trading setup.

When you can find a stock that performs like this, you owe it to yourself to get to know it well and trade it. We've traded IMAX dozens of times, for considerable profits, and only rarely for longer than a day or two. Eventually though, the predictable nature of its moves became more erratic, and we were forced to move on.

The Trend

This is actually a technical indicator, but we think this should probably be right at the top of any analysis of a company you are contemplating trading. Is your company in a general uptrend or downtrend? One of the most commonly heard phrases among traders of all types is, "The trend is your friend," and it's true, it is.

[fig 9.3]

The trend is defined like this: an uptrend means higher highs and higher lows. A downtrend means lower highs and lower lows. Looking at a daily chart of a stock's price, you can clearly see what the trend is. Interpretation can be as loosely defined or as exacting as you'd like—there are literally hundreds of patterns and methodologies you can use; and we'll touch on many in the Swing Trading chapter. For a company you like, you want to see a general uptrend. Seems obvious, but without taking a look at the chart, you just won't know.

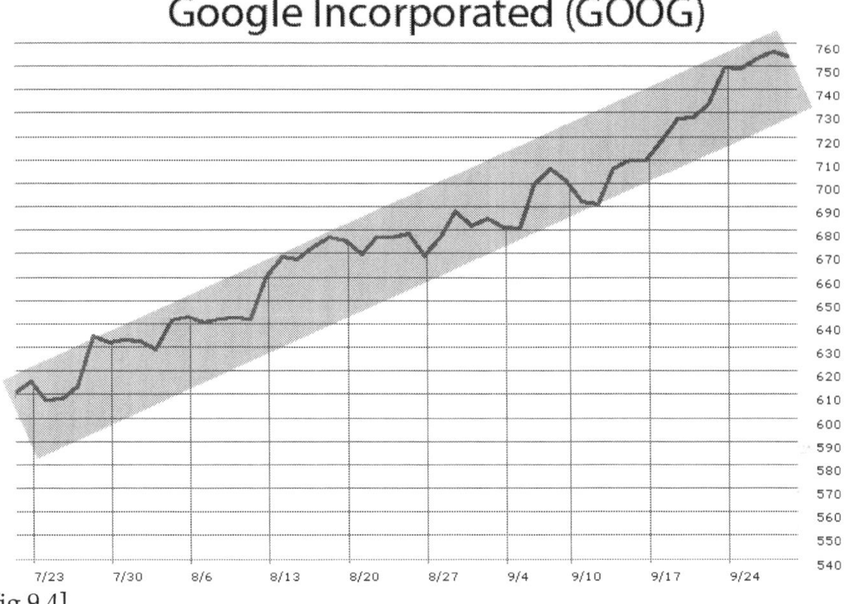

[fig 9.4]

Now Trade 'Em

So you've lined up your list of stocks, compared them to their competitors using some fundamental analysis, and checked out what their general trading trend has been. Now it's time to do something with all of this information. Are you ready? Great.

Cash—check! Watch list—check! Analysis—check!
Flight attendants, please prepare for takeoff.

The Strategies

We believe there are two fundamental trading strategies that the average Slacker can quickly learn, become proficient in, and make money at while still living a laid-back lifestyle. The two techniques/strategies are fading and swing trading. The former is simple as well as risky—both in theory and in practice—fading takes very little time and can produce quick profits. The second strategy will take a bit longer but swing trading can be a little less risky than fading.

Fading

Time is always at a premium, and we have young kids (Pat), wives (one each) and boats (one each) that need constant attention. On top of that, the beach is always steps away; and in perfect warm sunny weather, it's really hard to sit in front of a computer screen and watch stock tickers. So when we do take the time out to trade, we want it to be both quick and profitable.

"Fading" (sometimes mistakenly generalized as "day trading") is both of those things: quick and potentially profitable. We'll talk specifics in the next couple of chapters, but will give you the gist of it here.

But first let us clear up a misconception. Fade trading is not technically day trading. Day trading as most of us have come to understand it, (probably from the tech bubble trading boom), is more accurately characterized as "scalping." Scalpers are traders who look to make many tiny gains on extremely short-term trades throughout the day. They may make a hundred or more trades in one session—looking for just a few cents per trade. The downfall of this strategy, as the vast majority of day traders discover, is that when you are trading for pennies it only takes a couple of dime-sized losses to wipe you out.

Fading on the other hand is really uncomplicated—all you are really trying to do is look for puzzle pieces (stocks) that don't quite fit what's going on in the broader market or in their particular sector. For example, you are watching one of your favorite stocks lose four percent of its value while the DJIA is only down one percent—and there doesn't appear to be ANY reason why. If you are sitting there looking at your screen watching this stock drop, but you still love the company; and while searching the ticker's news feed you can't discern any good reason for the pummeling, then it *might* be the time to buy.

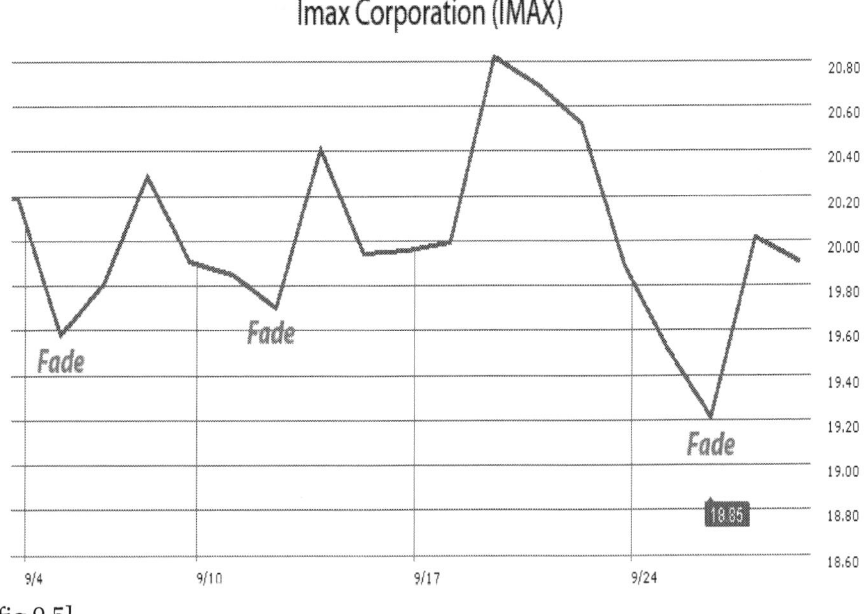

[fig 9.5]

Too often traders will sit on their hands during times like this, because they assume the market knows something that they don't (which is always possible). While on occasion this is the case; more times than not, the market doesn't know diddly—the market is a herd of sheep.

Why is your stock going down today of all days? Who knows—and that's the key to this strategy: you are looking for situations where there appears to be NO fundamental business-related reason for a drop. This stock may be dropping for a technical reason, or it may be getting beaten up because a mutual fund with a big stake needed to liquidate their position. Maybe options expiration is approaching, and the options traders are pressing the price lower to pin it at a certain strike price. Perhaps another company similar to this one had some bit of bad news that caused it to drop ten percent, in which case similar companies in the sector often take an exaggerated hit as well.

This little dip in share price could be for a million reasons ***other*** than because today, of all days, this company is no longer as good as it was yesterday.

These are the moves we look for, and when the beating appears to stall out, we step in and buy. When the rest of the market realizes nothing has fundamentally changed for this company, they often step back in and buy...which drives the price back up...and we sell—we profit. We "fade" the move. And in true slacker style, we usually only spend a day or two in the position at most—in fact sometimes we only stay in it for a matter of hours.

Swinging

Swingers-baby-yeah! Austin Powers would've been a great trader, right? Making big money fading in a short period of time (like in a day or two) means you need at least one of two things: high volatility (big moves) and/or a big chunk of cash you can risk. The less of one, the more you need of the other to make big gains. On the polar opposite end, long-term investors risk relatively little capital in any particular stock, but do so over a very long time period like months or even years. They hope that over that long period, they will see appreciation in the underlying company's value and be able to choose their exit at the most profitable time.

Swing trading is in the middle. You risk less capital on a single trade than a day trader would, but much more capital than the long-term trader does. You are in the trade over about two days to a week or so; and every once in a while, you hold your position for ten days or two weeks. The same principles as day trading or fading apply to swing trades, but there is less volatility required to make a profit. The major downside to swing trades is that you have to spend more time "working," and you know how we feel about that...

What to Choose?

Whether to fade or swing really comes down to market conditions and whether or not you have the time to watch your trade. Are you seeing really high volatility as the market is jolted by news of one sort or another? Then keep your trade short and consider putting more money on the line and fading. Are you seeing a definitive trend or a lot of excitement in the market about a particular stock and have high certainty about direction for the next week or so? Think about risking less money and swinging.

Options

Once you have an idea of what you think a stock is going to do price wise, the next decision becomes how to trade them. Do you just buy a stock and sell after it goes up? Do you short the stock and get out of the trade when it goes down? Are there any other "options?" Why yes, there is another option called, conveniently enough, an "option." (Most market jargon is very descriptive—so don't overthink it.)

In the following chapters, we are going to talk a lot about options trading and how they can be used to supplement our fading and swing trading strategies.

*The option's biggest advantage for traders like us is **leverage.***

Making big returns is all about the leverage. Trading a stock like Apple which is currently (as of this writing) trading around $600 a share takes a tremendous amount of capital. Sure you can trade just a few shares, but that may not earn you the kind of returns you are looking for. At a stock price of $600/share, if you think AAPL is going up $20 today and you want to make $100, that means you have to buy five shares for $3,000. $3,000 to make $100 in a day—not bad, but we can do better.

What if you could use that same $3,000 to buy control of 200 shares? If the stock goes up $20, you could make $4,000. Options are a tool that lets you do that kind of thing. Sounds interesting doesn't it? More to come.

Options are also a great way to trade stocks that you think are headed lower. A lot of brokerages won't allow short selling by customers without a certain amount of trading experience or—worse still—a certain amount of money in their accounts. Options can often get around this and allow you to play both sides of the market. Buy side (calls) for the companies you like and sell side (puts) for the pigs that you hate.

Did we wet your whistle?

Swing Trading

You've quit your job, sold everything you owned, flown to Tahiti, rented a one-room shack with a view of the beach, a bed, a rack on the wall for your surfboards, and you've pilfered some solid WiFi from the swank hotel across the street. You're paddling out early every morning and getting great waves, having fresh caught Snapper on the grill for lunch, and swinging in a hammock with a cold Hinano in your hand at night.

It's perfect—everything that you dreamed it would be. The only problem? Money. You spend too much.

You underestimated your burn rate by a few hundred bucks a month, a typical rookie mistake, you know; and now you're realizing that instead of two years funding, you've got maybe a smidge over a year's worth of dough. But this is it man! This is the life. You don't ever want to go home, or at least not anytime soon.

What to do, what to do? Repairing dinged surfboards isn't going to make you any money. Similarly, there isn't much call for a *Haole* to be a Customer Service Call Center Manager here on the island. You already live in a shack, so downsizing isn't really an option. You could probably drink less beer, but that isn't really an option either. There's only one thing left to do. Break out the Kindle, it's time to reread *Live on the Margin* and get to work.

So you do what, exactly?

When we tell people how we make money, they often say/ask, "So you're a day trader?" No. While we do use extremely short-term strategies from time to time (which we detail in the next chapter), the truth is that we don't like being married to our computers all day, and that's what day traders have to do. What we do most often is called *swing trading*.

We're going to guess you probably haven't heard much about swing trading. So what are we talking about? Well, day traders trade into and then close out of their positions during the trading day or maybe overnight into the next morning. Investors (and most retail traders) trade in and out of positions over the course of several weeks, months or even years. Swing traders are in between: we typically hold our positions for about two to seven days while trying to participate in a stock's current momentum or anticipate a move that's about to take place.

Why do we prefer swing trading over other time scales? It's probably the area of the market where an individual can bring the most skill. Day traders are busy racing algorithms and gambling on what the market makers are doing, and long-term investing is the domain of the fund managers and institutional investors.

Swing trading happens to fit in best with our lifestyle. Who wants to be glued to a computer all day like the day trader? Who wants to babysit low-return positions over weeks and years? There is also the question of profit. We need to make enough money to live on the margin!

Let's step back and take the wide view again...the view from 30,000 feet. Regardless of whether you are trading stocks or options or whatever, there are always the questions of:

- How much am I trying to make?
- Which financial instrument should I use?
- What strategy do I employ?

What you choose to do is dependent upon the answers to the following questions:

- What amount can I risk?—the more I risk, the higher the gain or loss.
- How much inherent risk can I take?—how volatile is this stock, and what is the downside if I am wrong?
- How long can I be in my position?—what sort of time do I have available?

Total risk = (how much capital you are risking) x (inherent risk) x (time over which you are risking)

Without delving into the mathematics, you can see that your total risk goes up if you risk more capital, and/or you take more inherent risk, and/or you lengthen the time you are exposed to that risk. So in general, to limit risk with any given amount of money—the higher the risk, the shorter term you want to hold the position. For example, if a stock is particularly volatile, you want to either not risk much capital, or you want to stay in the trade for a very short period of time.

Swing Trading Risk

Swing trading allows you to expose yourself to less risk than the day trader while using less capital than s/he does. At the same time, you are also exposing yourself to market fluctuations that are still within the realm of skill and thought—meaning you aren't racing against a machine algorithms used by HFTs ("high-frequency traders"). Instead, you are making predictions about the future state of the market and a stock and placing bets on whether you are right or wrong.

With a swing trade, you buy on Monday and you hold until Thursday or Friday or the following Tuesday or until the stock does what you think it will do. You enter a swing trade in *anticipation* of a move or continued trend; you are forecasting stock behavior for the next week or so. Things we generally look for:

- Upcoming earnings report,
- Reaction to a partnership/sales/biz dev./acquisition/ announcement,
- Reaching a technical limit of some sort,
- Or, anticipating that <u>none</u> of the above will happen.

For the biggest swing trade opportunities, you are looking for a *surprise* or a *catalyst* and one that's typically scheduled in advance. The more the market is surprised and the bigger the catalyst, the more volatility you can expect, and if you are on the right side of the trade, the higher the volatility, the higher the profit.

WHEN ARE SWING TRADES APPROPRIATE

As we have tried to hammer home, profit and loss in the market is all about making the right decision at the right time. So as a Slacker living on the margin, there are two things you need to consider: your conditions and the market's conditions.

You First

Trading profitably is as much about learning to control your own psychology as it is about picking stocks. You are living the digital-nomad lifestyle because you want to do what you want, when you want, and without worrying about money all the time, right? How are you going to do that when you have some or all of your liquid net worth on the line for several days at a time? The simple answer is that you can't. No one can.

So rule number one with swing trading is that you have to be in a location where you can watch the market for as long as you are in your trade—maybe not minute to minute, but at times during the day. You can't just set it and forget it like the long-term investor can. That means you need good internet for a week or more, which may or may not coincide with acceptable market conditions.

Some people may say they feel comfortable setting a limit order and taking off for their adventure, but they likely aren't taking enough risk or they have a high enough total net worth that they can sustain the potential loss. We think you have to be a little pickier to take big risks.

Market Conditions

Impatience will cost you money, so remember that not being in the market is a perfectly acceptable position to be in. In fact, being picky about market conditions is often more important than which particular stock you choose. There will be many times when sitting on the sidelines is the right place to be. We've seen several months strung together where we have been entirely in a cash position. There is nothing wrong with that at all. The following is an overview of when swing trading is best used.

Global Stability

Across the broad markets, we are looking for low volatility—we want things to be generally good or generally bad. We want stable trends, not a market moving sideways with the broader indices going up and down in huge moves on a day-to-day basis. If global markets are in general decline (bear market) or in a general upswing (bull market) over weeks and months, this could be a really good time to swing trade.

For example, when the DJIA is up 200 points one day, down 300 points the next, then up 120, then down 150, it's a very poor time to swing trade. When the broader market is moving erratically—like we've seen with the debt crises and international banking scandals, the retail investor and even the institutional investor can drive prices up and down quickly on low volume, completely overriding a signal that we might be trying to ride. There are ways to capitalize on these days, but in general it makes swing trading too risky.

It is much better to see the broader indices edging up or edging down with periodic corrections. DOW swings of 50–80 points are ideal, with general overall trends either up or down.

Sector and Industry Instability

If we want a predictable global market, we actually want the exact opposite for our chosen sector. We want to see upheaval and change, disruptors and innovators. We want controversy and consolidation, and financial distress or duress. We want to see emerging, disruptive companies and new business models replacing old tried and tested ones. We want to see shifting consumer demand and spending. We want to see investors confused, changing their minds, and reacting to every piece of information that comes across the media landscape.

We want an anxious herd of sheep! We want to see fear and greed in their eyes! These are the conditions when we tend to see higher volatility in a sector based on any given market signal or piece of information in the media. The market is nervous, itchy, and over-reactive, and that makes people irrational. That's a good thing.

This ever-shifting environment of change and disruption and innovation is exactly what has made technology stocks so attractive to traders over the last fifteen years or so. The VC (venture capital) funding model is constantly bringing new companies to market, changing the way consumers behave and how companies make money. There are always new and emerging technologies that replace the old, creating new demand and new efficiencies. Even more exciting is that recently, many of these newer public tech companies' products are easier to sample than ever before. If you are curious about a company's potential, it can be as simple as trying their hot new iPhone app.

Corporate Stability

So we want a virtual circus in any given sector or industry, but for our single chosen company, we want to see stability. These are companies that have a stable business model and strategy and their results tend to follow (or consistently exceed) analysts expectations. These are companies with stable leadership, consistent earnings or consistent earnings beats or disappointments.

The best time to trade this company is when they are at a point where the market is going to learn something new about them. Not necessarily something good or bad, but something NEW. Note that we didn't say that this particular company had to be doing well in their industry—there are companies in steady decline that are also good candidates for swing trades. It is just as easy to make money on a declining stock as it is to make money on one that's going up.

Picking Stocks for Swing Trading

Choosing what stock to trade and what instrument to use looks like a daunting task, however over a two to seven-day period, choosing what to trade gets a little easier. You need to know:

- If there is a clear catalyst or mover that will affect the stock within your trading horizon. We want a date or time.
- Current market consensus; we need to know what everyone else believes is happening with this stock.
- Possible trading range over your swing period. How low could this go? We want minimum downside with high upside obviously. If shorting, we want the opposite.

So of our stable full of companies that we know and understand, how do we go about evaluating the above characteristics? We have to look under the hood a bit. This is where a lot of smart people decide trading is just too complicated and where we tell you that there are all sorts of dolts and idiots out there making money, so you can too. Wink, wink.

Kicking Tires

When it comes to analyzing data to find trading opportunities, there are two broad schools of thought:

- fundamental analysis, and
- technical analysis

Neither should be used exclusively as they both have value. We don't even want to use the vocabulary since it looks so intimidating, but since you'll read the jargon elsewhere, we better stick with it. Let's use an example that might help illustrate the difference between fundamental and technical analysis.

Car Shopping

The fundamental analyst walks into a car dealership and says, "I want to buy the car with the best overall value based on *these* measurable qualities." He is looking at hard numbers and quantifiable terms that he can plug into a formula to compare one car against another. He looks at things like customer satisfaction ratings, horsepower, top speed, fuel economy, warranty, maintenance history, etc. He plugs it all into one or more equations and compares one car's numbers against another to choose a winner.

Our fictional fundamental analyst buys a Toyota Camry with an automatic transmission and a mid-range options package.

The technical analyst walks into the dealership and says, "I want the car that everyone else wants or a car that people don't want now, but may want again." He looks at graphical data like charts and graphs that show sales trends, average used car prices over time for each model, etc., and compares the effect of optional features, color, etc. He doesn't need to compare horsepower to fuel economy for each individual car—he is going to trust that the market has already built the importance of those factors into the sales trends for each vehicle. He compares the historical trends and patterns in the market for each vehicle to choose a winner.

Our technical analyst buys a Mini Cooper with no options package and a manual transmission.

Five years later, both analysts made good choices and bought cars that depreciated slower than the market average, even though they arrived at their choices through vastly different processes.

These two ways of looking at companies as well as trading and investing opportunities are not mutually exclusive. Remember you can cut down a tree with an ax or a saw. They both work alone, but they work a lot better when you use them together.

Fundamental Analysis

Balance sheets, cash flow statements, income statements, 10-K reports, etc. are the tools of the fundamental analysis trade. The idea is to try to come up with a company's "value;" or some sort of metric that helps you decide whether Company A is a better investment than Company B. It's important to remember that in reality, unless the company pays dividends, this fundamentally calculated "value," is very subjective.

If it were possible, using only fundamentals to make trading decisions would be really easy: if a stock is trading below its intrinsic value then it would be a good investment and a good stock to buy, and if it's trading above its intrinsic value, it would be a bad investment and a good stock to sell. Over the long haul that may work—unfortunately, that line of thinking doesn't reflect reality in the markets on a day-to-day and week-to-week basis. As swing traders that's what we need to focus on.

Even if the fundamental numbers are subjective and are not necessarily reflected in stock price, it's still really important to understand fundamental analysis. Why? Because other market participants follow these numbers and we want to understand what they might be thinking. You gotta know the terrain!

Technical Analysis

One picture, as they say, is better than a thousand words, and basically, that's what technical analysis is: finding patterns in graphical representations of data. Even though it sounds really scientific and mathematical, "technical analysis" actually involves a lot more "eyeballing," and less computation than fundamental analysis. It is all about pattern recognition—something your brain comes pre-wired to do.

For the longest time, technical analysis was seen as an art more than financial science, but with the advent of the online trading platform and one-click charting, technical analysis has become much more widely used.

Honestly, there are no hard and fast rules about technical analysis. There are new patterns and strategies introduced all the time. In this book, we are going to stick to the basics—of course there is a lot more you can learn elsewhere, and you should.

As we go through the following examples, remember that you will never find a stock with a perfectly formed pattern right out of a book. The idea isn't to fit a pattern from a book to what you are seeing in the market and then assume that your stock will behave like the model in the book does. Instead, the idea is to understand what the charts are trying to tell you about the stock and what the market might want to do next—you use the charts to tell a story about what's going on.

Here are just a few of the tools of the pattern recognition trade:

- trend lines
- support lines
- resistance lines
- double and triple bottoms
- moving averages
- breakouts (channels, flags, head and shoulders, triangles, etc.)

Trend Lines

Pattern recognition forms the basis of technical analysis. Trend lines are the building blocks and there are all sorts of trend line inventions out there, but they all have to do with smoothing data to pick out the important patterns.

Trends and patterns are all over the place, and you probably pick them out without even realizing it. Your brain is a powerful pattern-recognition machine!

Aunt Edna

You know how your generous and loving Aunt Edna gives you a sports-related gift every year? One year it's a baseball cap, the next year it's a vinyl catcher's mitt, then it's a football cleaner, then a furry bicycle seat cover. The value of the gift may go up or down a bit every year, but she more or less buys in the same approximate price range and in the same department and same genre year after year.

Her behavior makes Edna's gift buying kind of predictable, doesn't it? For example, in 2007 if you had no other data, what would you have predicted for 2008? Probably something cheap from the sports department at Target, right?

That's not what happens though. In 2008, she buys you a pitching machine. You may or may not know it, but Aunt Edna got her own credit card that year; one that Uncle Frank can't monitor. Her behavior changes substantially. The next year you get dugout tickets for your favorite home game. After that it's an hour of private lessons with a hitting coach and then she gives you a collectible jersey the year after that. Even with her new buying power, the value of her gifts year to year goes up and down just a little bit, even though the average price of the gift has made the range jump higher.

If we graphed Aunt Edna's gift expenditures over time, they would look a little something like this:

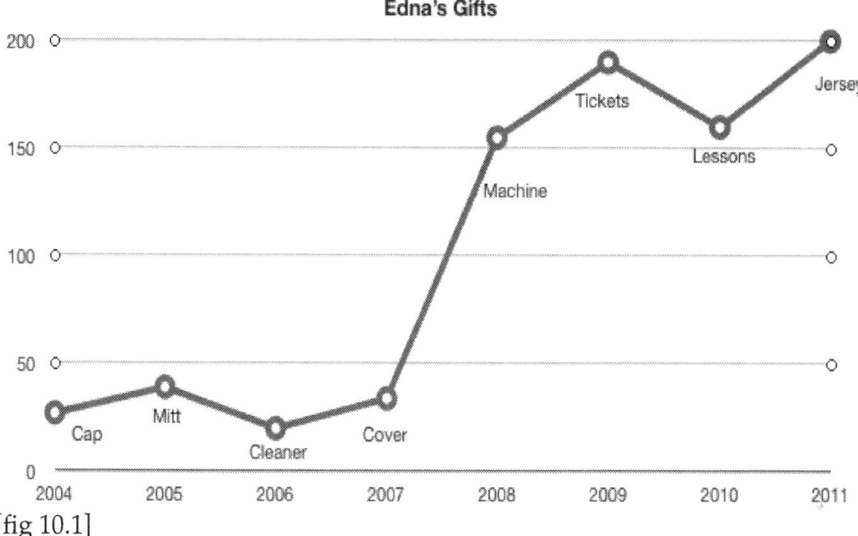

[fig 10.1]

Without doing any calculations, you can see pretty easily that Edna's gift expenditures fit a pattern. If you had to guess on her gift for 2012, it would be something sports related with a value between $150–$200, right? Tell us you see that…

You are a genius! How are you able to make such a crazy {sarcasm} prediction? What you have done, perhaps without even realizing it, is mentally defined *trend lines* on this chart. You just eyeballed it that time, so let's go ahead and draw some in:

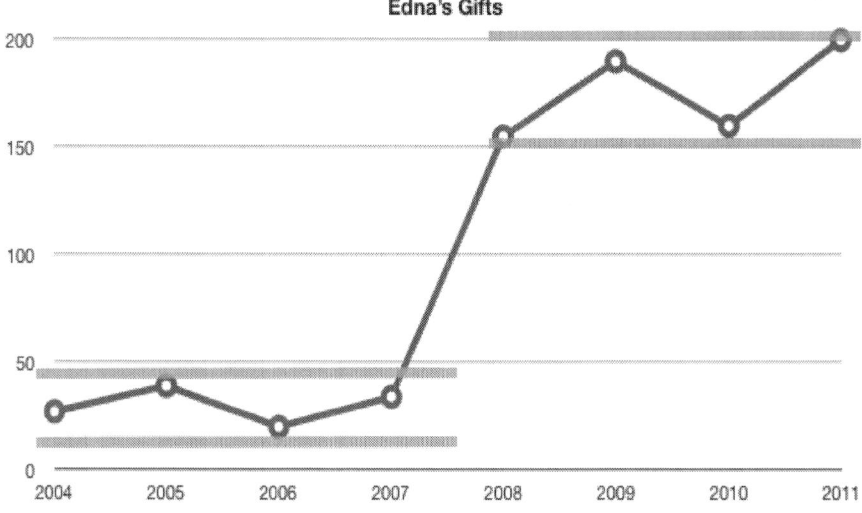

[fig 10.2]

Now all of a sudden, Aunt Edna's behavior looks much more consistent and predictable even though her drinking at the family Christmas party makes her anything but. Gift prices oscillate up and down over shorter periods, with the broader patterns defined by the extremes. Those overall patterns can be up or down or flat, and the oscillations inside of them can be increasing or decreasing or can remain steady. In real life, trend lines can actually be inclined, declined, converging, diverging, parallel, or whatever.

The area between the parallel lines is actually known as a "price channel," and it gives us a good idea about where Aunt Edna's next expenditure might fall. But you never know...Uncle Frank may take hold of that credit card and you are back to crappy gifts again or maybe even worse...a birthday card!

Danger Will Robinson!

A word of warning here—you always have to remember that when attempting pattern recognition of any sort, that you are imposing assumptions on top of real data and smoothing that real data out. You could be accidentally including or excluding important data points, and are probably missing important information that can make at least some of your pattern fitting—wrong. Take the chart below for example:

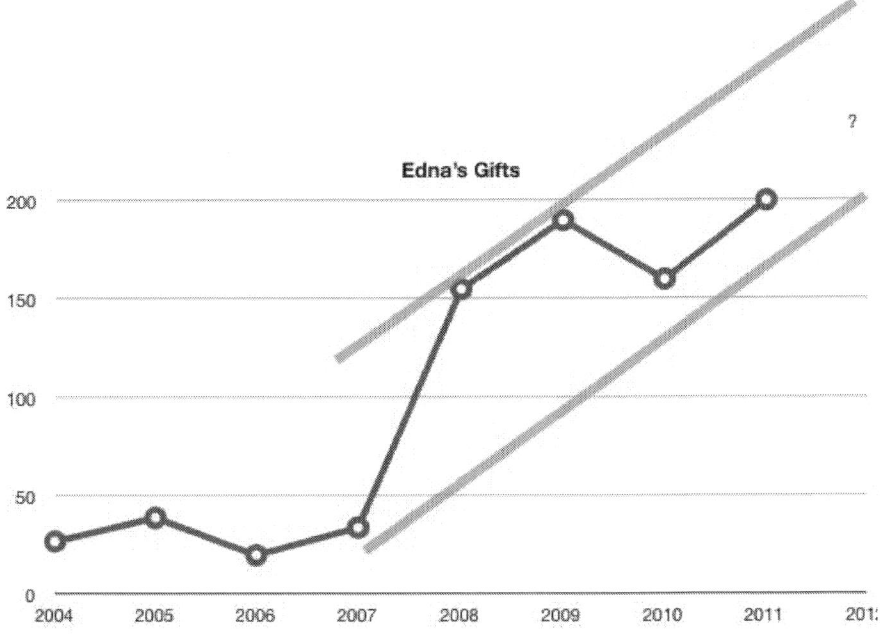

[fig 10.3]

If we create trend lines that include too much data like in the chart above, we will see trends and patterns that don't actually exist. For example, if we try to include 2007, when Edna didn't have a credit card with data from 2008 through 2012 when she did have plastic in her purse, we will be drawing trend lines slanting up. This pattern may push us towards predicting a more expensive gift in 2012; one that even drunken Edna won't buy with her new found wealth.

So when you are putting trend lines on a chart, whether mentally or actually drawing them in, you have to be aware of fundamental changes, announcements and news. The difference between knowing and not knowing that Edna got a credit card in 2008 could mean the difference between really really good or really really bad technical analysis and prediction.

Support Lines

Using our examples above, the support lines are the lines on the bottom of the two sets of parallel lines. These represent the level below which your Aunt Edna would feel like she was spending too little on you. Before her credit card, she would feel guilty if she gave you a gift that cost less than about $20. After her credit card arrived in the mail, somehow she decided to spend at least $150 on you every year. Anything less would make her feel like she wasn't taking care of you!

Strictly speaking, in the markets the support level or support line for a stock is the price at which demand for the stock is thought to be high enough to keep it from falling lower. Standard economic theory predicts that as the price falls, buyers become more inclined to buy and sellers become less inclined to sell. When a stock begins to fall towards a support line, the buyers start to say, "Hey, this is a good deal at this price, here's my money," while the sellers start to say, "I think I'll hang onto my stock at this price." The price has to rise or neither will get what they want, so it tends to find support at that price.

Support and resistance lines are somewhat arbitrary—they aren't necessarily solid and including all "lowest prices;" they are at your discretion as to where to put them. Think of them as soft boundaries.

[fig 10.4]

You look at a chart like this for Caterpillar (CAT) and it's pretty easy to see that every time this stock gets down to $80–83, it goes back up again. Each time it climbs out differently, but indeed, each time it goes back up. So having not checked any other data and seeing that this stock had reached down to $83 again, what would your prediction be? Obviously if you were going to stake real money on that prediction, you'd want to see more than just this chart.

Resistance Lines

Resistance lines are basically the opposite of a support level or support line; these are the lines on the top of the two parallel lines in the Aunt Edna example. Going back to your aunt's gift-giving analysis, resistance lines are the gift values above which she would feel like she was spoiling you. Before her credit card, this would've been anything over about $40, and after it would've been anything over $200.

In the markets, as the price of a stock goes up, sellers become more inclined to sell and buyers become less inclined to buy. The price eventually rises to the resistance level and demand falls off. As the price is going up, the seller says, "At this price I am ready to profit," while the buyers start to say, "Eh, that's too much for that stock, I won't pay that much." The price has to fall or neither will get what they want.

Caterpillar Incorporated (CAT)

[fig 10.5]

Take a look at the chart above. You can see that every time the price of CAT gets to $90–95, it falls. It falls differently each time, but it does fall. So if you saw no other data but noticed that the price had reached $90–95 what would you predict the price will do in the future? Exactly—support and resistance lines give you a nice basic starting point for your evaluation of a stock's price—it really is that easy.

Support and Resistance are Related

It happens a lot; over time, resistance lines will become support lines and vice versa. Let's say that a stock is bumping up against a resistance line over and over again for a few weeks or months. For whatever reason, XYZ just can't get above $30/share. Then it happens—the stock "breaks out" and closes above $30 for several straight sessions. It's very likely that this former resistance line will now become the support line, meaning that now it's much less likely for the stock to dip below $30.

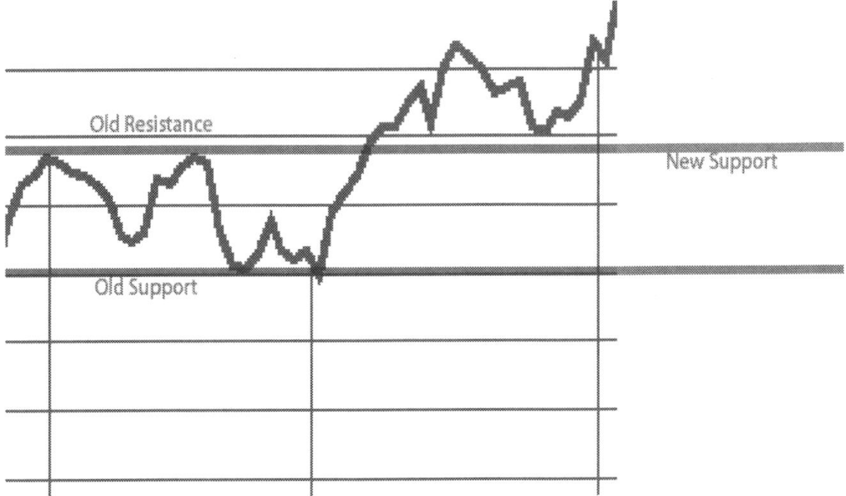

[fig 10.6]

What is going on is this; as the price goes above the resistance level, the signal to the market is that the factors that create demand have overcome the factors that create supply—if the price comes back down to this level, there will be an increase in supply of that stock. It could be anything: a new analyst price target, an earnings report, or some other announcement, but for whatever reason, the stock has cleared a psychological hurdle.

The same thing can happen in reverse; once a stock's price breaks *below* a support level, the broken support level can turn into a resistance level. This is called "breaking lower." If RSM stock has a support level of $85, but closes below $85 for the first time in a long time, it is possible that $85 will become a new resistance level. The break of support indicates that factors creating supply have overcome the factors creating demand. Therefore, if the price returns to this level, there is likely to be an increase in supply, which will lead to resistance. Again, this could be because of anything: analyst downgrade, earnings miss, etc.

Tops and Bottoms

It's really hard to time the market on a particular stock, and usually nearly impossible to buy at the absolute bottom or sell at the absolute top. When it does happen, you obviously only know it in retrospect, so it's a lot of wasted effort to try and catch the wave perfectly. That doesn't mean that looking for tops and bottoms is useless. There is actually valuable information at these inflection points because with swing trades, we are always watching for a change in direction or a new trend.

There are two very simple patterns you will hear batted about and they apply to market valleys and peaks. They are double and triple bottoms, and double and triple tops.

Double Bottoms

Stock price inflection points usually aren't as clean as a "V," like you see in the fictional example below; the low for a stock isn't usually a point at which it falls, falls, falls, falls, then reverses and gains, gains, gains, gains.

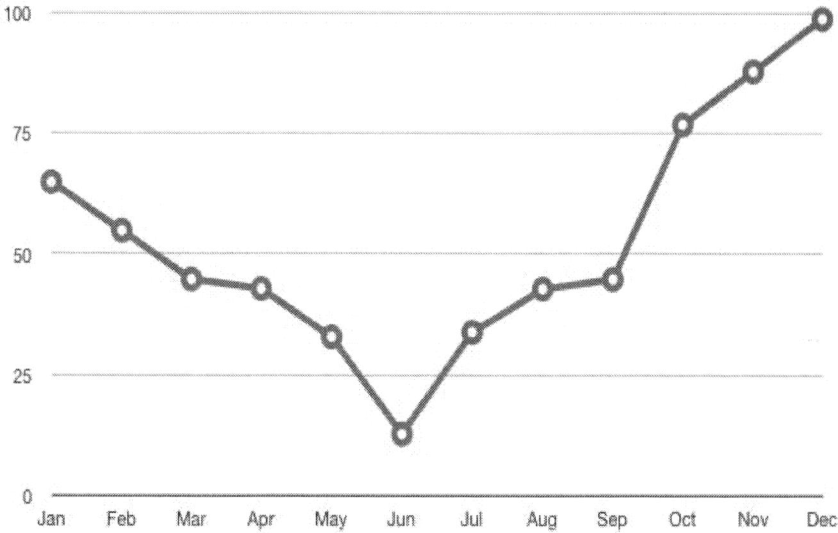

[fig 10.7]

This happens sometimes, but not often. The market isn't a machine (yet); it is composed of human beings, and their psychology tends to complicate matters a bit. There usually isn't some sort of decision made all at once where an unpopular stock suddenly becomes popular.

What is likely to happen looks a little more like this for our fictional stock XYZ:

- XYZ is out of favor for whatever reason. Could be accounting problems, earnings disappointments, or strategic disadvantages —it really doesn't matter. The stock is falling consistently over weeks or months.

- News about XYZ comes out to contradict the above sentiment: accounting issues resolved, earnings above expectations, a new strategic partnership gives the company an advantage over its competition.

- The first buyers come back to the stock, stopping the slide and driving the price higher for a few sessions. Some support builds on low volume. Short sellers may also see a risk in a reversal and buy the stock back.

- Sellers come back in increasing volume, but they still outnumber buyers, so the price slips again.
- Based on the strengthening fundamentals and perhaps a perception of being "oversold," the broader market takes note and buyers come back in, driving the price higher.

The chart may look a little something like this:

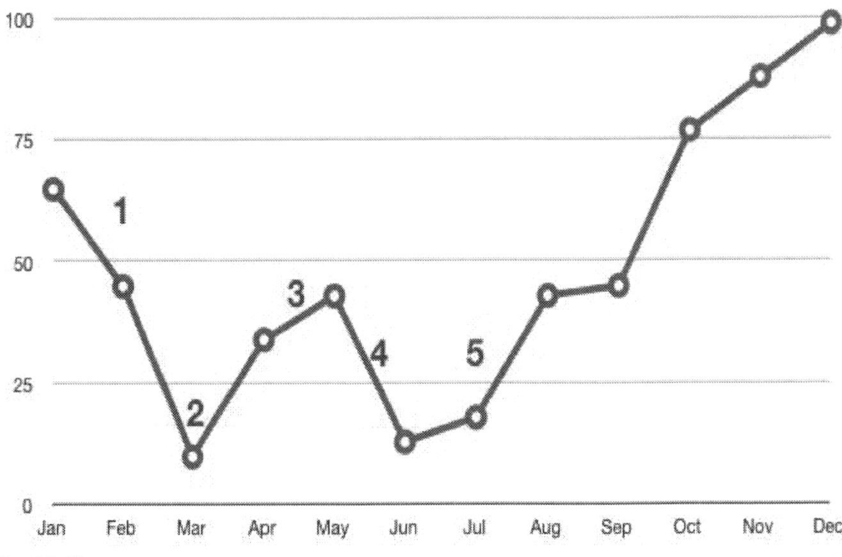

[fig 10.8]

1. Stock is in decline.
2. Price reaches a bottom when new information comes into play.
3. Price rises as buyers return, short sellers exit.
4. Profit taking.
5. Broader market support on greater volume drives price higher.

The reason this is called a double bottom is really because the price falls to a support level twice (at A and B), then rebounds. See fig 10.9:

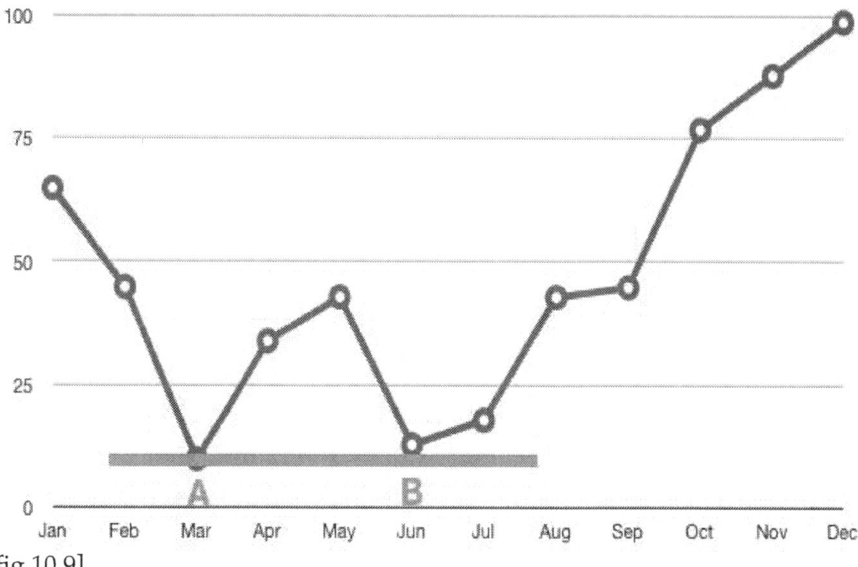

[fig 10.9]

When the stock price got back down to its support level at B, could we be certain that it was ready to move higher? Probably not. What about the next month; July? Probably not terribly certain there either. See below:

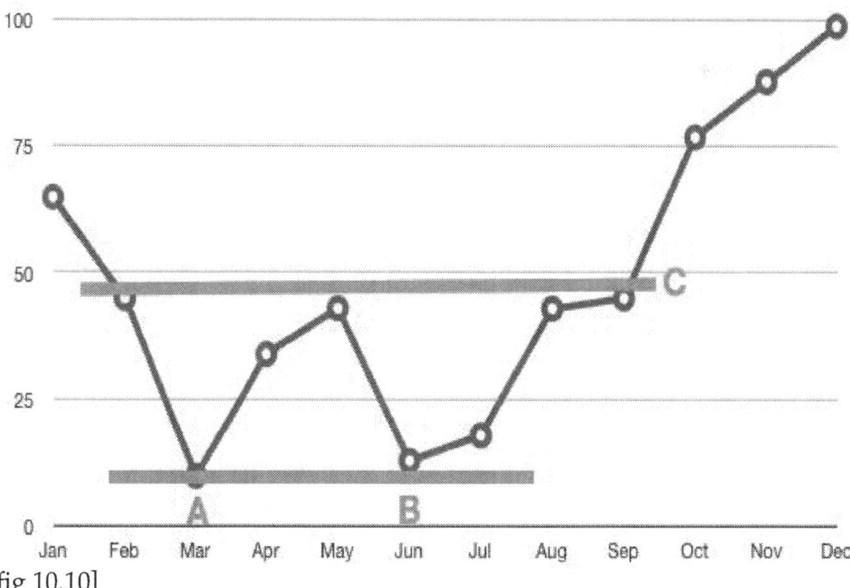

[fig 10.10]

It really wasn't until C that we could see that the stock had broken through its resistance level and was ready to move higher on a more consistent basis. What the market is telling us from a chart like this is that the game has changed for this stock for now.

Triple Bottom

The double bottom's big brother (or sister) is the triple bottom. This is where the support level is tested three times instead of twice. There is hesitation in the market as well as institutional moves that hamper the true inflection and final breakout. However, just like the double bottom, the triple bottom does break its short term resistance line before it moves broadly higher. This is called the *breakout*—a word you will hear a lot in trader chat.

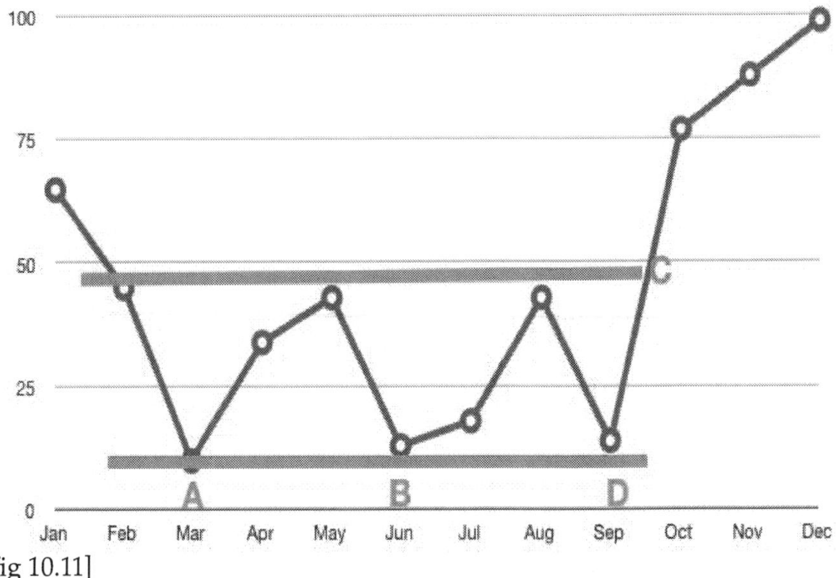

[fig 10.11]

This fine picture of the Loch Ness Monster is a good example of a fictional triple bottom. Instead of bottoming in June, we test the short-term resistance again in August before we get back down to our support price in September. After that we are off to the races.

The question, as always, is whether or not you can know at B whether you have hit the true inflection point, or whether you will bounce on the support line one more time or maybe again and again. The answer is that without more data, you really can't predict that. You have to treat a double or triple bottom as a neutral pattern until a breakout occurs. So the answer is that you can become a lot more certain that the bottom is behind you after mid-September (point C).

See, picking a "bottom" is really hard to do! Spotting a breakout, however, can be a little easier.

Double and Triple Tops

The patterns described above work in exact opposite for peak prices. Just take the same diagrams and invert them. Instead of a stock in decline that reaches a bottom, we are talking about a stock that has been going up but is reaching a high. It may test that resistance level two or three times before breaking lower. The same principles work in reverse.

Moving Averages

Even if statistics were not your strong suit in school, you are probably able to grasp the concept of an average; if you have two numbers and want their average, you add them together and divide by the number of numbers you are averaging. So the average of 4 and 6 is 4 + 6 divided by 2, which equals 5. Duh! A kid could do this. Now just imagine how easy it is when the computer does all the calculating for you.

With a series of data points—like you get from a series of stock prices—this averaging becomes really powerful. We need a way to simplify all of this short-term data wherever we can, and averages—specifically moving averages—are a way of doing that. Simple moving averages smooth out the day-to-day ups and downs by looking at past price behavior at a particular point in time, they then plot that average over time. Sounds more complicated than it is.

Simple Moving Average (SMA)

A SMA is a nice little tool available on most charting sections of your online trading platform that allows you to smooth out day-to-day price movements. The simple moving average simply takes a time series of prices, and averages them. For example, the 10-day SMA for 10, 15, 22, 33, 29, 37, 26, 39, 43, 45 is 29.9 (sum/10). So instead of looking at each day individually and trying to decide what it tells us about a trend, we can take several days together and smooth out the bumps.

Here is a real-world example. The chart below shows AAPL with a 10-day moving average. The two outside lines are a 6% envelope around the moving average. Why did we choose 6%? It's arbitrary, but what we're trying to do is envelop most of the daily moves—not all of them, but most.

[fig 10.12]

Once again you can see that on any given day, it's very likely that AAPL stock will trade within this price envelope of 6% of the moving average. So on an ongoing basis, moving averages are a lot like a moving support and resistance channel like we saw above with Aunt Edna's gifts. Notice that each time the price gets near the top or the bottom of the moving average envelope, the price tends to correct up or down.

Given the chart above, what do you think AAPL will do at the end of July? We'd really like to know actually—earnings come out tomorrow—and we are betting AAPL goes higher. How much higher? Well given this simple moving average, we'd bet as high as 640 and as low as maybe 575. Today the stock is trading somewhere near 600, so we're betting there's a greater chance that the stock goes up than down when earnings come out tomorrow. Of course the earnings themselves will decide if we are on the right or wrong side of that wager.

Exponential Moving Average (EMA)

The market has memory, and just like for any of us individuals, the most recent memories tend to be a little clearer and distant ones are a little foggier. Technically, we can apply this to moving averages as well. An exponential moving average (EMA) gives more weight to recent prices than to older prices; meaning that if a stock trades at $10 last week and $30 this week, the exponential moving average isn't $20, but rather skewed to the more recent price. Depending on the exponential and the number of data points, this might be $25 for our example above.

The next chart is what the EMA (we use the 30-day EMA a lot) looks like in practice. Figure 10.13 is the same exact chart as we have above for AAPL, but with a 30-day EMA with a 6% envelope:

[fig 10.13]

Notice on this chart that the higher the stock moves above its average, the more it "drags" the average. This is because of the longer averaging time of 30 days compared to 10 days, not because of the exponential. So when the stock is going up from February to April, it's trading well above the 30-day moving average. Lag is important, because if a stock continues to trade above its moving average, that means that it's going up faster and faster... exponentially!

Not many stocks can behave that way forever, and even mighty AAPL corrects in April. Even then, the correction doesn't spend much time below the 30-day EMA. When it does dip below in mid-May, it's important to note there were other outside factors in the broader market, like the debt crisis in Europe and new threats of Greek insolvency.

Support and Resistance on Moving Averages

Moving average lines very frequently act as support and resistance lines for many stocks. When a stock is generally trending up, it's supported by its 60-day average. When it's in decline, the price finds resistance at its 60-day moving average price. Not always, certainly, but often enough for us to say hmmmmmm... Check out the AAPL chart below with a 60-day EMA plotted:

[fig 10.14]

Notice anything kind of strange here? Most of the time, AAPL is trading above its 60-day moving average. There is that stretch in May during a broad-market sell-off, but after that it climbs right back up and (mostly) trades above that EMA. Most of the time, the 60-day moving average acts as a support level for the stock.

This tendency can help us identify swing trading opportunities. For example, when AAPL sank below its 60-day moving average in May and again in early June, it recovered pretty quickly. Buying on these dips can often make you a nice little profit!

Other Tools

There are other technical analysis tools you can look at, like stochastic indicators, Bollinger bands, and literally on and on and on and on, some of which we will talk about in the next chapter, and others that are beyond the scope of this book. But all these tools are used to do one thing: gauge the approximate past behavior of a stock and look for trends that you hope will continue going forward, or indicate a fundamental change going forward.

Apply this stuff to swing trading, please!

You'll notice from these diagrams that we are talking about patterns of weeks or months, and not the days to about a week that swing traders are concerned with—that's on purpose. As we look at potential swing trade opportunities, we need to know what the broad overall sentiment for the stock might be. Is it:

- In limbo waiting for some news to send it in one direction or another?

- In decline with nothing coming in the next week that might reverse that trend?
- In decline with news coming that might reverse that trend in the next week?
- Going up but there is no news coming that might reverse that trend?
- Going up but there is news coming that might reverse that trend?

Decision Time

So you are tied up to your slip or hooked up to your RV spot or saddled up in an internet cafe, and it's time to make some money. As swing traders, we have two distinct routes available to us:

1. Trade the range. Find a stock with a trading range we understand and buy on a dip.
2. Trade an inflection. Look for a stock poised to break out and potentially make much larger profits.

Option one is a relatively easy way to pad your account with a little bit of cash, but most of the time, we look for this second option.

Option #1: Trade the Range

Sometimes your travel schedule may limit your opportunity to trade on a big mover, and that's OK. Our overarching strategy in this book is to get to know a handful of stocks really, really well. Of that lot, there just might not be any big moves coming anytime soon. That's OK—chill out.

Don't be desperate—impulse buying leads to buyer's remorse—don't be that guy. It would be a big mistake to go shopping for new-to-you stocks just because they are making the kind of price moves that you want. Reading a couple of blog posts and scanning their financials on Yahoo does not an expert make. Just because there is high volatility in stock ABC that you don't know much about, doesn't mean you need to own it.

So without the volatility in the stocks we know well, we need to stick with the simple buy low, sell high strategy. We'll talk more extensively about "buying on a dip," in the next chapter with our short-term strategies. But the principle here for swing trading a range is pretty simple—you analyze your favorite stocks to find one where you can:

Step 1. **Identify** a clear target. Make sure there is no major scheduled news. That means no investor calls, no earnings announcements, no headlines expected that might move the stock radically. We want the stock to do its "normal" thing without drama.

Step 2. **Analysis.** Make sure the stock is trending. That means that it's gradually going up or gradually going down. We don't want a stock that's bouncing around.

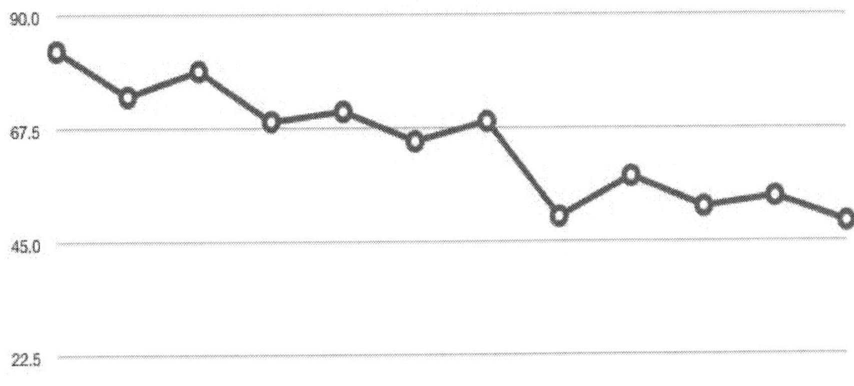

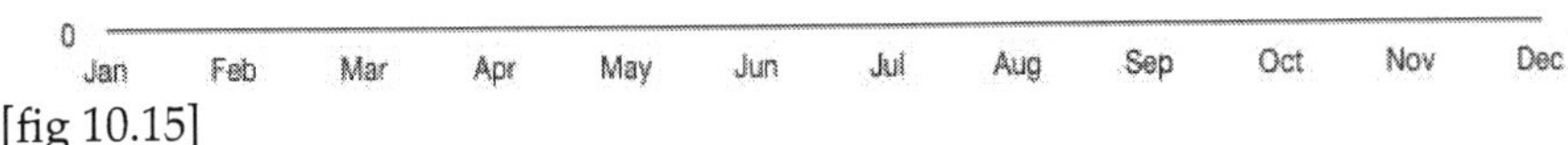

[fig 10.15]

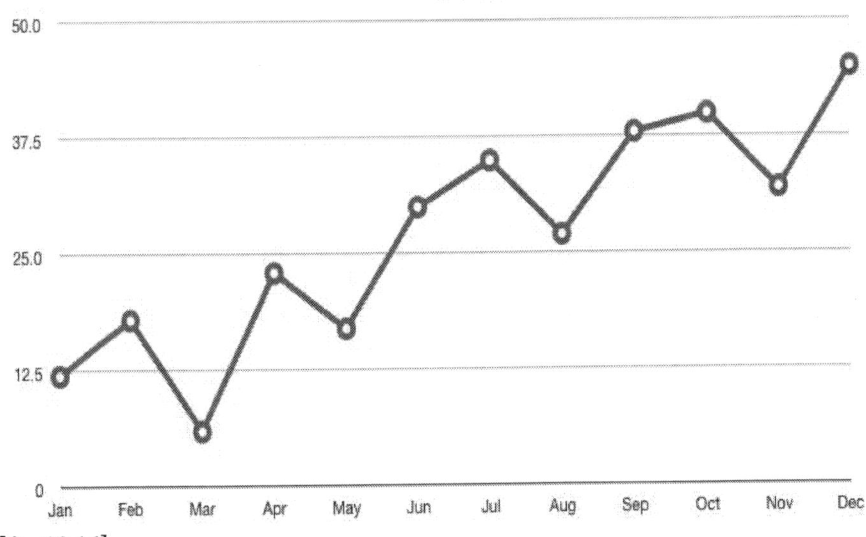

[fig 10.16]

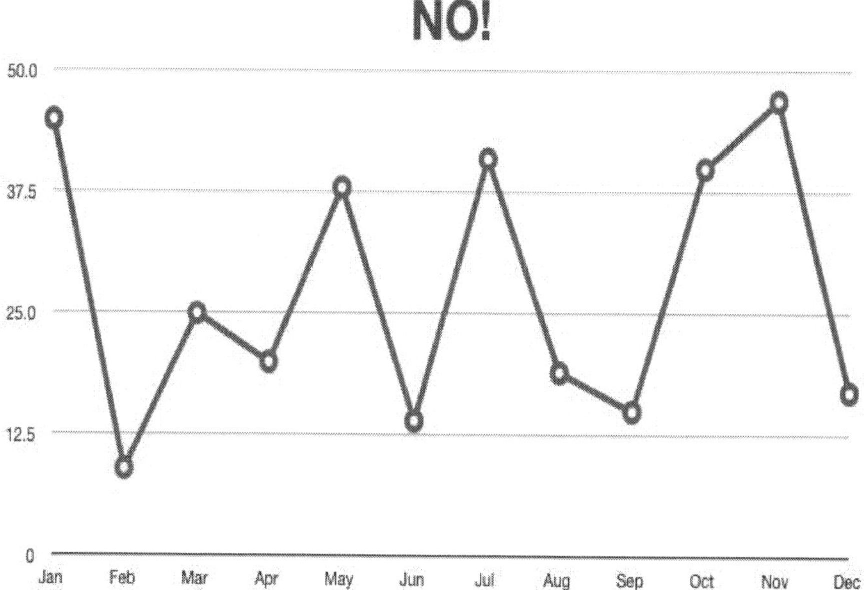

[fig 10.17]

Either of the first two examples would be good opportunities for a swing trade as you can easily see a general direction for the stock over monthly and yearly scales. At first glance, it looks like timing an opportunity isn't really all that difficult, but that's easier said than done because most stocks only trend about 1/3 of the time. That means that the other 2/3 of the time, they are in a *trading range*, meaning they are going up and down, up and down, up and down—as you see in the final example. As a slacker looking to trade only a few days a month, finding the right stock that happens to be trending is most of the work. The rest is somewhat mechanical.

Step 3. **Buy.** From the rudimentary technical analysis we talked about above, you should be able to identify the low end of the stock's weekly or biweekly range, so all you really need to do is buy it the next time it reaches near that low. If you can't buy near that low, then don't buy.

Step 4. **Hold** on and chill out. In the absence of any major unexpected news, once you are in your position you are just waiting until you have your profit. The price may oscillate over the next five to seven days, and it may go down before it goes back up—that's part of the game. If there's no fundamental change for the company; no unexpected news, no announcements, and no broad-market sell-offs, then just hold on and wait for it to go back up.

Step 5. **Sell.** The idea is that you sell it for more than you bought it for (duh!), but knowing when to lock in those profits and sell is the tough part. If we are long the stock and bullish, then we like to sell when it gets near the top of its

6–10% envelope on the 20- 30-day moving averages or moves to the top of its 14-day high. If you are bearish and have shorted, a good exit is when it reaches down near a support level like the 20- 30-day moving average line or its two-week low.

This strategy is embarrassingly simple—that's a good thing for the trader who is just starting out. This strategy will have you delving into your trading platform where you'll learn how to chart a stock, how to analyze that chart no matter how basically, how to buy a stock, and most importantly how to sell. You can risk as much or as little as you like, and in the process you will learn about your own trader psyche. This is a terrific strategy for getting your feet wet.

Now with that said, explaining this basic strategy to you is probably not worth the price of this book, so let's move on to the more interesting strategy.

Loving Volatility – The Big Moves

As swing traders, the most profitable opportunities occur by anticipating when stocks are going to break higher or lower. Breaks are any time a stock price makes a very large move compared to its weekly or monthly average volatility. For our purposes, we'd like to define a break as anything over either four percent higher or lower, although this is somewhat arbitrary. Two percent for Microsoft is almost a break.

Yes, this is difficult to do, but if it were easy, *"everyone"* would do it, and that's why *"everyone"* invests in mutual funds.

Here is the lowdown: the market works on distinctly different time scales depending on which market participants we are talking about. Day traders only care about what is happening during a particular day. They are in and out of their positions very quickly and have marginal effect on stock price. Day traders don't care if there is a broader price inflection—they just care about what is going on *right now*—this second. The day trader doesn't really care if he is getting in at the top or the bottom.

Institutional investors are the opposite: they make one or two trades a month in any particular stock. They have big price impacts, but the frequency is lower. They don't care about what is going on with the price on a day-to-day basis necessarily and they don't care if they time the market perfectly to catch the absolute bottom or top. They are in the stock for months, if not years, so they don't really care if they are getting the best price this week.

Like the three bears (or was it three little pigs?), as swing traders we are right in the middle. We don't necessarily care about the small price moves during a particular day, and we don't care about whether we are in a double or triple top or bottom. We only want to catch those inflection points, where the stock goes in one direction or another for a few days. If the stock tests its support or resistance level again next week or the week after, we could care less; we'll be on the beach buying drinks or paying our marina tab with the profits!

Breakout Patterns

Predicting big moves, the ones where we see a distinct "break" in price, is in essence the holy grail of swing trading. You can't do any better than predicting a stock will move out of its price channel to top new (or recent) highs or plunge to new (or recent) lows. A properly timed trade can yield very high profits.

Here are the basic patterns we are looking for to find a breakout or break in the price:

- channels
- flags
- head and shoulders
- triangles

Channels

We've already talked a little bit about breaking above and below resistance lines. In either case this means the stock is leaving its localized trading range and we call this trading range a channel. These are the easiest to spot: the stock is bouncing between a localized high and a localized low. When the price moves above a resistance line, it's possible that it will break higher. On the other hand, when it moves below a support line, it's possible it's going to break lower.

On the chart below, we have drawn in the overall channel for NFLX, but you can see channels within the broader channel, as well as the breaks higher and lower.

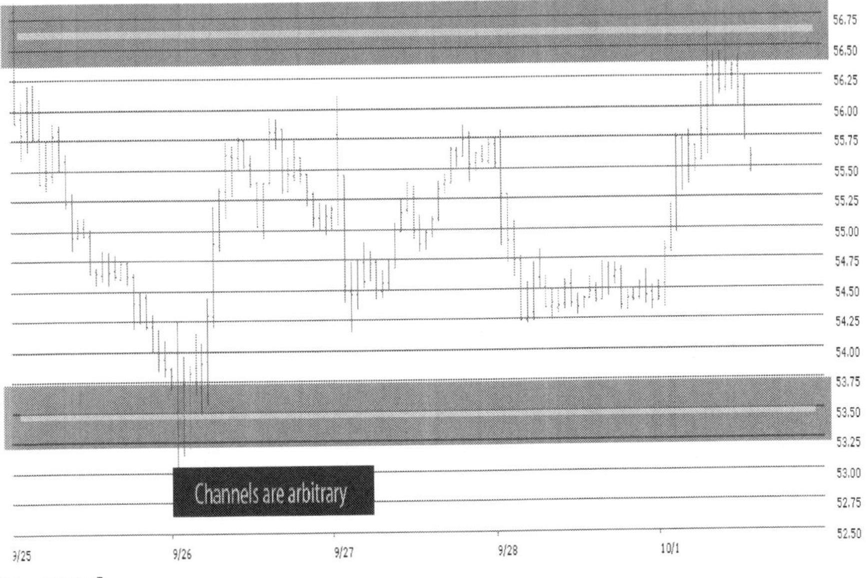

[fig 10.18]

What is going on? The stock is more or less in equilibrium with an equal number of buyers and sellers in the market at any one time. Volume (total number of shares traded) is relatively stable. Then, something happens; some new information or news spreads across the market. In the case of good news for the stock, buyers move in, driving the price through the resistance line. Other buyers see the opportunity and create momentum. The stock continues to move higher on increased volume. If there is bad news, sellers prevail and drive the price lower on increased volume.

Why? This may be an artifact of the digital age and sophisticated online trading platforms. At any one time, there are thousands of traders sitting on the sidelines watching any given stock. Everyone has watch lists like we've encouraged you to develop in this book. The more "sophisticated" traders set their software to notify them when the price of their watched stock goes above or below a predetermined level, usually a resistance or support level. Some even set long-term buy or sell orders based on these price channels. If their stock breaks out, they want in on it, and sometimes their trades are executed automatically.

How to swing trade it? Channel breakouts are probably the most likely to pay off on a one to three day basis, depending on the strength of any news. Because of the automated nature of the catalyst, it's best to ride this one like a day-trade or a one to three day trade and get out before the momentum falls away. For the option trader, it's critical that you get in early.

Flags

Once we describe the flag, you will see them on every chart you look at. Flags are basically small interruptions or reversals in an overall trend. They represent times of consolidation when the overall market basically hits "pause," while smaller volume trades are made. For example, a stock is trending overall higher, then it moves higher even faster, then out of nowhere it drops lower, then resumes the overall trend and continues to move higher.

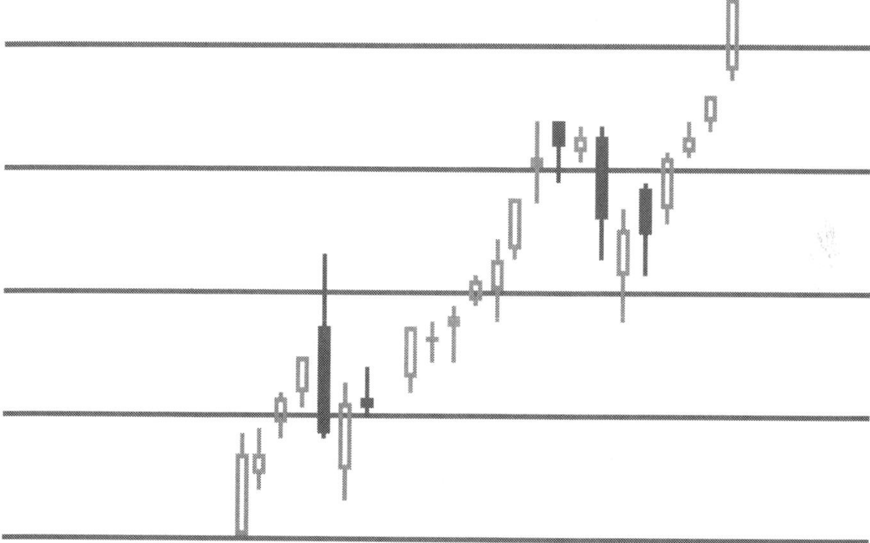

[fig 10.19]

What is going on? News or announcements likely play little or no role here. With a flag, the pricing trends are much more mechanical. If trending higher, buyers outnumber sellers (the ratio of sellers to buyers will determine how quickly the price goes up). Then buyers stop (or diminish) buying, while sellers continue at the same rate. Volume decreases (or continues almost unchanged) while the price breaks lower because the supply-demand balance has been disrupted. The market re-balances relatively quickly, and the trend heads higher once again.

Why? This happens because large investors like fund managers have to buy and sell in chunks over a period of days so that they don't move the market too far in one direction or another and cut into their own profits. In the case of a buyer where the stock is trending higher, they buy in blocks so they don't drive the price too high while they are accumulating. Eventually they run out of stock to buy while sellers in the market remain steady, so the price moves lower temporarily.

[fig 10.20]

How to swing trade? The best way to play a flag is to trade opposite the overall trend when you first identify the price move on waning volume. How long you stay in the trade depends primarily on how large the "correction" on lower volume is. Generally the larger the initial move, the shorter the duration of the flag before the overriding trend continues.

Head and Shoulders

Traders aren't a very sophisticated bunch, and chart pattern names are descriptive for a reason. This one looks exactly like you might expect: a large pointy thing on top with two somewhat less pointy things on either side of it. It looks a little bit like a head and shoulders. See figure 10.21.

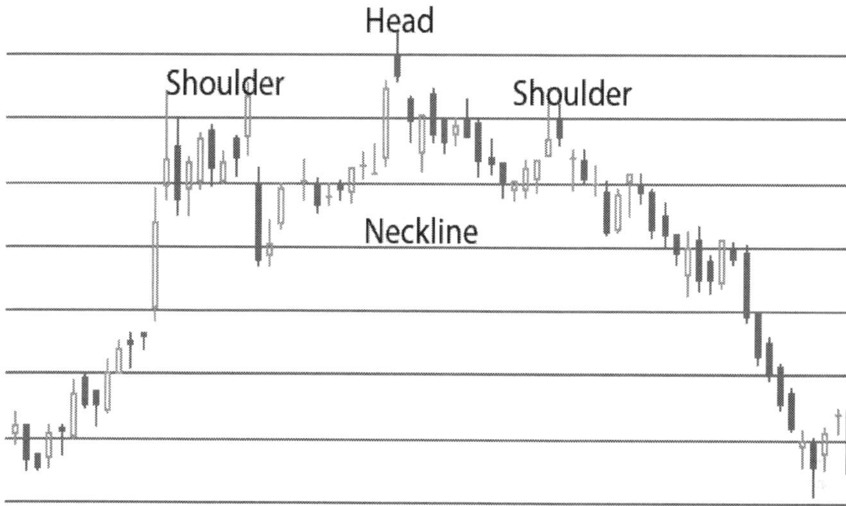

[fig 10.21]

This is generally an inflection or reversal pattern where an overall uptrend shifts to a downtrend. The duration of these reversals can be a couple of days to more than a couple weeks. Generally speaking this sort of pattern occurs most often when sector or industry shaking news has really turned the tables on one or more companies. Lawsuits and judgements will do this, earnings will do this, new product announcements will do this. You get the idea.

The market is confused and tentative—sentiment is all over the map—some are bullish, some are bearish, and most don't know what to think. What may have looked like good news for a stock becomes tepid, and then considered inconsequential, or maybe even bad news. It also happens when news is expected for a long time and then fails to wow the market.

What is going on here? This is one of the more complicated patterns to explain because the price moves aren't quite as important to recognize as the volume changes. First, the stock is generally going up, most likely on good news. Eventually, the market begins to slow down and the forces of supply and demand are generally considered in balance. Sellers start to doubt the stock or want to lock in profits, (where we see the first or "left" shoulder) and the stock slides a bit forming the neckline. Initially, tentative buyers who saw the announcement and still think it's a turning point for the company, think it's now time to return to the market and "buy on the dip," ultimately pushing the stock through to new highs, which is the top of the head.

It isn't long before the new highs are met and the profit takers begin to press the stock lower again (beginning of the right shoulder). Tentative buyers then step back in and the market rallies once more, but (usually) fails to get to the high that we saw at the peak of the head, forming the right shoulder. Buyers, seeing that there was never a legitimate reason for the run-up, cash-out and run for the exits; the trend reversal is complete—this stock is now out of favor.

Volume is a lot more important for this pattern than for the others. Volume generally goes higher as the speculators get in on what has become a "good thing." However once the price gets to the top of the head, volume goes way down. It's not that the market has changed its mind about this stock yet, but rather that new fans are no longer arriving to the party. When the price moves higher for the right shoulder, there continues to be very low volume. This last grasp for higher prices is just one last attempt for late arrivals to "get a good deal," and this really signals that the upside on this darling is gone gone gone. Volume then ramps up as the speculative buyers ditch the stock, pressing the price lower and lower. New selling comes in and previous buyers get out.

Why? This pattern happens because everyone likes a winner, no one likes a loser, and some announcements look better for a company at first glance. This is mostly a case of irrational exuberance—there is news of some sort of a partnership or perhaps a new exciting product is released, or maybe it's an analyst's upgrade. The stock appears in blogs, it gets talked about on TV—there is *buzz*. After the initial surge of interest, the market begins to question whether this really is a game changer for the company. Maybe this isn't as great a partnership or maybe the new sales figures are an anomaly and not indicative of growing product demand. Whatever. With no additional news or supporting announcements, the overall uptrend falters, albeit with some last gasps thrown in.

How to swing trade? There are a couple of methods here, depending on your time frame and historic volatility for this stock. If you are short on time, it's fine to get in when you first hear the news, even if you don't think it will benefit the company as much as the rest of the market appears to. Be prepared to sell at the drop of a hat though as you can never be sure when the initial surge in volume will disappear. You are hoping to sell at the top of the head, so enduring some shorter term downside is part of the ride.

The other way to play a head and shoulders pattern is to wait for the second shoulder and then short it. Selling short or buying puts are both great strategies here. We like to wait to see if there is a secondary announcement after the initial surge and volume is faltering. If the stock continues to fall even with a positive supporting announcement, our confidence in continued lower prices is even higher.

Triangles

We saved the best for last, because this pattern, when properly identified, is one of the clearest signs that a stock is about to break higher or lower through a resistance line. Finding the entry point is as easy as identifying the apex (corner) of a triangle. A triangle pattern is the convergence of trend lines after a stock has been trending for a while. We'll go through examples of uptrends and downtrends separately.

Ascending Triangle
This is a bullish pattern with an uptrend flattening to a break higher. This pattern is identified by an uptrend, followed by a flat resistance level, but an ascending support line. The stock goes up, meeting the support line before falling to a higher low than previously. This oscillation continues with higher and higher lows, but relatively consistent highs—forming a mini-resistance level. As the ascending support line converges with the flat resistance line, the stock breaks higher, usually continuing steadily higher like we see for Jive Software in figure 10.22.

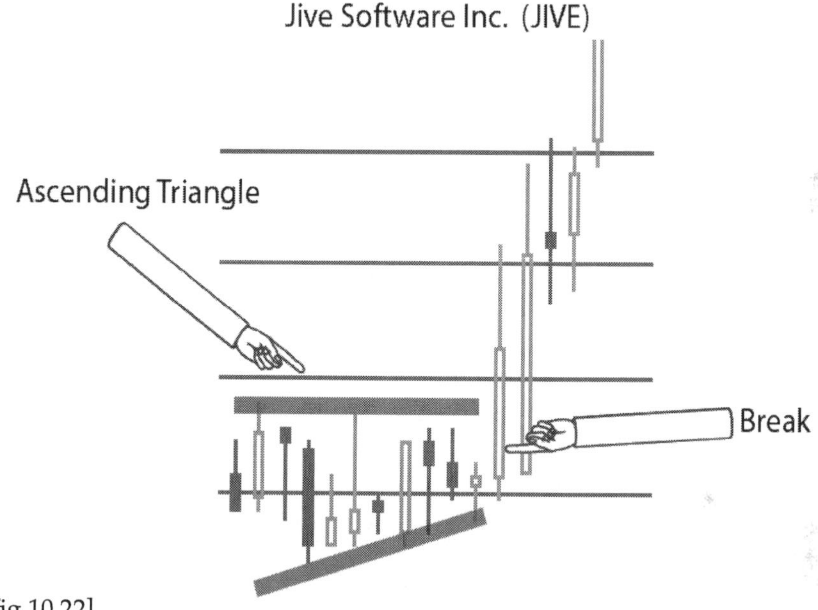

[fig 10.22]

What is going on? This stock has gone up for some time before leveling off, meaning that it was in favor and buyers were moving in, but eventually buyers and sellers reached equilibrium, and sellers began to take profits and leave the security for other opportunities. Volume is likely consistent throughout this pattern on a day to day basis. As the price falls, *new* buyers move in pushing prices higher, leading to more profit taking.

This time as the price falls, more new buyers are *slowly* moving in. This is why you don't see any volume spikes. The oscillation continues as sellers leave the security while buyers move in. Eventually, all of the sellers have left and buyers continue to move in, pushing the stock higher until it breaks through its resistance line and moves back into its original uptrend as momentum returns and everyone wants to get in while the gettin's good.

Why? In some ways, you can think of a triangle as a protracted flag pattern, but with more retail investors in play. The ascending triangle happens without major announcements most of the time. This is simply a case of the supply-demand economics for the stock falling into equilibrium while sellers get out because they feel that there is no more upside, and buyers move in because they believe in the fundamentals of the company. A lot of times, this will be accompanied by a broad market or sector rally.

How to swing trade? When the signal is clear, this is a no brainer. Go long the stock or call options as the highs and lows converge. The closer you are to the vertex of the triangle, the less time you have to wait for the upside. If you are in options, you have to lead this a day or two because this is an easy pattern for people to recognize and your calls will get expensive and cut into your profits. Once it has broken higher, you will want to get out quickly before volatility fades. If you are strictly in stock, you may want to wait for the break out to buy and then hold for a longer period.

Descending Triangle

This is obviously the opposite of the ascending triangle in every respect—this is a bearish pattern. The stock is in a downtrend, and there is a flat support line with a descending resistance line. The lows are relatively flat, but in this case the highs get lower and lower before the support line is broken and the downtrend continues. Agrium is an agricultural chemical fertilizer company.

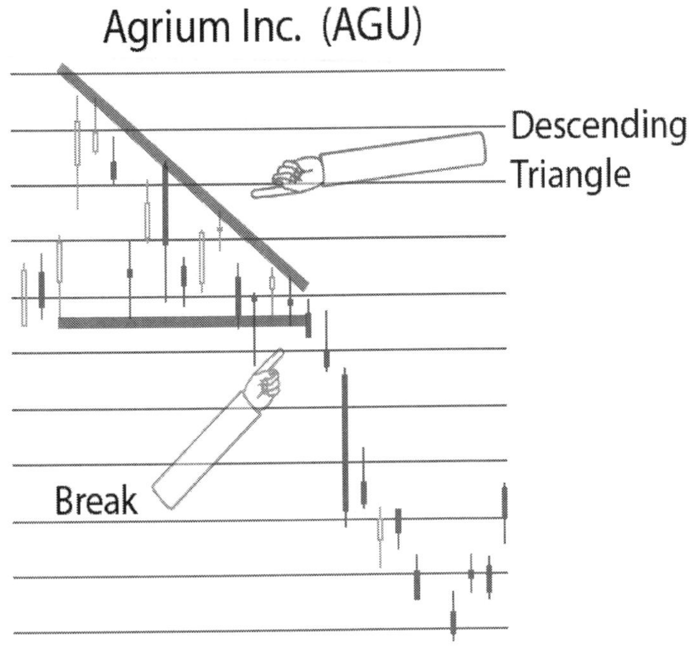

[fig 10.23]

What is going on? Like the ascending triangle, this is a bit of a protracted flag pattern, or more properly an "inverted flag." This stock was trending lower over a broad period before more buyers began to step in to create the support level. Again, there is a period of equilibrium with stable day-to-day volume. This is a "quiet time" for the stock. As new buyers are coming into the stock, sellers are leaving the stock for good. Eventually, the fresh blood (buyers) runs out, and sellers outnumber buyers, pressing the price lower.

Why? This is a sector in decline, a company in decline, or perhaps it's a faddish stock that ran way too high a few months ago and has been slowly bleeding for some time now. In the descending triangle (unlike the ascending triangle) there is likely some news, some catalyst that stops that decline. New buyers take note of the (relatively minor) positive sentiment in the blogosphere or on CNBC or whatever. Perhaps it's an analyst upgrade, or maybe a sales announcement. Fundamentally the company looks better on paper for some reason, however the market has memories of prior disappointments, and isn't eager to hop back on that train. New players, particularly retail investors take note of the new positive sentiment and move in tentatively, sensing the chance to catch a low, but the volume never increases and the momentum never swings, so the stock continues its decline.

How to swing trade? Well, as you might expect, this strategy is the opposite of the ascending triangle. Because downward movements are almost always more dramatic than upticks, the options trader wants to be particularly ready to buy puts ahead of the break and get out of them even faster. The options guy could be in this trade for as little as 24 to 48 hours. If choosing to short the stock, you have a much larger time horizon to work with; you can short earlier and can hold your position for a week or more sometimes.

Symmetric Triangle

This is the same idea as the ascending and descending flag patterns, but put together. Instead of a flat support level (descending triangle) or flat resistance level (ascending triangle), you have descending resistance and ascending support. Again, at the convergence point, the stock will break. The direction of that break is usually in the direction of the overall trend before the symmetric triangle formed.

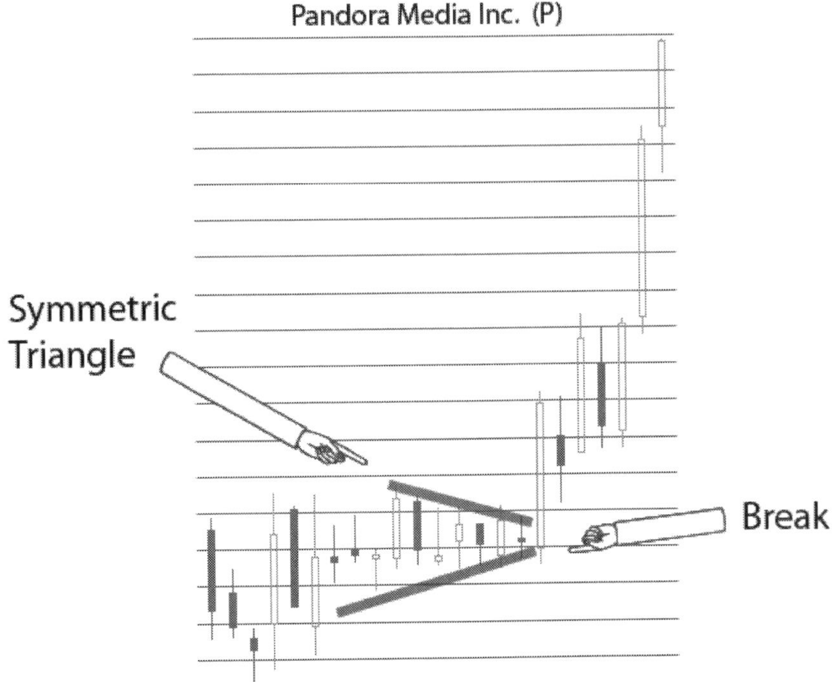

[fig 10.24]

What is going on? This is never as clean and easy to spot as the previous two patterns—it's always a confusing mess. There may be news, no news, whatever. However volume like with the other two triangle patterns is relatively consistent. The vertex of the triangle will become evident, but the direction of the break is usually a lot less clear.

Why? The market is confused about the company. The chart above is for Pandora Media. They basically provide personalized radio stations on the internet. At one moment they are the darlings of the new media space, then the market looks at their fundamental business model and gets frightened off —as a result, no one knows what to think about them, and their stock.

A stock showing a symmetric triangle pattern was usually in favor, then it was out of favor (or vice versa), and now there is a mixture of sentiment about what the future holds for this company—could be major growth, could be death and destruction. What starts to happen though is the fog begins to lift—people get more and more certain about whether they want to own this stock. Eventually however, the previous sentiment wins out, pushing the stock back into the original trend.

How to swing trade? We usually don't, and when we do, it's a gamble. What you can be most certain of is the timing of the move higher or lower, so this is most appropriately traded as an options spread, and maybe even a covered spread in which stock is held as well (things we will talk about later in the Options chapter). That way you may capitalize on the volatility without as much total exposure. This is a somewhat advanced move—it takes some skill and quite a bit of attention, and it may not be appropriate if you are focused mostly on slacking on the beach.

Institutional Momentum and Swing Trades

As we have talked about, it's really hard to time the market for a particular stock; trying to find good entry and exit points is always tough. No matter what pattern or opportunity you think you have identified, remember that you are a nobody trading with almost nothing. You are barely even a drop in the ocean. The big guys with their huge portfolios can come in and stamp you out and take your profits the minute after you make your move. The institutional investor's moves are both impossible to completely predict, but also incredibly important to be aware of.

The institutional investors are rarely just a single guy making a single decision to buy or sell huge blocks of stock. The actual traders are being told what to do by managers, who may even be following the direction of a manager above them. So what happens is the top dog says "let's get into XYZ," or "let's get out of XYZ," and it is up to the underlings to figure out how to do that with the highest profit or lowest loss. Because they don't want to move prices too much when they make their move by creating too much or too little demand, they buy and sell in chunks. This is called accumulation (buying) or distribution (selling).

So when you are contemplating your move and figuring out how and when to enter the trade regardless of the pattern, you want to be very careful to look at volume. If trading volume spikes in comparison to the stock's normal daily volume, while at the same time the price of the stock rises, you can make the assumption that large investors/institutions are buying. If volume is high and prices are dropping, institutions may be selling.

William O'Neil, author and founder of *Investor's Business Daily*, describes institutional investors as "elephants in a bathtub." When they get in and out of a stock they send big waves through the market.

Entry Point

So you have identified a pattern, see an opportunity, and have a strategy—what do you do? When do you enter your trade? Do you trade now and endure being premature, or do you wait for the herd to make their move and ride the wave? Regardless, if you are going long on the stock or short on options, or whatever, there are two schools of thought when it comes to entry:

- Lead the market. If you anticipate a move, then enduring some short-term downside for a later upside is fine. You may even accidentally time the bottom or top!

- Wait to be sure, then pounce when the first movers make their play. The downside is that you miss the big move at the beginning.

There is no right answer here. Depending on the situation, either one of these strategies can make sense. For the Slacker, the guy who doesn't want to spend a lot of time and energy babysitting their position, most of the time it makes more sense to lead the market a little. If you think that IMAX will surprise the market with earnings but you don't know by how much, it can make a lot of sense to enter your trade a few days in advance and check in after the earnings are released. You may even put in a limit order that will move you out of the position automatically once you have reached your predetermined profit or loss.

The longer we have traded, the more we have learned that you can waste a lot of time being unnecessarily greedy. Sometimes it's best to get into your position even if you don't buy at the low. You can then move on and enjoy the rest of your life while the market does its thing. That doesn't mean "set it and forget it," it means that once you have decided on your strategy: how much to risk and for how long, you can just check in from time to time until it's time to exit the trade.

Exit Point

Exiting your trade and locking in your profits is not as lackadaisical as the entry. The decision on when to sell is individual and will be made on a case by case basis. The most specific advice we can give when it comes to exiting a swing trade is:

- Sell when you have reached the target price you predicted before you entered the trade. If you haven't decided beforehand how much you think you can make, then you shouldn't be in the trade to begin with. When you have reached your goal, think about getting out, but don't get greedy. If it looks like there is still some momentum and you have time, then scale out, selling some of your position, then a little more, then the rest of it.

- Sell when you have reached your maximum loss limit. This will vary, but a loss of typically 15–25% of the capital risked is enough to get us to stop the loss. Because swing trades are longer than fading or day trading, enduring a little downside while you wait for the move you've predicted is just part of the game. However if we are down more than 15%, we typically decide we were wrong, cut our losses, and move on. Know your loss tolerance before you enter a trade, and stick to it. More on stop losses below.

- Sell when you have run out of time. If you have a week or two to trade while you wait out some bad weather, or your in-laws have come for a visit, or whatever it is, eventually it's going to be time to move on. If your position hasn't yet paid off, it can be really tempting to hold on for "one more day." You will be tempted to turn your trade into an investment and wait to see what comes later. Be careful here. If you are waiting for a catalyst or some sort of news to make the stock "pop," then you are better off just selling. If you really do believe in the long term value of the company and don't mind tying up the capital, then yes, go ahead and hold your long position in the stock. If it is an options trade, you don't have any choice, you have to sell—to do anything less is just inviting trouble.

Stop Loss

Good traders know how to make money in the market. Great traders know how to take a loss. That isn't haiku—that's reality. To succeed as a trader, you have to know how best to minimize your inevitable losses.

You will lose. Learn how to do it well.

We hope we have been able to scare you along the way with some dire warnings about losing money in the market. We aren't trying to cover our tails and avoid a lawsuit here. The fact is that you can and will lose money in the market—sometimes a lot of money. However, there are strategies you can use to help minimize those losses.

With swing trades, you are risking relatively large amounts of capital on a single trade as opposed to a long-term investment. That means that you can lose big and in a hurry. If you are trading options there is a floor to how much you can lose (which we will talk about later); you can't lose any more than the price of your contracts, so there is built in protection to the downside.

Employing a stop loss on a trade is a method by which you pre-define a level below which you don't want to own the stock or option. Depending on the brokerage, you will have different time periods over which you can set a sell order. The idea is that you set a price and if the security goes below that price, the brokerage will sell. This doesn't always work or work well, so here are some points to remember:

- Don't use round numbers. People are naturally drawn to round numbers. Retailers have known this for years; buyers are three times more likely to buy at $9.99 than $10. Floor traders, the guys who actually trade on the exchanges know this, too. So don't set your sell order for $10. Set it for $9.80. That way if and when the floor trader lowers his offer to $10 (or more likely $9.99) fishing for stop orders on a "dip" you won't get sold before the stock bounces higher.

- Don't set a sell order that's too close to the current or buy price. If the stop price is too close and the stock is volatile, it's likely that your order will get triggered and filled before the stock makes another move higher. If you are thinking of setting an order close to the market you are better off selling it now and being done with it.

- Don't forget to do it. Before you enter any trade, you have got to know how much pain you can endure. You have to set ahead of time your internal AND external stop loss. You may tell yourself ahead of the trade that you'll sell before XYZ gets down to $30, but once you are in the trade, you will find yourself hoping that it goes back up. Hope doesn't move stock prices. Markets do. Setting the actual sell order ahead of time is insurance against the fear of loss that can convince you, beyond all reasonable evidence to the contrary—that your stock is about to recover.

Summary

Swing trading strategies are the most appropriate for the trader who wants to participate in the market for just a few days a month or just a week or two every quarter. Now that computer algorithms and "high frequency traders" rule day trading, this is arguably the best opportunity an individual investor has to bring real skill to trading.

The patterns we've talked about represent just a smattering of what you should learn in order to be really effective and profitable. The best traders actually never stop learning. We encourage you to go beyond the scope of this book and explore further.

Fade Trading

"Day trading" and "day traders" have a bit of a stigma: homebound, bathrobe-wearing adrenaline junkies betting the farm on single stock moves where big money is won or lost in a matter of minutes. Some of that reputation is deserved because day traders do look to capitalize on small price moves. They have to bet big because they're looking for only a few pennies of upside, and they have to risk a lot of capital to make worthwhile profits. The day trader's fundamental strategy is to see a stock doing something and bet it will continue to do this same thing for the next minute, or hour, or hours. This usually means riding momentum that already exists and just going along for the ride.*

(*This is a very risky strategy because with a lot of capital on the line, unpredictable moves can lead to tremendous losses in a very short period of time.)

Frankly we don't like the "day trader" label because that's not a very good way of describing what we really do with our short-term trades. Plus, we haven't owned or worn a bathrobe in a long, long time. Where do you even buy a bathrobe?

Not Necessarily "Day Trading"

Strictly speaking, day traders don't finish a trading day with positions on (still in the trade). Instead, they are in, they are out, and they finish the day "flat." That's not what we do, although every once in awhile that's how it works out.

As we talked about in the last chapter, most of the time we are swing trading over two to seven days or so. This chapter is going to focus on shorter-term strategies most accurately called, "fade trading."

Fading

The definition of fade trading is to buy on a dip in stock price and sell when the stock rallies—it's as simple as that. Is it easy? Not necessarily, but at least it's not very complicated.

In identifying potential trades, we are looking for one-off price spikes—in other words, the stocks we are looking at are either range bound or trending when the price spike occurs.

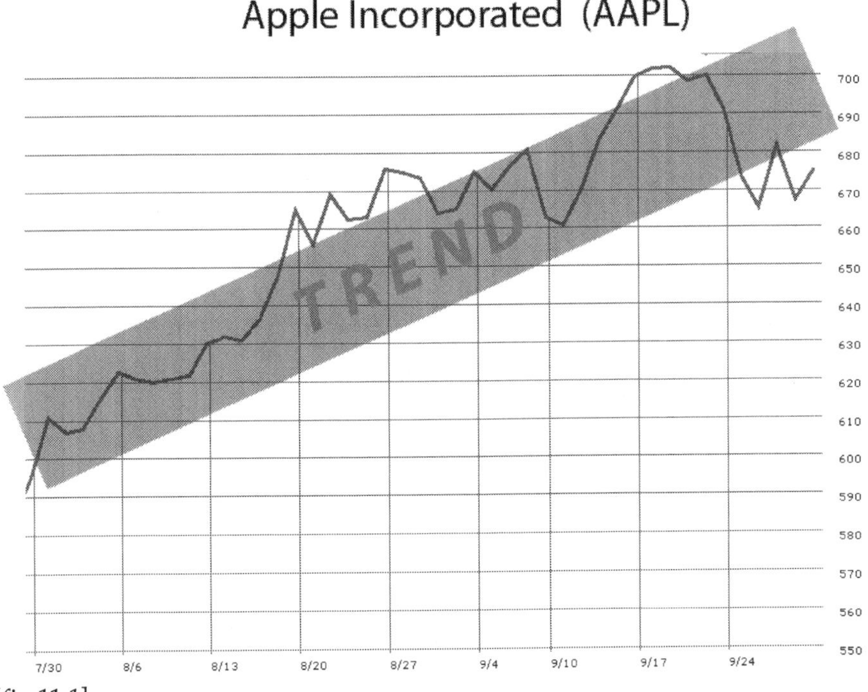

[fig 11.1]

You'll notice in the chart above that while there is an overall uptrend in AAPL over the last two months, there are certainly ups and downs on a daily and weekly basis. For the fade trader, these short-term, one to two or three day dips are where we can try to make money by fading. Let's zoom in on this chart toward the end of September:

[fig 11.2]

More than anything, we are looking for stock price movement that we deem *unwarranted* or an *overreaction*. These are situations in which we agree with what the market has been telling us about the company up to this point by pushing the stock price higher or lower.

However, when the stock spikes higher or lower *today* and there is no news, or news we don't think is very important, we aren't going to be swayed by the fear or greed in the market. In fact, we are going to bet, yes <u>bet</u> that the market is going to see that it has made a mistake and retrace the move that the fear in the market created.

Remaining unswayed by the herd mentality of the market and remaining independent and objective is key to this strategy, which is why it works best with companies that we believe in. The fade trade can certainly go both ways, but closely following our core group of stocks makes it easier to discern the noise in the market from a move based on real issues. We are not interested in companies with long-term problems and sharply declining trend lines. We are not looking to pick the bottom of a failing company whose stock has been in free fall. Stocks like those will rarely see sudden reversals to the upside like the core group of stocks that we follow will.

What do these moves look like?

Picture one of your core stocks just ticking away on a nice steady uptrend for a couple of weeks. Everybody and their grandma is on board riding this thing to infinity. Then a prominent analyst comes on CNBC and says they are downgrading the stock from buy to hold. Sometimes that's all it takes—the stock is down five percent within minutes.

This is exactly the kind of thing we are looking for in a fade trade. In the sections that follow, we are going to talk about how to recognize when these moves are setting up and how to take advantage of the trading opportunities, as well as what technical parameters we use to trigger our entry and exit of the position; but one of the primary things we like to see is a stock that drops even though the broader market is flat or higher—this is a situation where our stock appears to be trading against the market with little or no consequential news.

If the move down truly was unwarranted, the stock will likely rebound in a day or two, especially if the overall market is trending higher. Consider the chart below that compares Visa (V) to the Dow Jones Industrial Average (DOW):

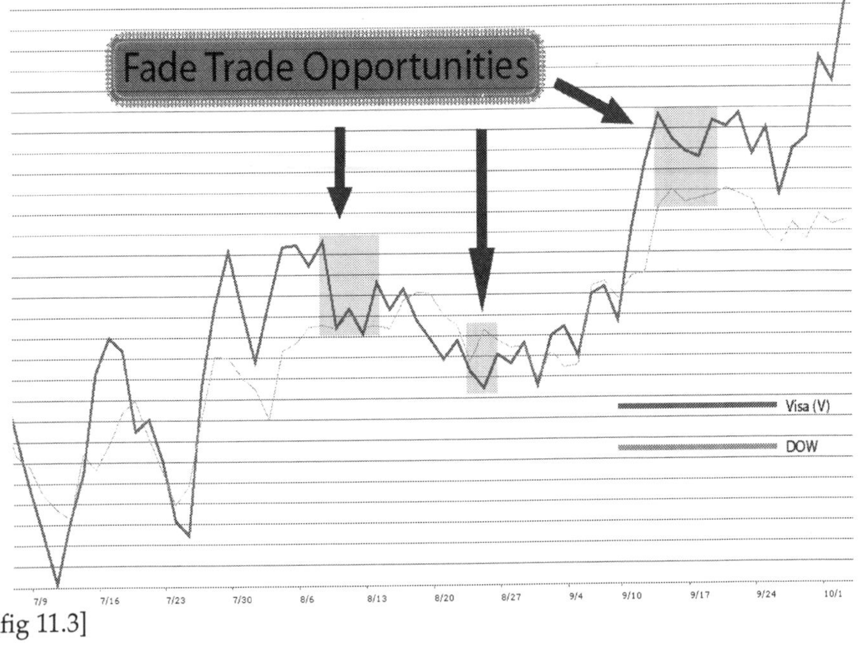

[fig 11.3]

Notice that in the highlighted areas this stock drops while the DOW remains flat or is up. This sort of negative correlation increases the likelihood that the market will "pull" our stock back up to pre-drop levels.

If the move doesn't come quickly, it doesn't come

These retracements—moves from the low of a dip or high of a spike back to the starting position—tend to happen rather quickly. We generally like to give them up to two or three days to make their move back up or down. If they haven't done it by day three, we can assume that the move is not forthcoming.

Why? Well, perhaps the news we disregarded as unimportant had a little more meat to it than we originally thought and all the chickens in the henhouse are clucking, or maybe the institution that originally triggered the sell-off is still selling, or even defending their short position. At the end of the day, the reason our stock hasn't retraced doesn't really matter; what matters is that we stick to our strategy and sell our position. We gave the stock two days to perform, it didn't do it, we move on and look for another opportunity. And there are always more opportunities.

Fade Trade Strategy
For beginners this is going to seem complicated at first—trust us, it's not. Computers do all the number crunching for us these days, so all we have to do is pull the trigger. We are going to introduce some vocabulary in this section like RSI, Bollinger Bands, candlesticks, etc. Don't be intimidated. We give you the vocabulary simply because you need to be able to find the right buttons on your trading platform. There are no calculations to worry about.

This strategy is a combination of technical analysis and news comprehension. The reason we have our core group of stocks that we follow continuously is because that gives us a frame of reference for digesting market moving news with an educated eye and without the overreaction that other market participants might have. When we get the news, we then turn to our charts and metrics to figure out how exactly to trade it.

Here are our rules for fading:

1. We see a significant stock price drop that we deem unwarranted in a market we feel has overreacted.
2. We choose a localized bottom by finding a clear signal that the rebalancing of sellers to buyers has been reached.
3. We see a trade that meets our criteria for signaling the localized downtrend has reversed.
4. We buy. We use market orders only for extremely quick movers, but otherwise almost always use limit orders (and especially when the bid-ask spread is wide).
5. We sell by scaling out to lock in profit (cover costs) and let winners run to increase that profit.

Alright, we can hear you thinking: *Golly gee guys that all sounds just swell, but how do I find a "clear signal" this and "limit order" that? Here's the part of the book where I get bored and turn on my favorite reality show... Give me some rules and tools you guys!*

Done! We are going to launch straight in, then go back and explain it all, so drop the remote and step away from the TV. We won't beat around the bush—this is going to sting for a second, but be patient because there's a lollipop at the end. Here are our rules for fade trading; this time in trader-speak:

1. We find an RSI below 30 if buying a dip or above 70 if selling a rally.
2. Start watching for a bounce when the stock price touches the 3rd Bollinger Band (BB).
3. We wait for a one-hour candle to close fully between the 1st and 2nd BB on its way back up or down.
4. Buy at the market price, but not with a market order. Use limit orders priced at the market for both stock and options. Don't chase, but don't try and save a few pennies by being stingy either; the move is already underway.
5. Sell strategy – Sell first half of position near the 20-day moving average, and second half at the second standard deviation BB on the upside (when long, downside when short). Stop loss limit should be just below the low of the move (the swing low). Once our first sale has been made, the stop loss limit should be moved up to the purchase price (break-even price).

Huh?

Okay, we just wanted to lay out the rules for you ahead of time. We'll refer back to our rules as we go through some examples. Now let's explain this in layman terms. This is going to seem like a lot, but really once you learn to navigate the charts on your trading platform you'll find it's actually very easy. It's not as if you have to do the math to come up with the Bollinger Bands by hand or calculate RSI. This stuff is all calculated with a click of your mouse on your trading platform.

Candles, Candlesticks, and Candlestick Charts

When you are contemplating a fade trade (after a dip), you should have one question and one question only on your mind: what are buyers going to do over the near term?—not sellers—there are ALWAYS sellers in the market when prices have been falling. Why is that the case? Because sellers have been pushing the price down, down, down, looking for more buyers. So when are the buyers going to show up again? If more buyers don't show up, the stock is going to continue to fall. If they return, the stock will stop sliding and perhaps go back up.

What we really need to know is where the balance of buyers to sellers is, and we use things like candlesticks to try and gauge just that.

A picture is worth a thousand words is probably our favorite cliché. We hate vocabulary and calculations and esoteric metrics as much as you do. If we have the choice between three paragraphs of text and a picture that can tell the same story, we're going to go with the picture ten times out of ten, and that's exactly what candlesticks and candlestick charts give us.

A candlestick chart is invaluable for the short term trader. In one little graphical snapshot, you can see not just stock prices, but the *price action*, i.e. what is going on with buying and selling pressures. You can see the high, the low, and depending on the time scale, you can see the open and closing prices (on an intraday chart, "open" and "close" are just time cycles of 15 or 30 or 60 or whatever minutes you define). Here is what it looks like and what it means.

Important note: In all of the charts used in this chapter the solid colored candlesticks are red, the hollow candlesticks are green.

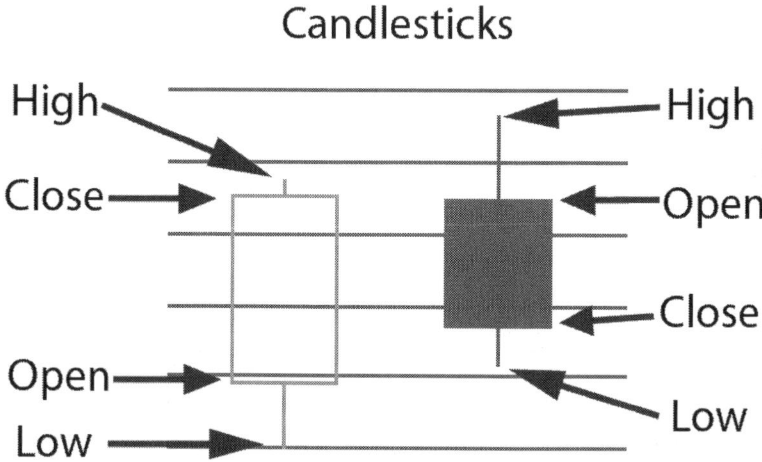

[fig 11.4]

The large rectangles (fig 11.4, green on left, red on right) define the price range between the open and close over the specified time interval. If green or hollow (or both, depending on your trading platform), it means the stock went up over that interval. If it's red or solid (or both, depending on your trading platform), it means the stock went down over that interval. The little lines coming off the top and bottom are referred to as *wicks* or *shadows*. They show the highest and lowest price paid over the interval.

How does this chart show pricing pressures and momentum? In general, the bigger the block part of the candlestick, the higher the buying or selling pressure. If the block is green (or hollow or both), it means that buyers were piling in to buy, and were willing to pay higher and higher prices to fill their orders. If the block is red (or solid or both), then sellers were piling in to sell, and were willing to accept lower and lower prices to fill their orders. The bigger the block, the higher the pricing pressure.

How about the little lines that extend from the top and bottom of the block part of the candle? Again, those little lines (also called "shadows") represent how high (top) and how low (bottom) the price went over the interval. So if the highest and lowest prices paid for the stock (long lines coming out the top or bottom) are far from the opening and closing prices, it means that buyers and sellers became *uncertain* as the price moved to the extremes—long lines mean that there was less price pressure above or below that particular closing level.

In the case of a long line on top, it means that buyers stepped in and bid the price up, but later the balance shifted to sellers and pressed the price lower. In the case of a long line on the bottom, it means that sellers drove the price down, but there was uncertainty and later buyers came in to push the price up again.

So at the end of the day, short lines on the top and bottom of the candle mean that most of the buying and selling pressure was near the highs and lows. In the case of a short line on top of a green block, most of the pricing pressure was from buyers—from people who think the stock is heading higher. In the case of a short line at the bottom of a red block, most of the pricing pressure was from sellers—from people who believe the stock is headed lower. Therefore, the shorter the line on the top of a green candle, the more momentum there is for the stock to go higher, and the shorter the line on the bottom of a red candle, the more momentum there is for a stock to go lower.

If there are long lines on the top and bottom of the block part of the candle, it means that buyers and sellers weren't sure what to do; that there is more confusion, less pricing pressure, and thus, less momentum. In trading jargon, these long-lined candles are called "spinning tops."

The Story

The best thing about candlestick charts is that they tell a story. Let's revisit our example above and try to make sense of what is going on with this stock. For simplicity, let's just say that these are daily candles for Monday and Tuesday.

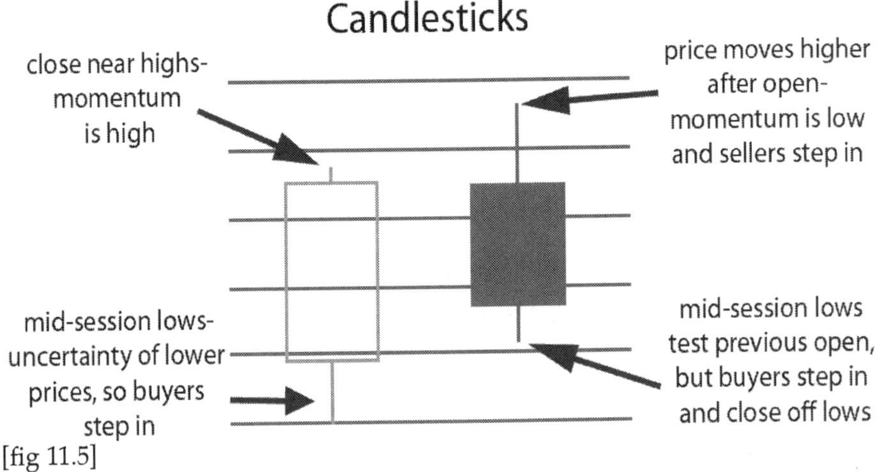

[fig 11.5]

In the first candle on the left the stock moved higher (green and hollow). The line at the bottom tells us that after the open, the stock moved lower before buyers stepped in to push the price higher. The short line on the top tells us that the stock closed near the highs for the day. This indicates that *buyers* were controlling the pricing action and there was momentum at the close.

The candle on the right (red and solid) shows us that the pricing pressure and price momentum continued into the next day, and as you can see from the longer line on top of the block, the price continued to head higher after the open. However, that upward momentum diminished and the buyers' enthusiasm waned, sellers took over pressing the price lower. The price then fell almost to the opening price on Monday (small line at the bottom of the solid red block, right side in fig 11.5), before buyers stepped in to press the price higher by the end of the trading session.

Relative Strength Index - RSI

We use candlestick charts to try and figure out whether the bulls or the bears are in charge; whether buyers or sellers are controlling the price movement on a stock. However that's overly-simplistic, because for every buyer who buys thinking the stock is going higher, there is a seller who thinks the opposite. At the end of the day we are talking about a system that's more or less in equilibrium with only a very small percentage of outstanding shares actually being traded at any one time. So we really need to have some sort of idea of how *strongly* a price is moving. The question is really one of how much momentum a stock price movement has.

Relative Strength Index, or RSI, is a technical indicator that's commonly known as a "momentum indicator" meant to show whether a stock is "oversold" or "overbought." An RSI below 30 indicates the stock is oversold, while an RSI above 70 indicates the stock is overbought (quite often traders look for RSI values of 20 and 80 to gain additional assurance that the market is indeed oversold or overbought). Most trading platforms have some sort of page or button that shows RSI, often directly below the stock's chart. This makes it easy to compare the stock price and the RSI for a given time period. Consult your trading platform's help section if you can't find it.

Oversold, overbought; what does that mean? In truth, these terms are extremely subjective. Obviously the person selling at the bottom of a stock's move down didn't think the stock was oversold or he would not have made that trade. The definition of oversold/overbought is when the price of a stock has fallen/risen sharply to a level below/above the stock's true value (another very subjective term). Overzealous buying and panic selling due to any number of news events can cause this to happen.

Despite the subjectiveness of these terms the RSI remains a very reliable indicator of price swings and is often one of the first technical indicators to signal an upcoming reversal of the trend, be it up or down. On its own it would be a strong trading tool, but combined with Bollinger Bands (that's next) we feel it is even stronger.

The RSI uses the closing prices of completed trading periods (we use one hour periods) in order to determine whether the bulls or the bears have the momentum. It assumes that prices close higher in bull market periods, lower in bear market periods, and then computes this as a ratio of the number of higher closes to lower closes during a certain period of time.

Statistics 101 - Bollinger Bands

After we look at the candlesticks to gauge the balance of buyers and sellers and the pricing pressure on a stock, and RSI to try to figure out the momentum in the stock price trend, we want to try to figure out how much volatility there is in a stock, i.e. how much upside or how much downside there might be going forward. This volatility indicator helps us define an envelope of future prices; how high or how low the price might go moving forward.

Before you get overwhelmed with the vocabulary, remember that we slackers like pretty pictures—give us a way to look at complicated data in a really simple, concise way, and we are going to use it. At the end of the day, all we are trying to teach you is what to look for in those pretty pictures.

Bollinger Bands (BB) are beautiful in their simplicity, and they give us a really clean way to measure volatility and that future price envelope we talked about before. Again, plotting Bollinger Bands is simply going to be a button or menu item in the charting system for your online trading platform—you don't have to figure anything out manually.

We are Deviants

Standard deviations are what Bollinger Bands are all about. Remember that statistics class you took in college? No? Well we do, so let us explain.

Bollinger Bands are based off of a simple moving average (SMA) which we talked about in the last chapter. As a quick reminder, an SMA is calculated by adding together the closing prices for a specific number of time periods (20 days) and dividing by the number of periods to give us an average. We generally use the 20-day SMA, though this can be adjusted up or down.

The Bollinger Bands are calculated by taking the standard deviations of this 20-day SMA. Going back to college statistics class again we know that the first standard deviation of a normal bell curve encompasses about 68% of available data while the second standard deviation gathers up 95%. Leaving the third standard deviation to suck up almost all the rest.

With stock prices it's a little different as they tend not to fall into a perfect bell curve (a normal distribution). A stock's bell curve is flatter and has bigger tails, meaning that only 88% of a stock's price during a specific time period falls within two standard deviations of the mean (20-day SMA). That leaves another 12% out there between the second and third standard deviations. These numbers should not be taken as gospel however, which is why we use other indications to signal when a reversal is actually taking place.

Okay, okay, slow down. A what is a huh? All right—example time: how about this?

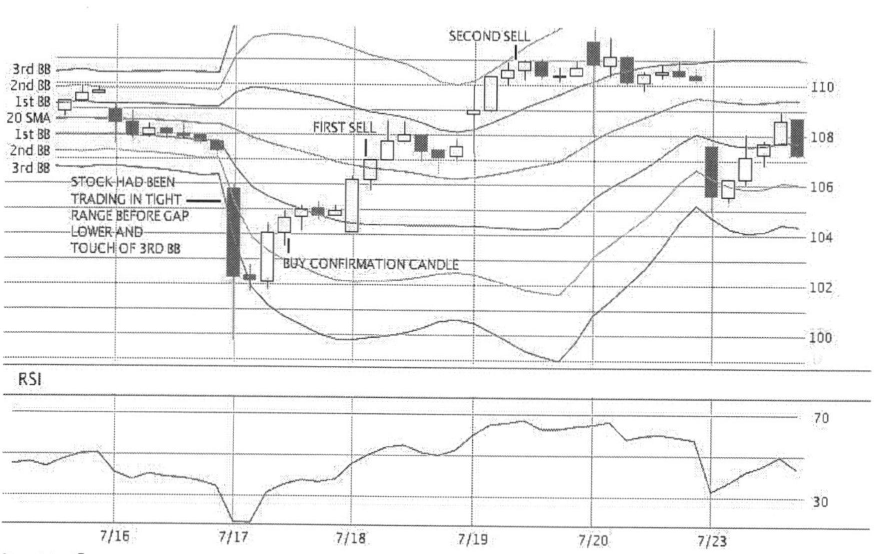

[fig 11.6]

This is a chart of Baidu, the Chinese internet search giant. Moving up and down through the middle of it is a 20-day SMA line. Both above and below that are your Bollinger Bands; first, second, and third standard deviation of the 20-day SMA. Look at those second standard deviation lines (the second lines in from the top and bottom); in between those two lines are, and will be, roughly 88% of the stock's moves during our time period.

Stop here and think about that a second: at least eighty-eight percent of the time this stock is trading between these two lines. That's pretty significant—the likelihood of future prices falling in between those lines is very, very high. So when you are looking at a plot of Bollinger Bands, you are really looking at an envelope of probability, and the distance between the top and bottom band gives you a really decent idea of how volatile the stock could be going forward in time. It won't absolutely trade in that envelope, but the bands provide us some decent guidance.

Now look out between those second and third deviations (outside two lines on top and bottom); these are the outliers—more or less the other twelve percent. When the stock gets out there we can begin to consider that things aren't quite normal. The stock needs to get back in between those 2nd BBs doesn't it? Yes, but not always right away. Which is why we introduce another rule—a condition that will signal to us that the reversal is underway and it's time for us to join in.

Step-by-Step Analysis

So step one: we need an RSI below 30. We've definitely got that; in fact the RSI ticks all the way down to 17. This stock is oversold here. (The RSI is the line chart at the bottom of the example above. On most trading platforms this is how it will appear.)

The next step is one that tends to go hand in hand with the RSI below 30, and that's a touch of the 3rd standard deviation Bollinger Band. In this case the stock opens around $106 before plummeting to $100 and tearing through the 3rd Band. Just as quickly as the stock dropped, it bounces. By the close of the first hour the stock is up above $102.

The next hour is spent consolidating at that $102 level before starting to tick higher the hour after that. This candle takes us from $102 on up to $104. Shortly after that we get our official confirmation of the move higher when the stock's candle closes (meaning both opens and closes; the rectangle of the candle) fully between the 1st and 2nd Bollinger Bands. We buy in somewhere around $104.50 and for the rest of the afternoon the stock slowly trends sideways.

Immediately upon buying we set a stop loss order at the low of the move—the swing low. In this case that would be at $100—though for most of us that would be too much risk on the trade—perhaps a better choice would be around $102, the support area if you were to take away that long shadow on the opening candle. Either way, we set a stop to limit our loss. By the close of the day the stock is sitting at $105.

In the morning the stock opens at $104 and from there it goes straight up. In the second hour of trading BIDU ticks up through the 20-day Simple Moving Average. Time for us to sell the first half of our position. At $106.50 we close out half for a two dollar gain. Nothing flashy about that, but a nice 24 hour profit.

With that first sell made we move our stop loss order up to break-even on the rest, $104.50.

After this move through the 20-day Simple Moving Average you can see how both the BBs and SMA turn into support and resistance lines. The hollow green candles run up and hit resistance at the 1st BB, then back down to where the solid red candles bounce off of support at the 20-day SMA. By the end of the day we've got a nice green (hollow) candle to send us home at $107.50 with half our position sold, profits locked in, and the trend higher still with us.

The next morning we get a nice little gap higher that takes the rest of our position to within mere pennies of the 2nd Bollinger Band. For the first four hours of the day the stock runs right up along the 2nd BB. The 2nd BB obviously has become a resistance level by the middle of the day as the stock starts leveling off. Hopefully we have already sold the rest of our position—

even if it never touched the 2nd BB it was so close for so long that we should've sold—don't be greedy. If not, we certainly would sell by the close; $110 represents about a five percent winner. There is no way we should be carrying this position home with us for a third night. We've made big profits on this fade; lock them up and look for the next trade.

This fade trade is really about as textbook as they come. These trades generally set up on the morning opens with gaps, followed by a two to three-hour period of setting up as the stock establishes the low and moves sideways or higher into the 2nd Band to confirm the bounce. The entire trade can take as little as a couple of hours occasionally, but generally twenty-four to forty-eight hours is more reasonable.

Market Movers

We spend most of our time out playing on the beach, or eating fish tacos, or reading books to our kids, or any number of things that don't include staring at charts on a computer screen. To identify potential trading opportunities, we look for market movers to tell us things might get interesting for any of our core group of stocks. What are we on the lookout for?

Market Mover - Earnings Report

Earnings reports come out quarterly. And thank goodness for that, as they provide those of us who aren't necessarily interested in spending our entire lives in front of a screen with a nice orderly schedule with which to watch our stocks for significant moves.

Trading <u>ahead</u> of earnings reports is a very risky business. You are basically trying to predict two things for which you don't have good information:

- What the earnings numbers will be.
- What the market is expecting those numbers will be.

Getting it right can pay off in a really big way, but if you are wrong, it will cost you big as well. Fortunes are made and lost every quarter on the basis of these reports—much like fortunes are made and lost every night in front of roulette table. We say it again here lest you forget: this is gambling. And while we are not immune to trading ahead of earnings reports, we aren't advocating it either.

Instead we want to point out, especially if the earnings report is a surprise (either beating or missing expectations) to the market, that there is the potential for significant moves immediately following the announcement. By using our fade trading strategies, we may be looking to capitalize on those moves <u>after</u> the earnings come out.

When earnings reports move a stock radically, quite often there is overreaction as those who were on the wrong side of the trade are flushed out en masse. After the initial hysteria, as the traders who were squeezed out either by margin calls or their own pain threshold leave the market, things tend to level off quickly. The market will absorb the earnings information and we may see a reversal of the initial move. By following our rules for fade trading we can spot opportunities here.

Market Mover - Analysts

When an analyst changes his rating or price target for a stock, the immediate market reaction can be pretty amazing. One analyst, one word, and boom, millions, if not billions of dollars are immediately added to or subtracted from a company's market capitalization. How is this possible?

Here is a quote from the Financial Industry Regulatory Authority (FINRA) website:

"...a large number of analysts are employed by institutions whose financial stake in their recommendations may go well beyond their accuracy."

They are not mincing words here: analysts are employed by large financial firms—banks—that are anything but neutral parties. Of course some analysts are unaffiliated with the banks, but the customers for their "independent" reports *are* the banks. And you can imagine that the banks aren't in the habit of paying for reports that would be detrimental to their bottom line.

You should assign zero authoritative credibility to analysts reports—they are opinions, and it is entirely possible, perhaps even probable, that they are biased opinions. Their reports are marketing—pure and simple. That doesn't mean that you should disregard them—not at all. It's just that you should be extremely skeptical of what they have to say.

Think about it this way: when an analyst issues a "buy" rating, it's because they or the people who pay them want you to buy. When they issue a "hold" rating, it's because they want you to not sell. It's the same story with "sell," "accumulate," etc. They are (or may be) trying to manipulate you into doing what they need done.

Put another way, if a bank's analyst believes a stock is going to go from the current $80 per share up to $100, why are they sharing this information with the general public—the *non-paying* public? I'm not a customer of theirs so why are they giving me this incredible stock tip? The answer is that there is no good reason for them to do so. They've got millions, if not billions, of trading dollars at their disposal, so if they truly believe this is where the stock is going why don't they just buy as much as they can and earn that 25% profit for themselves? The answer more than likely is that they **already** own the stock, don't really believe in it any longer, and want to exit the position at the best possible price. Think pump and dump. We are not saying that this is the case each and every time, but think about that line of reasoning and see if it sounds plausible to you.

Does that mean we should ignore these analysis, forecasts, expectations and recommendations? Never—what we should do with these reports is trade them. They create big moves even though they may mean little or nothing in the grand scheme of things for the company and its stock. This makes it ripe for fading, because regardless of whether or not we agree with what an analyst has to say, in the very near term, the market will believe these opinions as fact. Any substantial move in a stock based solely on an analyst's report should be scrutinized for a fade trade.

Here is a great example:

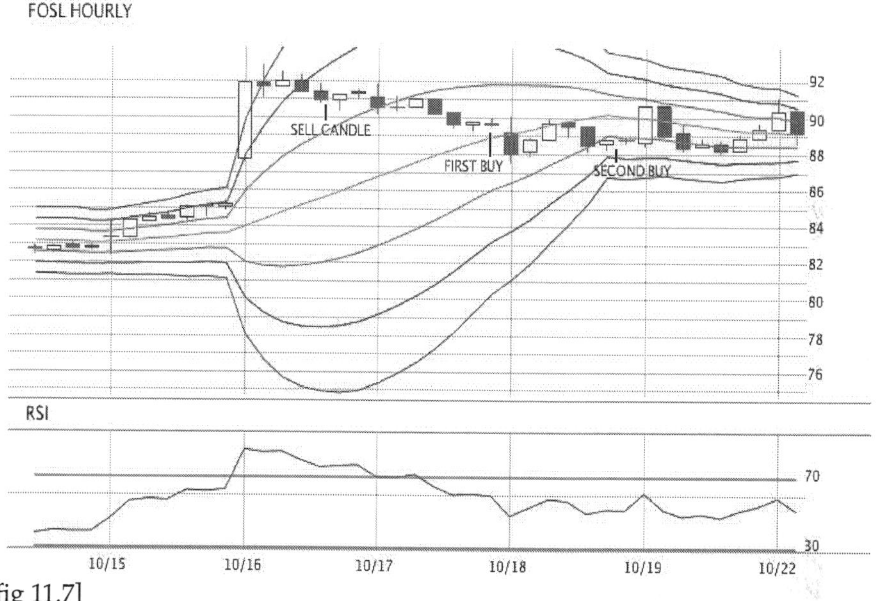

[fig 11.7]

In this Fossil (FOSL) example the stock had been trading in a pretty tight range with low volatility until the morning of the 16th when Citigroup upgraded the stock to a buy rating with a price target of $100. That's all it took for the stock to jump 9%. You'll see this sort of thing time and time again. Every single day in the market, stocks jump around like this based on nothing more than a piece of paper written by a who-knows-who analyst at such-and-such bank.

This is the reason that fundamental analysis of a company can only take you so far in trading. It's not as if Fossil suddenly did something that improved its worth by 9%; it didn't increase profits or lower expenses overnight. It didn't sign a huge contract guaranteeing it millions of dollars a year in additional revenues. No, none of those things happened; instead a pencil pusher said he thinks the stock will someday be worth $100, and the market said, "Let's buy FOSL!"

Soooooo, what to do about it? Well that's what we have rules in place for. Now that we have seen this stock bust right through the third standard deviation Bollinger Band, it's on our radar. And look, the RSI on the 16th is at 85—way overbought. We think that this is an overreaction to some ho-hum news, and that the stock will probably correct lower over a few days.

The charts on these fade trades often look just like this one. First we get that big initial gap open. The stock opens higher than the previous close and then continues to be pressured higher as buyers rush in, not wanting to miss out. The first hour sees frantic activity and high volume.

Then the news is digested and the craziness subsides. The next couple of hours the stock consolidates around the high of the day, moving sideways from there until midway through the trading day when the early longs begin to realize that the fun may be over and start taking their profits.

This is when we get our candle that both opens and closes between the 1st and 2nd Bollinger Band. We enter a short position (likely through the use of put options which we will discuss in the next chapter) just as the late buyers start to realize the error of their ways. They bought the top and now want out before their losses mount.

In this case the selling pressure never really mounted—as it often does—instead we got a slow, steady decline over the course of the next couple of days as the market for FOSL found itself a new equilibrium.

At the market's close on day one the stock is trading just a smidgen higher than where we sold. We didn't trade this move, but think there is only about a fifty/fifty chance we'd have held onto the position overnight. There just didn't seem to be much conviction in the reversal; which would give us reason to close the position for just a small loss. On the other hand this is a stock that wasn't trading with a lot of volatility prior to the move, which might indicate to us that there isn't a lot of risk in holding the position overnight.

If we had held overnight we would've seen the stock continue to meander lower the next day until by the close we were starting to see some decent profit on our trade. Again, this would've been a coin toss deciding whether or not to continue with this position or not. Probably take the small winner and move on.

On day three (if we were still in) we'd have had a sizable winner in the first hour of trading, then watched as the stock grinded away sideways. You can see on the chart that after two days of sideways tight-range trade the Bollinger Bands are coming back together, indicating that volatility has decreased. Obviously right?

Now, late in the day on the 18th a green candle comes very close to hitting the second standard deviation Bollinger Band, which is our price target for the trade. It didn't quite touch, but this is the third day of the trade and we've got a decent little profit; we would definitely close this position by the end of the day. We don't hold these grinding trades forever. A day, two, *maybe* three, but that's it.

Market Mover - General Company News

New product releases, exclusive content deals, building contracts, whatever the case may be, can trigger unexpected high volume moves as well. The nice thing is that these days traders know within minutes when these developments occur.

To be honest we don't know what traders did before instant online and cable news. We suppose that back then it was still possible to strictly be a technical trader. You sat at home with the morning *Wall Street Journal*, looked up your stock, drew a candle on your graph paper, got out a ruler and drew in some lines, then decided where to have your broker place your order when you called him.

Nowadays the world is plugged in. Investors want to know what their company is doing; not next week, not tomorrow, but right at this moment. Because of this ability, even technical traders have had to become a combination technical/fundamental/news trader. Nobody can just sit back and trade based solely on technical indicators with no idea as to what is going on in the news, just like nobody can trade by only looking at CNBC headlines (though I'm afraid many do).

Today, short-term traders need three eyes: one on the charts, one on the fundamentals, and one on the news. What would that be—a Triclops? Well even with only two eyes it is still easier than ever to keep watch over all the elements using these fancy computer gadgets of ours. Point is, don't narrow your focus too much.

Gap Opens

A gap open occurs when the stock's opening price is either higher than the previous day's high price, or lower than the previous day's low price. On a bar or candle chart there will be a "gap" in the bars. These generally occur because of any one of the market mover items listed in the sections above.

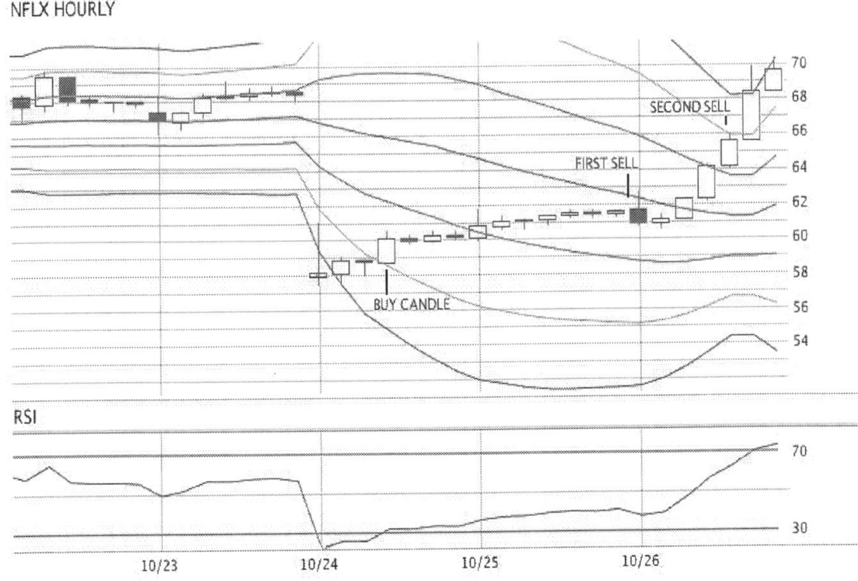

[fig 11.8]

Gaps are easy to see on a chart. Here is an example of a large gap lower open. Netflix reported earnings after the close the day before the gap. One of their numbers, new subscribers, came in significantly lower than expected, and the stock paid the price for that in the morning. But then look what happened—here we see it again—the market overreacts, then comes to its senses.

After the opening gap lower, the stock immediately started moving back up, and within a couple of hours we had our buy signal. The RSI had dropped well below thirty and was on its way back up—at the same time we got a green candle closed inside the 1st and 2nd Bollinger Bands. We bought in at right around $60 and placed a sell-stop around $58, the low of the move.

For the rest of the day and through the next, Netflix stock climbed slowly higher. Very slowly. By the close of day two you had a choice to make: sell half now around $61.50, just below the 20-day Simple Moving Average, or hold the full position overnight into Friday. Friday would definitely be the last day of this trade either way. No way we were going to be taking this home over the weekend. Whether to hold or sell half in this case really just depended on your risk tolerance. Nobody could fault you for locking in some profits, however small, after two days in the position.

If you held the position overnight, you were rewarded on the open when the stock ticked up through the 20-day SMA. Your sale would've been around $62.50. Your stop price would've been moved up from $58 to $60 at this point, though in the end it wouldn't matter. The stock went parabolic on Friday hitting our 2nd standard deviation BB within a couple of hours. Position closed at $66 for what was, all in all, a perfect fade trade.

Traders have an old saying that "the market abhors a vacuum; therefore all gaps must be filled." This isn't always true—if it were there would never be a gap—but it's true often enough that a gap should always be right at the top of your watch list.

More Fade Trade Examples

Fade trading is really a very simple system. Especially once you've discovered exactly how your charting software works through your trading firm and established the RSI and Bollinger Bands as your default chart setup. After that it is simply a matter of watching for the stock to set off our signals.

[fig 11.9]

Here is an example of a fade we made while sitting at Nick's kitchen table writing this book. On 9/26 Apple stock gapped lower on the open through the 2nd Bollinger Band. Within the hour it traded down to just shy of touching the 3rd BB. At the same time the RSI was showing well below thirty indicating that the stock was oversold. Although it didn't actually touch the 3rd BB sometimes you need to leave yourself a little wiggle room. It was close enough for us to consider watching for a reversal and a fade trade.

The next hour the stock flattened out and traded within the 2nd and 3rd bands, indicating that a reversal was possible but still unconfirmed. In the third hour we got the confirmation as the candle closed fully within the 1st and 2nd BBs. At that point we bought at-the-money calls.

The stock continued to climb and we sold the first half of the position at the 1st Bollinger Band. The reason we sold here instead of at the 20-day SMA (per our written rules) is that the morning gap had not quite filled and then the stock started to fall again. Gaps (in this case the gap is the difference between the opening price and the previous day's closing low) often fill, but they can also provide significant resistance or support. In this case the stock approached that level and it acted as resistance, the momentum of the upside move was stopped there.

We then sold the remaining half at break even after the stock failed to clear the 1st Bollinger Band and dropped heading into the day's close. There seemed to be little incentive to hold the position overnight. As it turns out our stop loss order at the bottom of the swing low would've been triggered in the next day's opening hour. Immediately after which we would've seen significant gains. This happens sometimes, and is one of the reasons trading can be frustrating. It's also a reason that many traders have a hard time sticking to their rules. Psychologically however, this is an example of SPPP (selective potential past performance) because the stock could just as easily have continued lower against our position. We need to stick to our rules.

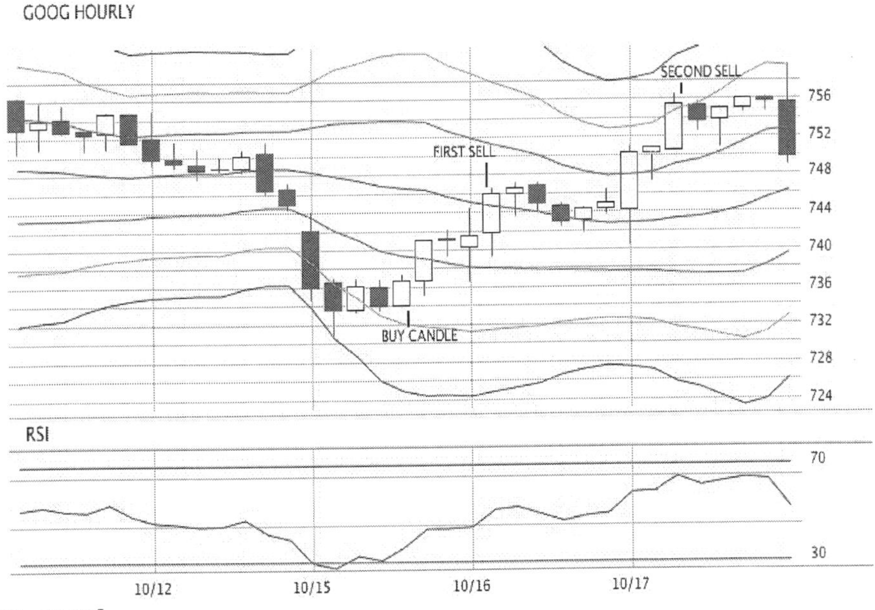

[fig 11.10]

Another example. This time Google on 10/15. The stock hits the 3rd BB shortly after the open while at the same time the RSI ticks below 30 indicating oversold conditions. The next hour the stock flattens out right on the 2nd BB and the hour after that we get a candle that closes fully within the 1st and 2nd BB; meaning that both the open and the close of the candle are within the two Bollinger Bands. But because this candle closed with a higher open and lower close we wait for further confirmation which comes the next hour when the candle reverses to a lower open and higher close. This is our buying opportunity.

As a rule we look for our confirmation candle to be in the direction of the reversal. In other words we want to see a green (hollow) candle as confirmation for an upside move, and a red (solid) candle for the downside.

You can see that in this case the stock traded higher nicely for two days with only one small blip in the uptrend.

Our exit strategy is to sell half of our position at the 20-day SMA and the balance at the 2nd Bollinger Band. In this case we reached both of our targets with little to no sweating. We bought in at around $736, sold half our position the next morning at the 20-day for $744, and reached the 2nd BB the morning after that, selling the balance at $754. Textbook.

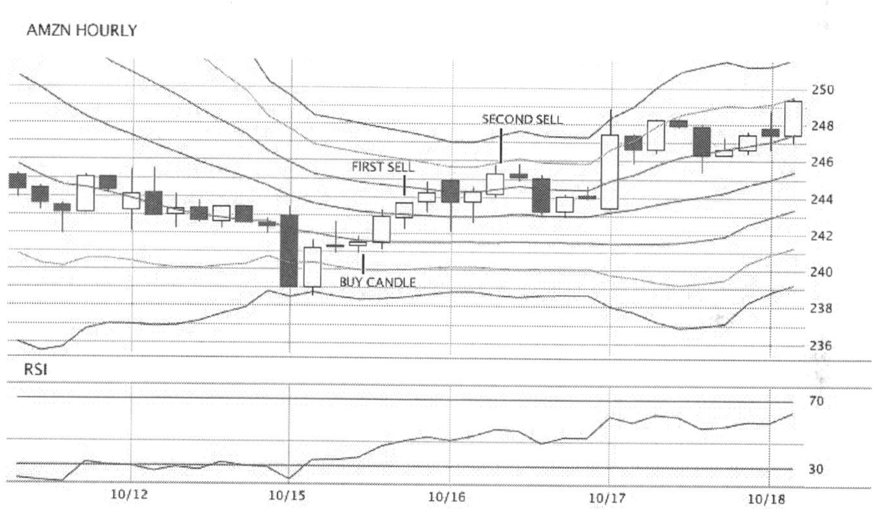

[fig 11.11]

Here is Amazon's chart from the same time period. Let's walk through it.

On the opening of the 15th we get a big fat red candle indicating that we had a pretty steep sell off after the open. In the next hour we get our touch of the 3rd Bollinger Band, the first step we need to get a fade trade underway.

At the same time, the RSI was right around 30. It had spiked to 20 on the open but had been steadily climbing since then. Looking at that fat red candle it was pretty obvious the RSI would indicate oversold conditions; the fairly sizable hollow green candle in the next hour would've also indicated to us, even without looking at the RSI, that the selling pressure had eased considerably.

In the next hour there was a very thin red candle with its open and close between the 1st and 2nd Bollinger Bands. A candle this thin indicates that only a few cents separated the open and close of the time period (one hour). You may very well have decided that was close enough, and entered the trade there, or you may have followed the rules to the T and waited another hour, at which point you would've gotten the green candle between the bands that we were looking for.

From there it was only one hour before the 20-day SMA got tapped and we sold the first half of our position.

With that half sold we moved our stop on the remaining half up to our original purchase price. When we say "our stop" we don't necessarily mean that we actually set a stop order. What we do mean is that we set our *mental* stop at that price. We often trade options instead of stock. Stop orders for options are only recommended on very rare occasions, like when your appendix bursts in the middle of a trade. "Please Doctor, just one thing before you put me under. Tell my wife I...I need her...I need her to enter a stop at $11.85."

Why? The spreads in options are too wide and the volume too low. Market makers will take you to the bank if you try that. With stock you can use stop orders if you are so inclined.

The sale of the remainder of this position came the next day when the price ticked up and tapped the 2nd BB. However, it was such a close call on that one before the stock dropped back down that it is likely you didn't get the sale off in time. The stock dropped a bit from there but never approached our stop. The next morning we got our fill at the 2nd BB in the opening hour. This was a perfectly played out fade trade.

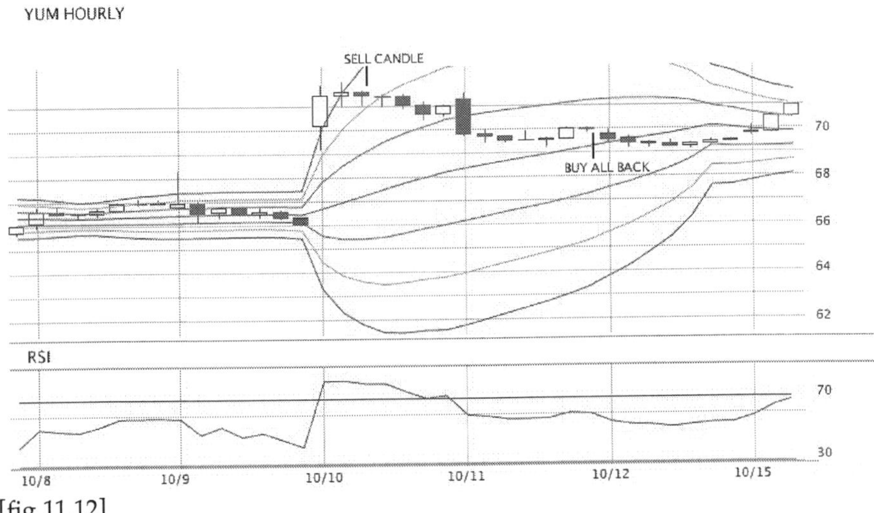

[fig 11.12]

This is a chart of YUM after reporting solid earnings; exactly the sort of earnings move you will see time and time again, and even though we didn't get a full follow through on this trade we still made a nice profit.

Earnings beat analysts expectations due to healthy profits in China. Apparently the Chinese love themselves some Kentucky Fried Chicken. The morning after the announcement the stock opened with a big gap higher right through the 3rd Bollinger Band which also caused the RSI to spike to well above our 70 threshold, indicating overbought conditions.

Two hours later we got the closed red candle we were hoping for, indicating the move lower was about to begin. And it did—slowly. We took this position home with us overnight.

The next morning we got a nice move lower in the opening hour before the boredom overtook us. By the close it was clear that this stock was not going to make a significant move lower and that in fact it was probably building a new support level here. While there appeared to be little risk in holding the position overnight there also appeared to be little incentive to do so; we closed the whole position for a small win.

Advanced Bollinger Bands

What you see above are the Bollinger Bands Basics. Don't trade them until you get really comfortable and understand what you are looking for. On top of that, there are a few other things we should know about Bollinger Bands.

One is that the reason we wait for the closing candle between the 1st and 2nd BB is that a stock's price can, and often does, "climb" a band. What you may think at first glance is going to be a classic reversal can instead turn into a trend.

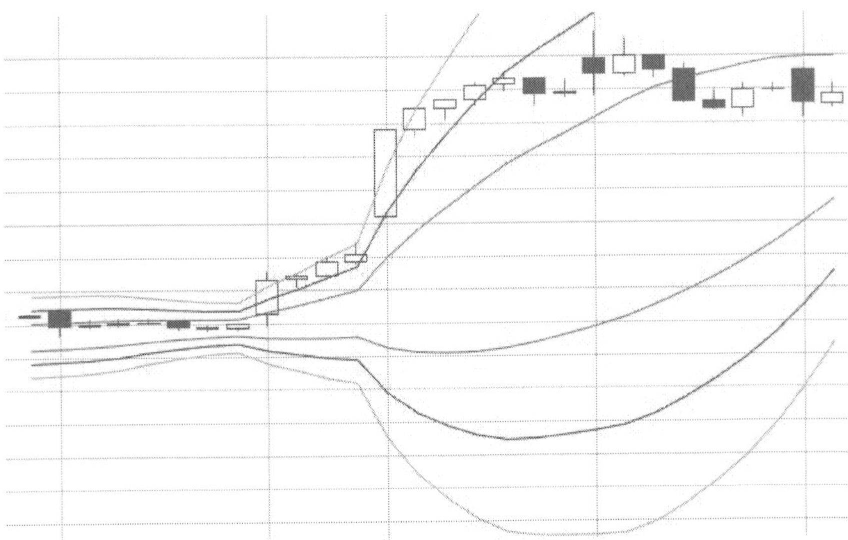

[fig 11.13]

You can see in this chart that the stock was trading in a tight range before breaking out to the upside and ticking through the 3rd standard deviation Bollinger Band. The candle after the breakout moves sideways at which point you may start to think the stock is setting up for a reversal, but then the next hour is higher again, and the one after that—all of them climbing up that 3rd standard deviation line.

This is why we must always wait for the confirmation candle.

Along these same lines is the fact that *closes* outside of the 3rd standard deviation BB can often be a continuation signal as opposed to a reversal signal. This is true in the above example.

What this all means is simply that a touch of the 3rd BB is not an indicator of either a reversal or a breakout. A touch of the band is only a signal to you that one of these things may be about to occur and that more information as well as confirmation is needed.

Volatility

By looking at the width between the upper (say the 2nd standard deviation line above the SMA) Bollinger Band and the lower (2nd standard deviation below the SMA) Bollinger Band you get a visual picture of a stock's volatility. Bollinger Bands narrow during times of low volatility and explode outward during periods of high volatility. Narrow bands equal little price movement (range bound), wide bands equal considerable price movement.

Range bound trading eventually gives way to a new trend, be it higher or lower. Bollinger Bands can indicate for us when a stock is range bound and therefore a likely candidate to experience a high volatility breakout, but they can't tell us which way that breakout is going to be, or even when it might happen.

Entry—Goldilocks and the Three Little Candles
Pat reads so many bedtime stories to his kids these days that he is able to zone out while reading them and think about something else—like candles. When it comes to identifying a reversal, we need to see candles that are neither too hot nor too cold, but rather just right.

Let's step back for a second: the first thing we are looking for in a fade trade to signal a reversal may be coming, is a touch of the 3rd Bollinger Band. When a stock gets that far outside it's bound to correct. But that doesn't mean it's going to happen each and every time; which is why we wait for a closing candle back up between the 1st and 2nd BB as our confirmation.

But let's try and be even more clear on what that means. (Note: In all of these examples the RSI was either above 70 or below 30 at the point that the candle hit the 3rd standard deviation.)

This Candle is Too Cold

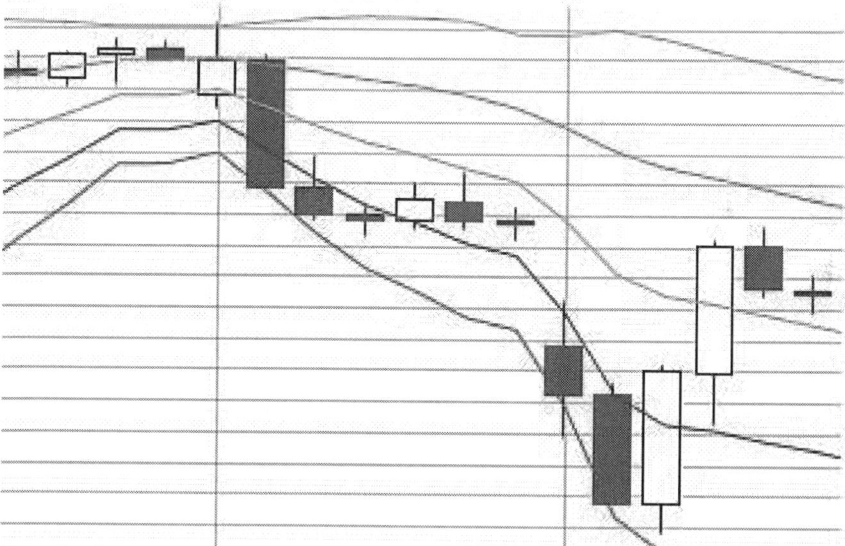

[fig 11.14]

In this chart we have a candle reach down and tap the 3rd Bollinger Band—okay, time to start looking for that reversal candle. But it doesn't come; the next hourly candle drops further, as does the next. Then we finally get that green candle in between the 1st and 2nd BB. By now we are significantly below the original breach of the 3rd BB. Does this hollow green candle signal a reversal? No.

When we have a stock hit the 3rd BB we are looking for an almost immediate halt to the stock's price drop (or rally). When a second and third candle continue lower (or higher) we consider the possibility of a fade trade over with. A green candle four hours later at a considerably lower price than the original touch of the BB is not indicating a reversal. More likely it is simply a lull in a trend, and that's exactly what happens in fig 11.14.

This Candle is Too Hot

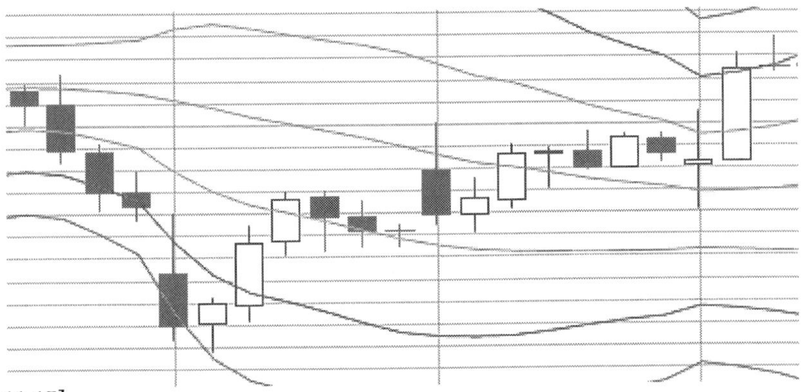

[fig 11.15]

What about when the stock hits that 3rd Bollinger Band and then immediately turns and runs higher? This one becomes a bit more subjective.

In figure 11.15 the first candle after the touch turns green (closes higher than it opened). That's a good looking candle and seems to be getting a nice fade setup going for us. All we need is that closed candle between 1st and 2nd BB. The problem in this case is that the next candle opens below the 2nd BB and then proceeds to run well above it. Our requirement is not met, but...

Yes, but...the closed candle between 1 and 2 hasn't been met, but an experienced trader would be watching the move on that candle near the end of the hour and would be feeling pretty good about this being a solid reversal.

The fade is clearly underway at this point. If you wait another hour you've got the confirmation candle you need, but by now the stock is so far off its lows that it could be considered too late. If you were to enter on that late candle your stop loss limit at the low of the move would be pretty far below your purchase price. You'd likely be taking more risk than you want by this point in the move.

These are the kinds of decisions that you'll need to make every day as a trader. Some people say stick to the rules no matter what. Which is great and all, but will leave trades like this one undone. If you had entered the trade near the top of that second green candle you'd have had a slight winner at the close of the day despite the pullback. On the open the next morning you'd have hit the 20-day SMA for your first sale, then rode a nice winner through the rest of the day. The morning after that you would've hit the 2nd Bollinger Band to the upside to close out a very profitable trade.

We've got rules in place, but as you progress as a trader you will have to determine your *own* set of rules in order to reach maximum profitability.

This Candle is Just Right

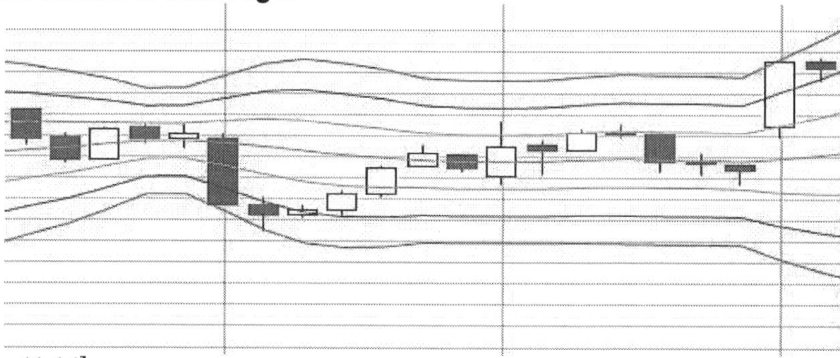

[fig 11.16]

What does a perfect entry look like? Well fig 11.16 is pretty much a textbook move. We get a big fat red candle on the open leading into a lower candle that just taps the 3rd Bollinger Band before stalling out in the next hour. Then the reversal begins.

Two hours after the first touch we get a nice green candle situated smack dab in the middle of the 1st and 2nd Bollinger Bands. We buy here. Next hour is up again, and the hour after that we hit our first price target. After selling half our position we trend sideways into the close.

After holding the balance overnight we open day two a smidgen lower before rallying a bit more. Then the day becomes a challenge as the stock ticks lower for a couple of hours to the close. This is one of those dilemmas that traders face; do we close the position or hold overnight? We've still got a small profit on this second half of our position and we could just lock it in. On the other hand we've already taken some profits and we are still higher on this second half so maybe the risk overnight is worth it.

That decision could go either way, and at that point there really is no wrong choice, but the next morning it turns out that holding overnight was the right play as the stock gaps higher and quickly blasts through the 2nd Bollinger Band where we sell the balance of our position. A nice two day trade.

Another Entry Example

Sometimes what appears to be a perfect entry just doesn't pan out. In fig 11.17 we had a nice gap down through the 3rd Bollinger Band on the open. The next candle climbed upward, and the third candle of the day gave us the confirmation we were looking for to enter the trade. Things looked OK for an hour or two before turning south. By the third red candle in a row, leading into the closing bell for the day we should have realized that this trade just wasn't working out. With all those red candles there was too much risk in holding overnight. We still had a very small winner at the close so the only prudent thing to do was to close out the trade.

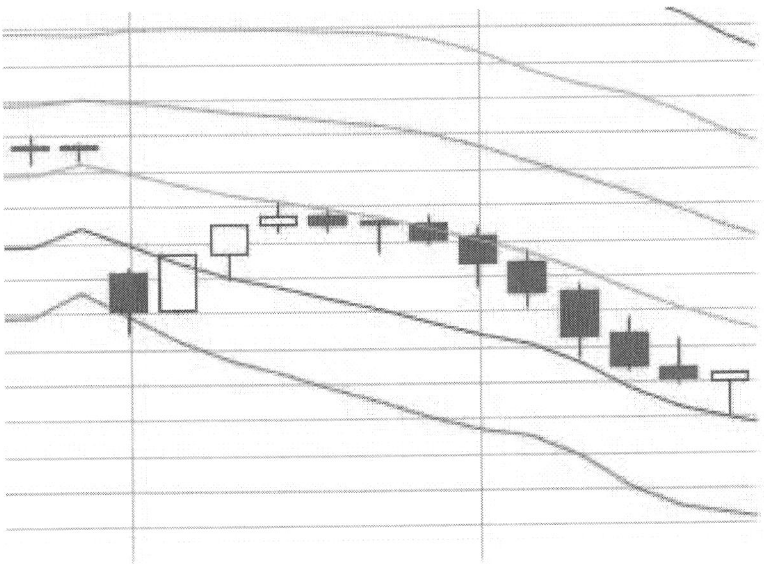

[fig 11.17]

If for some reason you did hold this one overnight it should've been painfully obvious at the open that there was no reversal in the cards with this move. Close it out now, don't wait for your stop to get hit!

Fade trading based on these pricing discrepancies is easy. It requires little from you, the slacker trader, other than a solid knowledge of your core group of stocks, the ability to act decisively when you see and understand the right signals, and most importantly the ability to manage your risk.

Exiting a Fade Trade - The Winners

While we have specific rules in place for getting out of trades, in reality there are any number of things that could lead us to breaking those rules.

First, the rules. Rule number one is to sell half the position at the 20-day Simple Moving Average. If we bought correctly, this should lock in a tidy little profit, and anything from here on is just gravy. This is the easiest one to follow as it doesn't usually represent a huge move. It's a move that's easily attainable if you are onboard a legitimate fade trade.

Rule number two is that we sell the balance of the position when it hits the 2nd Bollinger Band above the Simple Moving Average (when fading a dip lower; below the SMA when fading a spike higher).

This second sale is usually the one that requires more interpretation on the part of the trader. There are two things that can cause us to break this rule; momentum and time.

When we are in a trade we should obviously be paying close attention to it. What we are going to do during this second leg of the trade is watch for signs of exhaustion. Really all this means is that we are going to watch the chart, looking for candles that have stopped their upward momentum and begun moving in a sideways pattern.

A sideways pattern can be especially telling if 1) it's bouncing off of an area of resistance; the 1st Bollinger Band for instance, and 2) if the RSI has stalled out at 50. An RSI of 50 is often used by traders as a resistance line during a bounce. The reason is that RSI of 50 is essentially telling us that there is a balance between buyers and sellers. If more buying doesn't come into the market the stock is either going to stall out here or sellers will get back in charge and the RSI will begin dropping (along with the price).

In this case it is important to recognize that the bounce is having trouble and begin weighing the risk/reward ratio accordingly. When this happens you may want to consider selling the position right there, or moving your stop loss price up in order to let this sideways pattern play out without leaving all the risk on the table.

And then there is time. Remember, we are supposed to be doing this while "living the dream." We are slackers who want to be outside enjoying life, not sitting in front of a computer screen worrying about squeezing an extra fifty bucks out of a trade.

Day one of a trade we've hopefully seen some upside momentum. Day two we hope to see the momentum continue. On day three we're closing out our position, pretty much no matter what has happened. Fade trades shouldn't take longer than this. If they have, the most likely reason is that the stock has found a new equilibrium price. The move has stalled and the stock price probably has an equal likelihood of increasing or decreasing. By day three the risk has increased beyond the reward.

Exiting a Fade Trade - The Losers

Taking a loss, as always, represents the most crucial aspect to becoming a successful trader. This is a fade trade; there should be no emotional attachment to the trade. Therefore getting out of it when it goes against you should not be difficult at all. Of course taking a loss is always difficult, but with the rules we have in place for these trades all the emotion should be taken out of the equation.

Immediately upon entering the trade we establish the low of the move as our stop loss level—our maximum loss. If the stock had already bounced significantly off of that low, creating a gap between the low and your entry price that requires too much risk you can maneuver the stop upwards, perhaps to the 3rd BB, or to the low of the second bar after the stock touched the BB. Or, if the stock has bounced too much, perhaps you need to consider whether to make the trade at all.

When a trade goes in our favor we still need to manage our risk. Once that first sale is made at the 20-day Simple Moving Average we move our stop loss order from the low of the move, up to our actual entry point for the trade—our break-even price for the balance of the position.

Being an ex-pit trader, I (Pat) could go on and on about taking a loss. How crucial it is to success in trading. But I'm also a sailor, and taking a loss as a sailor is every bit as crucial.

With about eight hours worth of sailing experience under my belt I set off with my wife to sail from Florida to Bimini, in the Bahamas; famous haunt of Hemingway himself. Now this isn't a big trip—only about sixty miles—but it does cross the Gulf Stream; a treacherous stretch of water in the wrong conditions. With the strong current running north, any sort of north wind can cause huge waves.

We had been waiting and watching the weather and finally decided to go for it. At three a.m. we picked our way out into open ocean. Within an hour we were deep in the shit. The weather was much worse than we had anticipated, and the waves—especially to our rookie eyes—were tremendous. We plunged onward as things got worse, much like a rookie trader will watch a loser with his butt cheeks clenched—praying for the pain to stop and the turn-around to begin.

When one of our engines overheated my trader instincts took over at last—it was time to take a loss. We turned the boat around and spent eight hours fighting the current and the huge waves all the way back to where we had begun the day. It's demoralizing taking a loss like that, but absolutely necessary. The weather didn't improve, and there is no telling what would have happened to us had our other engine crapped out (remember we were sailing novices at this point, sailing often meant motoring).

My wife and I went to bed that night in a safe harbor, licked our wounds, and waited a few more days for calm weather to descend. When we jumped back into the Gulf Stream the next time the water was like glass—not a ripple upon it—until the bottle-nosed dolphins arrived to swim in our bow wake all the way to Bimini. A winning trade.

Fading a Spike Higher

Throughout this chapter we've spoken mainly about buying on dips. As we have a core group of strong stocks that we like, this makes sense. The stock dips for some reason that we deem unwarranted so we buy it back for a fade trade as it fulfills our fade trade requirements/rules.

However, fade trading works every bit as well on price spikes higher. In fact with our core stocks we can easily see spikes higher even during an overall upward trend. A good earnings report that beats analyst expectations, a new and much higher price target for the stock by a big name analyst, a new product announcement; any of these things could cause a spike in the price of our favorite stocks.

Remember though that just because they are our favorite stocks does not mean that every spike higher should automatically be labeled as the new fair value price. Perhaps that new product is expected to have much lower margins than previous products, or traders come to their senses and realize that the analyst that raised his price target is really just an idiot whose bank owns millions of shares in the stock.

Whatever, doesn't really matter; what matters is that we focus on the spike higher and watch it—just like we do on dips—for a reversal. All our rules apply to the upside the same as they do to the downside. As you can see from a number of examples scattered throughout the chapter.

Here is How it Works in True Slacker Fashion

And what's our favorite thing about fade trading? Very little time commitment, and that works well with our travel schedules! Here's an example:

(Pat) When my daughter was one and a half and my wife was eight-months pregnant with number two, they flew to Puerto Vallarta where the new baby would be born. Meanwhile I was to sail the boat down by myself from San Diego. Basically I wanted to do this as quickly as possible to join the family before it got any bigger. After eight days of sailing, as I rounded the corner of Cabo Falso in the final stretch to Cabo San Lucas it was more than a little disappointing to drop my sails and realize my transmission coupler had broken. Three hundred miles from Puerto Vallarta and I had no engine.

I had a fishing boat tow me into the marina and then spent the day frantically racing around town with a transmission mechanic trying to figure out a fix. By nightfall we had gotten the needed part fabricated and were set to install it the next morning.

That morning I woke early and hopped online to see what was shaking. I saw immediately that one of my core stocks was getting beat up. Down four percent with the market down just one percent. A scan of the news revealed not one single mention of the company, yet there it was just coming off the 3rd BB with the RSI under 30. When I saw the market start to tick up—and got the confirmation candle I was looking for—I bought a pile of call options. Just thirty minutes later I exited half the trade with a $700 winner.

The stock had been down for no discernible reason, and had quickly retraced its losses when the market had gone green. In minutes I had covered my boat expenses for both the marina and the repair, and by that afternoon was sailing across the Sea of Cortez bound for Puerto Vallarta still holding half the position with a stop loss order in place that at worst would still net me another $500. Upon arrival I fired up my laptop and found that the stock had continued its run; I closed the position for another $1,100 and met my family a doubly happy man.

Paddling Out

We put this section at the end so that we wouldn't add to the confusion that some readers might be struggling with; deciding when fade trading is appropriate is as much a part of success as learning to use technical tools like Bollinger Bands and candlestick charts.

Okay, we concede that if this is the first time you've been exposed to these things, it probably looks *a little* complicated—but after you try it out with your practice (paper) trading account for a while, the buy and sell signals are just going to start jumping out at you. It's really like anything in life; the more you do it, the more comfortable you will become with it.

Look Cool for a While

Doesn't matter if you are a kook (newbie) or total shredder, do you just grab your board, toss it in the water, and start paddling out? No way, bradda, you gotta stand on the beach and look cool for a little while; you gotta scope the scene. Which way is the swell coming in? How far apart are the sets? Has the sand moved around and changed the break since yesterday? Who else is out there in the lineup? Is it crowded? Are the locals talking quietly and grabbing a bigger board off the rack? You gotta know what's up.

That goes triple for the stock market. You can't just arrive at your destination, fire up the WiFi, and make a trade. Well, maybe you can if you're a genius like the two of us, otherwise that's not a great idea. These are real dollars we're talking about, and you'll be better served by watching the waves for a while before committing to a barrel.

The Market Open

On days when you are able to log in and watch the opening of the market there are a number of important bits of information that you can glean that may tell you a lot about what's in store for the session.

The market open doesn't actually start with the opening bell. It starts with the after-hours and overnight trading and what is happening in the international markets. These foreign exchanges often give us some hints on our opening momentum. If Asia closed down and Europe is down, unless there are other forces at work in the U.S. markets, it will likely open down as well.

And remember, the market does not begin from the previous day's close and gradually move on from there. The market can simply open four percent lower, you don't always get a chance to get in or out right where things left off the day before. So how do we go about interpreting the market open?

Well, just like there are support and resistance lines for stocks, there are support and resistance lines for the major market averages. If after the opening flurry of trades, the DJIA, the NASDAQ, the S&P 500, etc. settle into the middle of the trading ranges defined, we'll expect that today will be a range bound day (neglecting any major economic announcements like employment, GDP, or Federal Reserve). We can probably assume that the day will be a quiet one for the overall market—we can't predict that for sure, but it's our first indication.

After looking at the overall market we do the same for our stable of stocks. If they are all sitting in the same general position as the overall market it's a safe bet that today will be a good day to close the laptop and head out for some adventure—no work to be done today. We may miss an opportunity here and there, but it's important to remember that our time is worth something too, and days like this are meant to be spent doing something else.

If on the other hand the market or one of our stocks opened up near our trend lines, or even through them, we need to grab a cup of coffee, pay attention, and delve a little deeper into what is happening. In other words, we're going to have to stick around.

Opening Volume

Another interesting indicator we can use to help us decide a day's importance, is volume. Both for the state of the general market as well as our individual stocks. A general rule of thumb is that increased volume leads to increased volatility.

When we say increased volume we are talking about volume compared to previous mornings' volume because morning volume (and closing volume) is almost always higher than the rest of the day.

Whew. That was a mouthful. So what does this really mean to us as traders? Well, as traders who are only interested in trading if there is something really *worth* trading, we view volatility as our friend. A stock with low volume and thus low volatility is only very rarely going to see the large spike moves that we are always hoping to see.

High volatility also indicates to us that the big players are in the market. High volatility is a byproduct of high volume, and that volume has to come from somewhere. It isn't coming from you and me. Retail investors like us are small fish. We may generate the greatest *number* of trades, but the institutional investors generate the greatest *volume,* and therefore have the greatest impact on stock price per trade.

High volume near the open therefore indicates a greater chance for a larger than normal change in price. Low volume indicates we are more likely to see a range bound day—meaning the stock will go up and down during the day, but the difference between the high and the low will be smaller.

So...at the "end of the beginning" of the day, a low volume open in the middle of our trend lines gives us all the information we need to pick our board and head out for a session. Whereas high volume and an opening price near our trend lines tells us we best check our cash balance and get ready for some fireworks.

Too Hot to Trot

Fading really is a fairly simple strategy—it's true: you can be in and out quickly and make a tidy little profit if you are on the right side of the trade. The problem is that it can look a little too easy. You're in port or hooked up in the RV park or you have a few hours at the internet cafe, and you are ready to make some quick dough. If you don't see any opportunities with your core group of stocks or the market isn't really showing you the signs you want to see, you are going to be tempted to *make something happen* with stocks which seem to fit the patterns and signals we described above.

Don't stray! Fading is simple and easy, but it doesn't work if you don't know and understand a particular stock and you can't evaluate the market news which is sparking the spike higher or lower to begin with. You must have the confidence and discipline to discern the real opportunities from those that look "just close enough"—those will cost you.

Options Trading

We very seldom trade stock—we invest in stock. If we are trading, it is most likely through the use of options.

Options are financial *derivatives* of stocks, and while they are deeply linked, trading options is very different than trading stocks. When you buy stocks, you simply want them to go up in value. You hope they go up quickly of course so that you can profit and move on, but when you buy a stock you don't really have to consider how long that move higher is going to take. You buy XYZ at $80 and if it only goes to $83 by next month, you can always decide to hold it a bit longer if you think that it will continue to go up in value.

Options are a completely different beast that offers you the chance for much higher gains (and losses) in a much shorter period of time. With options you aren't just forecasting whether you think the stock will go up or down, but you are forecasting the time period over which that move will take place.

With an option, you need to be confident not only that the underlying stock will go in the direction you think it will, but you have to successfully forecast how long that move will take. Options are time dependent, and stocks are not.

What are they?

Options are contracts with specified terms that give you the right to buy or sell a specific number of shares of stock, at a specific price, at a specific time in the future. The value of this contract goes up and down as the stock goes up and down, so we have something of value that we can trade; we have a separate market (the options market) that depends on the underlying stock's market price.

Limited Downside Risk

One huge benefit to options is that they limit how much we can lose; they limit our downside risk. With stocks, you theoretically have unlimited downside risk, because companies do fail, and when they do, their stocks go to zero. Because an option is a contract that gives the holder the right to buy (or sell) at a certain price by a certain date, the downside risk is only what you paid for that option, called the *premium.*

Consider the example of fictional stock BADD. Let's say that we bought the "$25 call option" for $4 (more on what that means later). Our total cost basis is

$400 (each contract price is multiplied by 100 because it is for 100 shares of stock). Let's compare that to buying 100 shares of BADD at the current share price of $25. In figure 12.1 we have plotted profit against share price to show you what happens as the stock goes up or down:

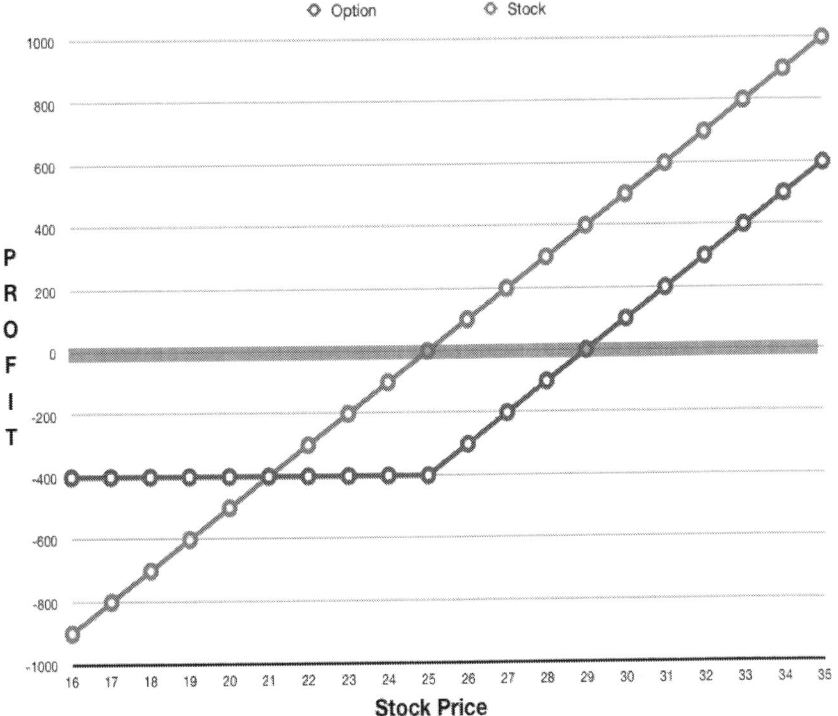

[fig 12.1]

You can see that if the option expires at or below the $25 "strike price," we lose our $400 premium, but that's all we can lose. On the other hand, if we bought the stock outright, our cost basis is $2500 and theoretically, we could lose it all. If the stock goes up we make a little money on the stock. If the price of the stock rises above $29 per share, we make money on our options.

We are going to guess you aren't impressed yet, so let's look at fig 12.2 and the percentages gained or lost on the stock vs. the options as the stock price goes up or down:

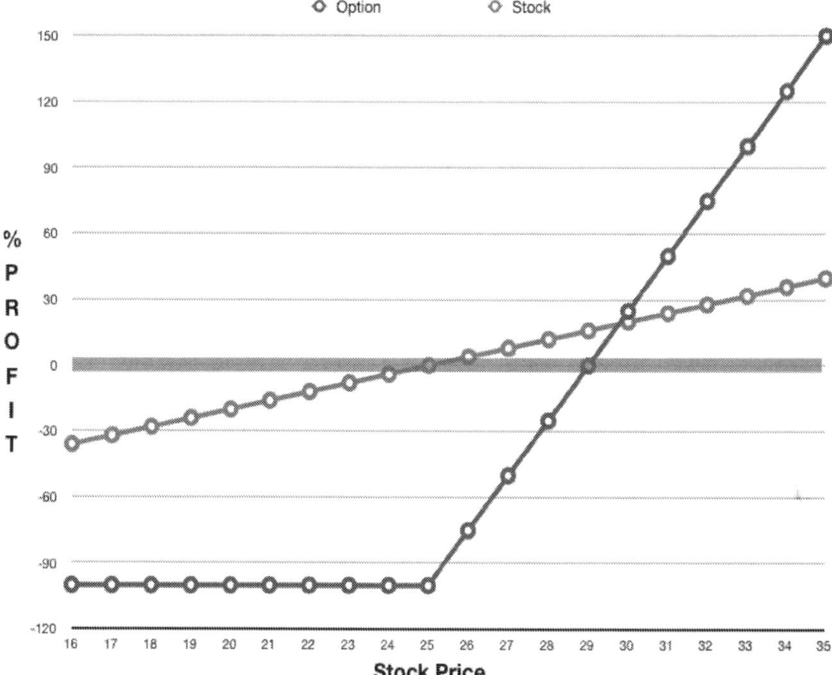

[fig 12.2]

When you look at the percentages gained or lost on fictional BADD and compare options to stocks, the profit looks a little more impressive. In the case of our call option, the percentage gain goes up really fast compared to owning the stock outright.

For example, if the stock goes up to $31, we make $200, which is a 50% return on our $400. If we bought 100 shares of stock outright for $2,500, we'd only be making 24%. At a stock price of $35, the stock purchase makes us 40% profit while the option would earn 150%.

You may be seeing the benefit of options already. We told you in the introduction that we weren't satisfied making small percentages on our money. Options boost our horsepower significantly so our money can work a lot harder!

Leverage!

We love trading options and using them as an alternative to outright stock purchases because they give us that one thing we are always looking for: leverage. So let us start by explaining what options are and then move on to how you can use them. For the purposes of this book we are going to concentrate strictly on stock options.

Now we really wish there were an easy way to explain options to somebody who is starting from scratch, but there isn't. We're going to give it a try because it's a worthwhile addition to any trader's arsenal.

CALLS AND PUTS

This is where it all begins. Read this and digest it. If you get a little confused or lost, just slow down and read it again. We guarantee you will have to stare at this section a little bit and re-read it a few times. At some point, it's just going to "click," and you will say to yourself, "Ahhhhhh, I get it!" Everyone who has never been exposed to options before has the same reaction that you are about to, so be patient with yourself. Here are the fundamental definitions and concepts:

Call Options

You buy a call option because you expect a stock's price to go up over a certain period of time. A *call* gives the holder (you) the right to <u>buy</u> 100 shares of the underlying stock at a specified price within a specific time period. A call option really has three components you are paying attention to, and they are all important:

- The price the call is trading at (what you pay for it), sometimes alternatively called the "premium."
- The "strike price" which is the price you would be able to buy the underlying stock for if you "exercised" the right to buy the stock at or before expiration (which you most likely will never do).
- The date at which the option expires.

So immediately, you can see that an option is completely different from the stock itself, but it's dependent on the underlying stock price. Instead of buying stock in XYZ for $50 per share, you might be buying the "XYZ May 50 call" for let's just say $2 (it is important to note that because the call gives you the right to buy 100 shares, purchasing that single contract at $2 really costs you $200—that's just the standard nomenclature because one option contract is for 100 shares). That means that for $200, you have the right to buy 100 shares of XYZ at $50 on the third Friday of May (for monthly options, it's always the end of the third Friday of the month—that's the standard expiration day), no matter what the actual stock price ends up being that day.

How Money is Made on Call Options

To put it in its simplest terms, if you buy that $50 call and the stock goes up to $60, you have a $10 profit (minus the cost of the call, which was $2 per share) on each share at expiration; you have the right to buy the stock at $50 despite it being worth $60 on expiration day. That ten dollars is actually $1,000 since each call (or contract) is equivalent to 100 shares of the underlying stock. So to continue with our example of the XYZ May 50 call you purchased for $200, you just made $800 ($1,000 - $200). Bingo—that's leverage in action.

Put Options

Let's say you think a stock is going to go down in a certain period of time. A *put* gives the holder the right to sell 100 shares of the underlying stock at a certain price within a specific time period. You are locking in a price at which you can sell the stock.

Again, at its simplest, if you buy a $30 put and the stock goes down to $25, you have a $5 profit, multiplied by 100 since each option contract is equivalent to 100 shares, or $500 on one put, minus what you paid for the option, which is called the *premium*.

Expiration Date

There are more terms that you need to be familiar with. One of the most important being the expiration date. This is the last day that an options contract is valid. In order for an option buyer to exercise their right to either buy (calls) or sell (puts) the stock at the option's strike price they must do so on or before the expiration date. Options held through the close of expiration day will generally be exercised automatically by your brokerage if they are even one penny in-the-money. Normally the options expiration date is on the third Friday of every month, but there are weekly options available as well (we don't trade these very often, so we aren't going to get into them).

As you get closer and closer to the expiration date, there are fewer and fewer days for the current stock price to rise (in the case of a call) to the price the option can be exercised at, so the value of the option goes **down** over time, all other factors remaining equal. This is called *time decay,* and it tends to accelerate as the expiration date draws near because as the days tick away there is a smaller chance of getting to the strike price.

Strike Price

This is the price at which the stock can be bought or sold. For instance, if the stock is trading at $25 and you want to be able to buy the stock at $30 anticipating a large increase in the stock's price, you would be purchasing the $30 calls. Thirty dollars being the strike price.

It's really important to note that you will probably never (unless you want to) exercise your option to buy at the strike price before the expiration day—you will be trading into and out of the option before that happens. So at the end of the day, strike price is really a measure of where the stock is today (or the day you buy it) compared to where you think it will go by a certain date—the expiration date. As you can see, you need to have a forecast in your mind for what the stock will do over a specific period of time—there is no "buy and hold" strategy in options trading.

The further away (above for a call and below for a put) a strike price is from the price the stock trades at on the day you buy it, the lower the chance of it actually reaching that price by expiration day. For example, if the stock is trading at $10 today, and you buy next month's $50 call option, obviously there is a really really small chance of that stock making it to the strike price.

If a stock is trading at $10 today and you buy next month's $11 call, there is a much better chance of it reaching that value.

So which option should cost more to buy today when the stock is trading at $10: the $11 call or the $50 call? See, this is easy—of course it's the $11 call.

There are three terms regarding strike price that should be understood: at-the-money, in-the-money, and out-of-the-money. This is all jargon, but this is the sort of thing you are going to come across on all of the trading websites and financial news, so you might as well learn them now.

At-the-Money

An at-the-money option has a strike price very close to the price of the underlying stock. So if a stock trades at $400 (or close to it) and you buy the $400 option, you are buying an at-the-money option.

Out-of-the-Money

An out-of-the-money call option has a strike price above the current stock price (below in the case of a put option). In the case of a call option, an example would be when the current stock price is $400 and you buy the $420 call. The $420 call is out-of-the-money, a $450 call is *further* out-of-the-money.

In-the-Money

An in-the-money call option has a strike price below the current stock price. For our $400 stock, the $370 call is in-the-money and the $320 call is "deeper" in-the-money. An in-the-money put has a strike price above the current stock price.

The Premium—How Option Prices are Determined by the Market

The stock's price, the strike price, the implied volatility, and the number of days remaining until expiration all contribute to the price of an option, and the price of the option is called the *premium*. It's beyond the scope of this book to fully explain the pricing, but there are some obvious points that can be made and understood.

First, the closer the strike price is to the underlying stock's current price the more expensive the option will be. This is because it's more likely that the stock can move beyond the strike price and end up in-the-money, or profitable at expiration.

Also, higher volatility equals a higher premium, and vice versa. A more volatile stock makes it more likely that the stock can move beyond the strike price and end up in-the-money.

And lastly, the more days remaining until the expiration date, the higher the likelihood that the stock can move beyond the strike price, and thus the higher the premium that must be paid. For example, if the stock is at $23 and you want to buy a call at the $25 strike price it's far more likely the stock price could move through that strike price if there are ninety days left until expiration instead of only two days left.

The current stock price, the expiration date, the strike price, and stock volatility are the four main factors (there are a couple others) that determine risk, and risk is what determines the price (premium) of an option. The higher the risk of a given outcome, the higher the price. See, at the end of the day, options are a form of insurance, and it costs a lot more to insure against a sure thing than it does to insure against a low-probability outcome.

Options are a Form of Insurance

For any option you buy, there is someone out there who sold that option. The seller is insuring him or herself against that outcome actually happening. If you are buying a $100 option, someone is selling you that option and profiting by the premium you pay because they are betting that the stock price never reaches $100. Why are they doing it? Well, we don't need to confuse you with something you will probably never do yourself, but what the seller of the option is probably doing is called, "hedging." In essence, he is selling some of his risk.

Let's draw a couple real world parallels from the world of property and life insurance. For example, if you are a healthy, young, non-smoking woman, your life insurance premium is going to cost a lot less than it will for an overweight, middle-aged smoker. This is because the insurance company has a lower risk of loss with the young healthy person than with the old unhealthy one—they know they have a greater risk of paying out the policy for the old smoker dying than the young non-smoker, so they charge more for the older person.

Here is another example. Is there a higher risk or a lower risk of flood damage to a house located on a hill in a desert than to one located on a riverbank in a flood zone? Right, easy answer there too, so flood insurance is going to cost more for the house on the water. Premium paid is directly tied to risk.

So if options are all about paying a premium for (and hopefully profiting from) risk, then we need to think a little bit more about risk and how it is measured for options.

The Greeks

When we were talking about fundamental analysis in previous chapters (things like P/E ratios and return on equity, etc.), what we were trying to do was introduce you to some concepts and tools for understanding businesses, how they are performing, and how to compare them to other companies in the same market. In essence, what we wanted you to try to do was start thinking about businesses in the ways that the rest of the stock market thinks about them and start to form your own opinions to see opportunities where stocks might be over or undervalued.

However no matter how much research you did or how well you knew the company, you didn't know then and can never know for certain if those companies and their stocks will go up or down in value. Your research may help form an opinion and help you make your own forecast about the future, but there is always a risk you are wrong.

The "greeks" are some of the analysis tools you need to understand to try and decide if the options (calls and puts) for those stocks are an opportunity or not—whether the risk taken is worth the premium paid. These greeks are some of the tools to help you evaluate risk, and understanding them is essential, because options are full of risk (remember, risk can be a good thing), and if you don't understand the risks you are taking, you are going to make bad decisions and lose all your money. That = not good.

Delta

One first time option trader's mistake is thinking that if the stock price goes up a dollar, the (call) option price for that stock will go up a dollar. That would be really nice, but that's not usually how it works. Instead of going up $1, it will go up some percentage of $1. An option's *delta* measures the sensitivity of the option's price to a change in the underlying stock's price. That's a mouthful. How about this? For a one dollar change in the price of the stock, an option's price will change by x amount. That number x is called the delta.

Some traders prefer to think of delta as the probability that an option will expire in-the-money. The problem with this is that it relies on the assumption that each day the odds of a stock going up or down is a coin flip, fifty-fifty. It's not. But as an easy way to think about delta, this works well enough. In the table shown in fig 12.3 you would say that the out-of-the-money $25 call has a 10% chance of being in-the-money at expiration.

Two important details are: a delta's value can range from zero to one, and an in-the-money option's delta will be higher than an out-of-the-money option. Say it again to yourself a few times and it will sink in.

ABC stock at $20	Strike	Delta
Out-of-the-Money	$25	.10
At-the-Money	$20	.50
In-the-Money	$15	.90

[fig 12.3]

Let's say this through an example. Stock ABC has a current price of $20. The $20 call has a delta of .50. Essentially telling you the option has a 50/50 shot of being in-the-money at expiration. The $25 call (which is "out-of-the-money") has a delta of just .10 showing that it's less likely this call will be in-the-money at expiration.

Another way to try and understand delta is from the point of view of a pit trader.

I (Pat) was a soybean options pit trader in Chicago. When a broker would receive an order he would yell out the option he wanted a quote on and we pit traders would yell out a bid and an offer. Essentially what we pit traders were looking to do was to profit on the bid/offer spread. We worked under the assumption that we knew the exact true value of an option and would price our bid and our offer slightly below and above that true value. The difference between the true value and our bid/offer was, in effect, the premium that we were charging in order to assume the risk of the option.

Okay, so say I bought 100 at-the-money calls with a delta of .60; what does that mean? Well I bought calls, so I make money on them if the price of the underlying commodity (soybeans) goes up.

But I didn't know when I gave the broker a bid/ask quote if he was going to be selling me calls or buying them. In other words I wasn't actually looking to take a directional position in the market. I wasn't specifically looking to buy calls because I felt that soybean prices were going up; I was giving a market in order to try and profit from either buying below what I felt the true value of the option was or selling it above that value.

Since I didn't simply want to be long 100 calls in the soybean market I would look to hedge that risk that I had just purchased; the risk that soybean prices would fall. To do this I needed to know the delta. In this case the delta was .60. So to hedge my 100 calls I needed to sell 60 (100 x .60) soybean futures contracts. At that point I was ***delta neutral.***

Think that through. For every one dollar the price of soybeans increased, my 100 calls would increase in value by $60. On the flip side though, I had sold 60 futures contracts that would've lost $60 in value. I neither made money nor lost money, I am ***perfectly hedged****. If the price of soybeans went up I would make money on the calls but lose the same amount on the futures, and if the price of beans went down I would lose money on the calls but make the same amount of money on the futures. So what's the point you wonder?*

Well there were two other ways to make money other than simply owning the calls and hoping the price of soybeans went up. One was to scalp the calls. Scalping in the case of the pit trader would mean to buy the calls at the bid price and quickly sell them at the offer. In practice this wasn't all that common because the odds that another order would come into the market for the same option, but to buy it instead, was unlikely.

Usually what would happen instead is that the pit trader would look to sell different options, generally at a nearby strike price, for slightly less than the offer price. So it's not a true scalp but works in much the same way. Scalping is not a trading method that's at all profitable for you and me sitting at home on our computers. There is no way to consistently buy at the bid price and sell at the offer price. There is no "edge."

I was not a scalper. I wasn't fast enough, and I didn't see enough profit in it. Some guys were trained as scalpers and spent their entire careers in the pits trying to squeeze a tiny profit out of each trade. For some it worked, for most it didn't.

The other way to make money while at the same time being hedged is to trade the volatility.

Implied Volatility

As we talked about above, the price of an option is based on a number of factors such as current stock price, strike price, days until expiration, interest rate, dividends, and volatility. "Implied volatility" is the expected volatility of the stock price between now and expiration. In other words, is the stock going to move around a lot or a little?

Determining implied volatility is crucial in determining the value of an option. If a stock has low implied volatility, meaning traders expect that the stock will not move around much, then the price of options will be lower. Why? Because, in the case of an out-of-the-money call, there is less chance of the stock moving far enough for the call to become in-the-money.

And if the implied volatility is high, then the premium charged for that same out-of-the-money call will be higher because the chance that the call will become in-the-money is greater.

Going back to our soybean example from above, if we were hedged delta neutral then the only way outside of scalping to make money off of those 100 calls would be for implied volatility to increase. An increase in volatility would lead to the same option being more expensive. Thus we would be able to sell them for a higher price than we bought them for, even if the price of soybeans hadn't really moved. In essence you are trading volatility, not soybeans, stocks, or whatever the case may be.

This is a really important point to make. With options (keeping all other factors constant) the higher the volatility, the higher the option price. So to profit, you want to look for opportunities where the market thinks there will be less volatility than you think there will be. When a stock makes a big move up or down in a way that the rest of the market was not anticipating, the option will see bigger moves due to the increased premium caused by higher implied volatility. On the flip side, the smaller the stock move or the more anticipated that move is, the smaller the change in option price. Make sense?

A common scenario is for volatility to have a run up in anticipation of a report or other big news event. As the volatility increases the premium (cost) of the options increases. The uncertainty drives this, so what often happens is that the report/news comes out and suddenly the uncertainty is gone. Now regardless of whether the news caused a big move or left the stock flat the implied volatility comes crashing back down, dragging the options premiums down with it.

Gamma

If delta is a measurement of how much an option's price changes in relation to how the underlying stock price changes, you might want to know what sort of trends delta has. You want to know if the option price is becoming more or less sensitive to the underlying stock price. If an option has a delta of .10 but increases to .20, what does that tell you? That means that the option is becoming more sensitive to a change in stock price—which means, by extension, that the market is more and more concerned with the fact that the stock price is making (or could make) larger moves. This rate of change of delta is called gamma.

So where is delta going to change most? It is going to change most when you are at or near-the-money, meaning when the option strike price is very close to the current stock price. In general, gamma is going to be highest at-the-money and lower the further you get both out-of-the-money and deeper into-the-money.

Vega

Vega is the greek that brings implied volatility to life and gives it some meaning. Vega represents the amount that an options price changes based on a 1% change in volatility. Options are more expensive when volatility is high and get cheaper when volatility is low, so when calculating what an options price would be at a different volatility level we add the vega when volatility is increasing and subtract it as volatility decreases.

For example, XYZ is trading at $40 and the $45 call is trading at $1 with a volatility of 25% and vega of .10. If volatility were to increase by 1% to 26% we could expect the price of the option to increase to $1.10. If however volatility were to decrease 3% to 22%, we would expect the price of the option to drop to $.70 ($1 - (3 x .10) = .70).

Theta

We mentioned above that an option is going to decrease in value over time as we approach the expiration date, so it would be really great to have some sort of measure of how fast that time decay is happening. For that we have *theta,* which measures the rate at which an option's value decreases over time. All options have a time value built into their price. Obviously the more time left before expiration the greater chance that the underlying stock price can move in the right direction to make your option profitable, hence the higher the option price. If there is only one month left for your $20 stock to move $5 the chances of that happening are far less than if there are six months left.

When trading options with expirations more than a couple of months out it's fairly easy to ignore theta because time value doesn't change very quickly. But with only a month or two to go before expiration it's something that needs to be taken into consideration as every day that goes by, regardless of what the market is doing, you will lose some money to time decay on your long options positions.

Fade Trading and Greeks

While all of these greeks are important in understanding options as a whole, they become less important when using them in fade trading, where we are in and out of trades quickly. Almost always within two days.

If your option's expiration date is beyond a week or two away then theta becomes unimportant because it just isn't going to make that great an impact on your one or two day trade. And also, very generally, you won't see that great a fluctuation in volatility in such a short time period so gamma isn't quite as big an issue, though it cannot be ignored because volatility can change quickly around important announcements and it is always a risk in options trading. It is an unknown, whereas time decay is a known factor.

Delta is probably the most important greek for the fade trader who uses options. You always want to be cognizant of how an option is behaving in relation to the underlying stock. If you see one of your favorite stocks dip a couple percent more than the sector or the major indices and you think it will bounce back in a day or two, you want to make sure you buy options with a high delta to capitalize on the move you anticipate.

REAL WORLD EXAMPLES

We realize that what you just read was probably a bunch of gibberish. So how about a couple of simplified real world examples?

For years now you've been an avid Apple computer user. You use their laptops, their iPods, and now you've even bought yourself an iPad. You like the company and you like their products. You might even consider yourself a fanboy. (Warning: becoming overly enamored with a company can lead to trouble. Remain subjective!)

The stock has been sitting around $600 a share with a P/E ratio of about fourteen. You think this is cheap. You see that Apple Computer continues to innovate, and most importantly, your brother Ferdinand who has never owned an Apple product says he is going to stand in line for the next iPhone release. You are bullish, but you don't really have the capital necessary ($60,000) to buy the hundred shares of the company you wish you could.

In addition to all the other Apple greatness, you believe the rumors swirling around that the company is about to release an iTV. You aren't entirely clear, as nobody else seems to be, what this means, but you are confident that if anybody can revolutionize the television it's Apple. You are full-on bullish Apple. This stock is headed for the stratosphere in your opinion.

This is frustrating. You really believe if this iTV announcement comes out in December as the rumors indicate, that the price of Apple's stock will jump to $750 share. But as it is right now you could only afford to buy five shares. So even if you were to do that you could only expect a profit of $750 ($150 x 5) on a massive move like this. It would be sad to be so right about a stock, have it make a huge move, but still only make a small profit.

This is the kind of situation where the leverage of options comes into play.

What you could do instead of buying those five shares is that you could buy a call. Remember—a call option represents control of 100 shares of the underlying stock.

In this instance what you are looking for is a very big move. Therefore you decide to buy a December 700 call. This is a full $100 higher than the current stock price, but by buying the December expiration it gives Apple stock three full months to make that move. In addition it expires on the third Friday of December, which is three weeks later than the rumored iTV announcement that you are banking on in the first place.

The cost of this option is $2.00. That's per share, so $2.00 x 100 shares equals $200. That $200 is the premium you pay for the right to buy 100 shares of Apple stock three months from now at $700 per share.

Say that you were right. Apple does come out with an iTV full of features that nobody expected, and they did it two weeks before Christmas. The stock price soars to $750 on options expiration day. You would realize a profit of $50 per share, the difference between the $700 strike price and the actual $750 stock price. $50 x 100 shares is $5,000. Minus the $200 premium you paid you walk away with a $4,800 profit on your one option contract.

What if there had been no iTV; what would have happened then? Well, nothing. On options expiration day your call would've been worthless as the price of the stock was below the price that you had reserved the right to purchase it at. In this case you would only have been out the premium you originally paid, $200.

So you have to like the risk/reward of a play like that don't you? Risk of $200 to a reward of $4,800. Twenty-four to one. Of course there is a reason for that. <u>Most options expire worthless.</u> Two-thirds by many estimates. And even that two-thirds number is misleading as the majority of options owned at any given time are within a strike price of the actual value of the stock, not ten strike prices away from the stock.

Let's give another example of exactly how a call option works as you can see in fig 12.4. As we write this Exxon stock is trading at $92. That means if you wanted to own 100 shares of XOM it would cost you $9,200. Not an insignificant sum to most of us.

The alternative to laying out nine grand is to buy a call option. Remember one option is equivalent to one hundred shares of the underlying stock. If you were to buy a call with a strike price of 90 you would be in-the-money, meaning that if you were to exercise that option this moment you would own 100 shares of XOM at 90. The cost of this option with an expiration date six months away is just $400.

What you've done by buying this call is given yourself unlimited upside potential for the next six months, until expiration. If Iran and Israel go to war and Exxon stock goes to $120 you will have made a profit of $30 per share times 100 shares, or $3,000, minus the premium paid for the option of $400. Success with moves this large should always be considered highly unlikely, of course, but it serves the purpose of this example.

The other, more important thing you've done is managed your risk. If you buy 100 shares of Exxon, your risk (theoretically of course) is the total amount, $9,200, because companies can go to zero. Again, this is unlikely, but it's not so unlikely that the stock could drop twenty dollars resulting in a loss of $2,000.

Instead what you've done is limit your risk to $400—the premium paid for the call option. You can not lose more than this.

So how do you **lose** in this case?

Well, there are two ways. Assume that you hold this call for the full six months until expiration. The first risk is that the stock goes down. If the stock price at expiration is below $90 your call option expires worthless. Why? Because your call gave you the right to buy 100 shares of Exxon stock at $90. If the stock is at $80 you obviously wouldn't exercise your right to buy it at $90 in that case, you would just go out and buy the stock at $80 if that's what you wanted to do.

An important point relating to the above is that if you had owned the stock outright instead of owning this call option your loss would've been $1,000. A far larger loss than the cost of the call. However if Exxon had been at $89 at expiration your loss owning the stock would've only been $1 per share, or $100. The loss on your call would be the full $400. This is how an option's leverage can hurt you.

The other way to lose is for the stock not to have gone up more than the price you paid for the call, divided by 100. Because you paid $400 for the call option you need the price of the stock to go above $94 before you will be profitable on the trade. If the price were still $92 at expiration you would exercise your right to buy the stock at $90, netting you $200; but taking into account the $400 that you paid for the option you would still have a $200 loser.

So how do you **win** in this case?

The purchase of the call option for $400 was essentially a bet that the stock price would move above $94 in six months. If the stock were to go to $100 on expiration day you'd have a profit of $600. If you had owned the stock outright your profit would've been larger, but you would also have had more risk to the downside. This way you limited your risk to $400 and you substantially reduced the money you would originally have had to put up in order to control 100 shares of the stock.

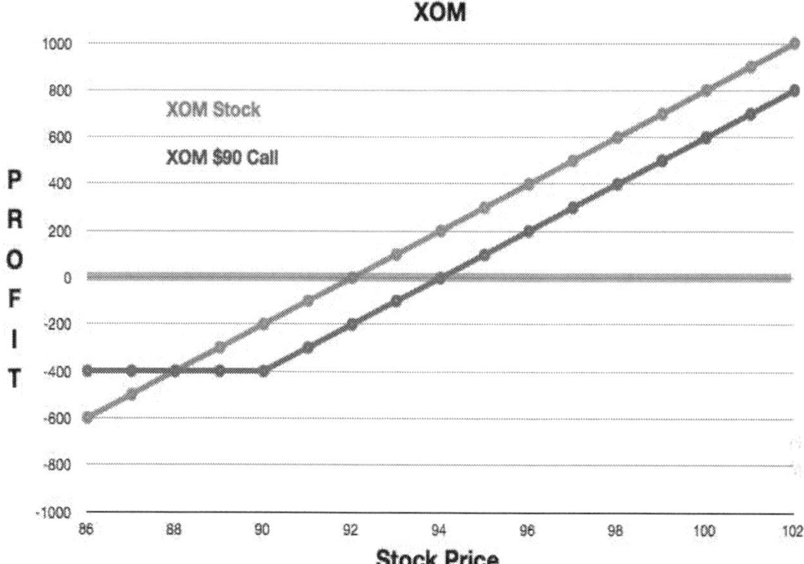

[fig 12.4]

There are limitless option strategies, and we will talk about more of them in a bit. The most basic to execute is the long call, as we've been talking about here. Its benefits include:

- Limited Risk. Your only risk is the money spent on the call. You can never lose more, no matter how far the stock price falls.
- Unlimited Profit Potential. By buying a call you stand to profit if the stock rises; and just like owning the stock outright, your profit is theoretically unlimited.
- Lower Cost of Entry. You can control the same number of shares for a much lower entry price.

The downside is:

- Total Premium Loss. If at expiration the price of the stock is below the strike price the option is worth zero. Even if the stock price has increased since you bought the call, if it hasn't increased above the strike price it's worth zero.
- Time Decay. Every day the option is worth a little less, until expiration day, at which point it is worth exactly the difference between the strike price and the stock price.

- Options represent a much smaller market than the actual stock itself. There are fewer players which leads to wider bid/ask spreads. This isn't so prevalent in steady stocks such as Exxon, but a popular high-flying stock like GOOG will generally have a market for their stock only a few cents wide; the options for the same stock will often have a market twenty cents, thirty cents, or even a dollar wider. This can eat into your profits or add to your losses.

Leverage

If you are *living on the margin,* options trading has a lot going for it—leverage being the most important. Leverage is what makes the world go round.

It's important for all traders to understand what leverage means. The most common example of leverage for most people is a home loan. Let's say you want to buy a house for $200,000. To do so you need to put ten percent down, or $20,000. The bank then finances the balance of $180,000.

So on day one you've got $20,000 in equity that cost you $20,000. Now one year later home prices in the area have gone up and your home is now worth $220,000. The equity in the home is now $220,000–$180,000, or $40,000. A 100% increase despite the fact that the loan balance hasn't increased.

	Today	In 1 Year	Change
Home Value	200k	220k	10 %
Loan Balance	180k	180k	0
Equity	20k	40k	100 %

[fig 12.5]

This is a very basic example that doesn't take into account payments made on the loan or the fact that home prices are extremely subjective right up until the day you actually sell your home.

How does leverage work with options?

Let's take a look now at the leverage that options create for you when trading. We'll use TRV stock as an example, as you can see in fig 12.6. The insurance giant is currently trading at $64 and you feel confident that they will continue to climb. To buy 100 shares would cost you $6,400, and for every dollar the stock price increased you would make $100.

Now let's say that instead of buying 100 shares of the stock you buy a call with a strike price of $60 and an expiration date six months away for $6.00. This means that instead of paying $6,400 for control of 100 shares of the company's stock you have paid $600.

Six months down the line the share price of TRV has indeed gone up, to $72 on option expiration day. Let's look at the gains you've made.

Had you simply bought the stock for $64 you'd have made $800. That's a 12.5% gain. Not bad right?

But what if you had purchased that call? You bought the $60 call, so at expiration that would be worth $12 ($72 stock price - $60 strike price). With a $600 investment you'd have made $600, or a 100% return.

While the actual dollar gain may have been smaller, the percentage gain on investment was much higher. That is leverage and that's why trading options can be such an attractive approach for those of us living on the margin.

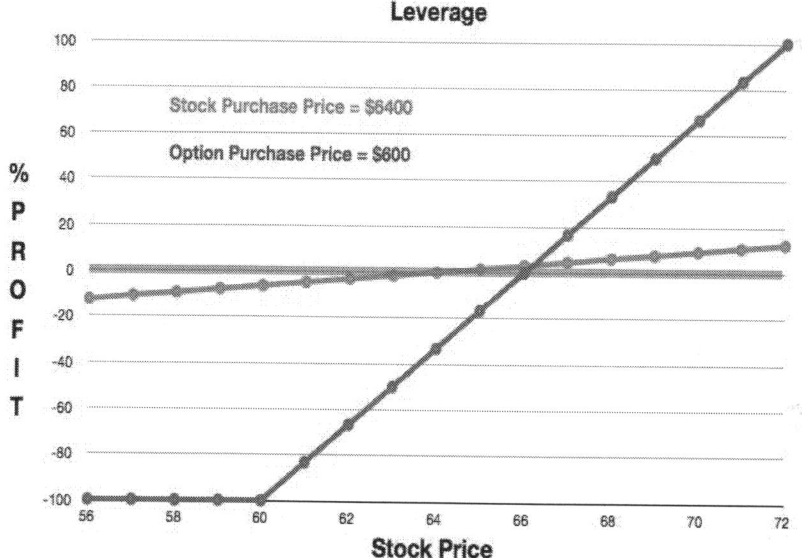

[fig 12.6]

The Risk of Leverage

Trading options and using leverage sounds so appealing that it's important to remember that leverage works both ways. In fact if you google *"Options Trading,"* you will find millions of websites touting the magic of leverage without so much as glossing over the risk. So what is that risk?

Take the example above again. Now you've made the same trade but this time the stock doesn't go up, and on the expiration date it's sitting at $59.

If you had purchased those 100 shares outright you'd have a loss of $500 at this point. The stock cost you $6,400 and is now worth $5,900, a percentage loss of 7.8%. However you would still own the stock and be in a position to profit if it were to go up again.

What happened with your option purchase? Well you bought the $60 call, so at expiration it's worthless. Your loss is 100%. So while you may have limited your dollar outlay to $600 you also put yourself in a position to lose it all despite a relatively small drop in the price of the stock. You now own no stock and are not in a position any longer to profit if TRV stock price increases.

Newbie Mistakes

One trap that a beginning option trader can find him or herself in is overleveraging. For instance maybe they'd be comfortable buying three hundred shares of ABC stock at $25—a total cash outlay of $7,500 to own the stock. But then they think, *wow I could do that or I could buy these $22 calls for only $375 each. I can buy twenty calls for the same $7,500, but now I'll control 2,000 shares of the stock!*

Brilliant right? So what's the problem? The problem is that if the stock drops just three dollars to $22 by expiration day the call options expire worthless. A total loss of the $7,500. If they'd bought the stock they'd have only lost $600. An extreme example maybe, but you can see how the potential for equity abuse is there.

Those are the real risks of option trading. It's easy to feel complacent about a trade because the dollar outlay can be so small, however, as a trader looking to make a profit you need to be hyperaware of percentage gains and losses. You also need to consider that if you are only comfortable holding 300 shares of ABC stock you should only be trading options that control the same amount, but for less money.

How do we use options?

Okay, so options seem like the right fit for us. Now how do we go about choosing which one? Which strike price and which expiration date? Well, online options trading platforms supply what's called an "options chain." Why "chain?" We don't know, but it's a place where you can see all the different options that are being traded. Which one to choose is important—this can be the difference between profiting too little or losing a lot. Option chains look like a confusing mess of numbers at first, but the longer you stare at them, the more you can glean about the current state of the options market for a particular stock; you can see where the action is and where you might want to buy.

The images on the following pages are screen captures of the Google (GOOG) option chain. You are looking at the options available (in $5 strike price increments) within $25 of the day's closing price, which on Sept. 24, 2012 was $749.38 (nice run, Google!). On the left-hand side are the call options, and on the right-hand side are the put options. In the middle are the dates and strike prices for three series: at the top are the "28 Oct 12" monthly (October 2012) options, below that are the Nov 12 options, and below that are the Dec 12 options. If we wanted to, we could expand this display to show calls available for the next couple of years or show the options deeper in-the-money or further out-of-the-money. Pat has been known to trade options more than a year out!

Bid	Ask	Int	Ext	Chg	Vol	OI	Pos	STRIKE	Bid	Ask	Int	Ext	Chg	Vol	OI	Pos
28 Oct 12 [Days to Expiration: 25]																
38.20	38.50	25.33	13.02	10.70	1469	1661	--	**725**	13.30	13.60	0.00	13.45	-4.90	572	844	--
34.70	35.20	20.33	14.62	10.15	963	1291	--	**730**	14.90	15.30	0.00	15.10	-5.45	576	1232	--
31.50	32.10	15.33	16.47	9.60	743	1359	--	**735**	16.90	17.00	0.00	16.95	-5.95	634	346	--
28.50	29.10	10.33	18.47	9.10	1201	959	--	**740**	18.80	19.20	0.00	19.00	-6.45	2559	2747	--
26.10	26.20	5.33	20.82	8.70	2773	1482	--	**745**	21.00	21.40	0.00	21.20	-7.00	1843	105	--
23.20	23.50	0.33	23.02	7.95	2144	1902	--	**750**	23.30	23.70	0.00	23.50	-7.60	511	532	--
20.60	21.00	0.00	20.80	7.30	572	499	--	**755**	25.70	26.20	4.67	21.28	-8.30	45	92	--
18.20	18.60	0.00	18.40	6.65	545	1039	--	**760**	28.30	28.80	9.67	18.88	-8.90	2066	100	--
16.10	16.50	0.00	16.30	6.10	445	489	--	**765**	31.10	31.70	14.67	16.73	-9.55	620	32	--
14.10	14.50	0.00	14.30	5.50	765	1014	--	**770**	34.30	34.80	19.67	14.88	-10.00	143	142	--
12.30	12.70	0.00	12.50	4.95	543	1023	--	**775**	37.50	37.90	24.67	13.03	-10.60	627	66	--
Nov 12 [Days to Expiration 53]																
42.60	43.20	25.33	17.57	11.15	202	221	--	**725**	17.70	18.20	0.00	17.95	-4.45	103	337	--
39.40	40.00	20.33	19.37	10.65	351	469	--	**730**	19.60	20.00	0.00	19.80	-4.85	74	186	--
36.40	37.00	15.33	21.37	10.25	123	187	--	**735**	21.50	22.00	0.00	21.75	-5.25	124	630	--
33.50	34.10	10.33	23.47	9.90	348	513	--	**740**	23.60	24.10	0.00	23.85	-5.70	346	328	--
30.80	31.20	5.33	25.67	9.35	93	166	--	**745**	25.80	26.40	0.00	26.10	-6.15	135	24	--
28.30	28.60	0.33	28.12	9.00	764	865	--	**750**	28.30	28.80	0.00	28.55	-6.50	583	18	--
25.70	26.10	0.00	25.90	8.45	512	66	--	**755**	30.70	31.30	4.67	26.33	-7.15	14	2	--
23.50	23.80	0.00	23.65	8.00	294	294	--	**760**	33.50	34.00	9.67	24.08	-7.50	136	3	--
21.40	21.70	0.00	21.55	7.60	67	202	--	**765**	36.40	36.80	14.67	21.93	-8.00	17	3	--
19.40	19.70	0.00	19.55	7.15	113	487	--	**770**	39.20	39.90	19.67	19.88	-8.45	40	19	--
17.50	17.90	0.00	17.70	6.70	26	72	--	**775**	42.10	43.10	24.67	17.93	-9.80	0	0	--
Dec 12 [Days to Expiration 88]																
47.50	48.20	25.33	22.52	10.65	55	551	--	**725**	22.40	23.10	0.00	22.75	-4.85	148	53	--
44.20	45.20	20.33	24.37	10.25	305	653	--	**730**	24.30	24.90	0.00	24.60	-5.30	46	95	--
41.40	42.10	15.33	26.42	9.90	32	296	--	**735**	26.30	27.00	0.00	26.65	-5.60	112	64	--
38.60	39.30	10.33	28.62	9.60	59	402	--	**740**	28.40	29.10	0.00	28.75	-6.05	161	7	--
35.50	36.50	5.33	30.67	8.95	342	153	--	**745**	30.90	31.50	0.00	31.20	-6.30	48	3	--
33.30	33.90	0.33	33.27	8.80	773	906	--	**750**	33.10	33.90	0.00	33.50	-6.75	147	11	--
30.80	31.40	0.00	31.10	8.35	78	259	--	**755**	35.60	36.30	4.67	31.28	-7.25	9	9	--
28.50	29.00	0.00	28.75	7.95	253	457	--	**760**	38.20	39.00	9.67	28.93	-7.65	7	7	--
26.20	26.80	0.00	26.50	7.55	239	246	--	**765**	41.10	41.70	14.67	26.73	-8.05	11	12	--
24.10	24.70	0.00	24.40	7.15	360	553	--	**770**	43.90	44.60	19.67	24.58	-8.50	10	8	--
22.10	22.60	0.00	22.35	6.65	362	904	--	**775**	46.80	47.70	24.67	22.58	-8.90	19	10	--

[fig 12.7]

From left to right, you can see the current bid price for each call option, the current ask price, Int means the intrinsic value (the difference between the strike price and the current stock price), Ext means the extrinsic value (the difference between the intrinsic value and the option premium), Chg is the option price change for the day (green positive, red negative), Vol is the volume or number of trades made today, and OI is the open interest (how many options are open). Pos is positions and there would be a number listed if we had a position in one of these options. Strike is strike price. Continuing left to right, we move into the put side of the chain.

The shaded lines are the "at-the-money" options and they are there just to break up the numbers and make it easier to read.

Here are a couple of generalities to take note of right off the bat: notice that as we look at options that are further and further out in time, the premium price for the same strike price gets higher and higher. You'll remember that's because the further out in time, the higher the chance that the option will expire in-the-money. For example, you can see above that the asking price for the Oct $750 call option expiring in 25 days is $23.50 while the December 2012 $750 call is $33.90 because it's expiring in 88 days. You might also notice that the intrinsic value of out-of-the-money options is zero.

Call side of the option chain:

Bid	Ask	Int	Ext	Chg	Vol	OI	Pos	STRIKE
				28 Oct 12	[Days to E			
38.20	38.50	25.33	13.02	10.70	1469	1661	--	**725**
34.70	35.20	20.33	14.62	10.15	963	1291	--	**730**
31.50	32.10	15.33	16.47	9.60	743	1359	--	**735**
28.50	29.10	10.33	18.47	9.10	1201	959	--	**740**
26.10	26.20	5.33	20.82	8.70	2773	1482	--	**745**
23.20	23.50	0.33	23.02	7.95	2144	1902	--	**750**
20.60	21.00	0.00	20.80	7.30	572	499	--	**755**
18.20	18.60	0.00	18.40	6.65	545	1039	--	**760**
16.10	16.50	0.00	16.30	6.10	445	489	--	**765**
14.10	14.50	0.00	14.30	5.50	765	1014	--	**770**
12.30	12.70	0.00	12.50	4.95	543	1023	--	**775**

[fig 12.8]

What else do you notice from the call side of the chain? How about the change in option price for the day—GOOG was up $15.39 at the close. Notice that the deeper "in-the-money" a call is, the larger the change in price for the day. For example, the $725 call went up $10.70 while the $775 call only went up $4.95. That's because delta, which we explained above as being the correlation between stock price and option price, is higher for deeper in-the-money options. When the stock went up, the deeper in-the-money calls went up more than those at- and out-of-the-money—they have a higher delta.

How about Ext or extrinsic value? It is highest at-the-money ($23.02) while deep in-the-money and far out-of-the-money, it is much less ($13.02 and

$12.50, respectively). Extrinsic value goes up and down based on several factors, such as how much time is left before expiration and how volatile the underlying stock is. Time decay is the most important factor to consider in extrinsic value, because volatility is priced in.

Put side of the option chain:

STRIKE	Bid	Ask	Int	Ext	Chg	Vol	OI	Pos
ys to Expiration: 25]								
725	13.30	13.60	0.00	13.45	-4.90	572	844	--
730	14.90	15.30	0.00	15.10	-5.45	576	1232	--
735	16.90	17.00	0.00	16.95	-5.95	634	346	--
740	18.80	19.20	0.00	19.00	-6.45	2559	2747	--
745	21.00	21.40	0.00	21.20	-7.00	1843	105	--
750	23.30	23.70	0.00	23.50	-7.60	511	532	--
755	25.70	26.20	4.67	21.28	-8.30	45	92	--
760	28.30	28.80	9.67	18.88	-8.90	2066	100	--
765	31.10	31.70	14.67	16.73	-9.55	620	32	--
770	34.30	34.80	19.67	14.88	-10.00	143	142	--
775	37.50	37.90	24.67	13.03	-10.60	627	66	--

[fig 12.9]

The put side of the option chain for GOOG (again, we are just zoomed in on the upper right of that first image) shows the mirror opposite in many ways. You can see that Chg is negative because the put options went down that day as the stock price went higher. Remember that for put options, "in-the-money" and "out-of-the-money" are just the opposite of calls because a put gives you the right to sell the stock at the strike price and in the case where the stock price is going up, put option prices typically fall. Int and Ext values mean the same as for a call, and the same goes for Volume and Open Interest.

Other Chains and Platforms

No matter what trading platform you are using you will find they all look pretty much the same as what you see above, perhaps with different colors or control buttons. They are all going to contain at least the basic information needed to make a trade and watch your position as the market fluctuates.

Using these option chains to buy or sell with an online brokerage is very easy. The OptionsHouse platform, for example, allows you to click on the bid or ask price and a little window pops up that allows you to buy or sell. You set the number of contracts, the type of order, it confirms you have the buying power to do so, you confirm with one click, and the order is in. If it's a market order, the trade is made in a few seconds and appears in the positions section of the interface with the cash deducted from your account. It is all very slick.

Back to Decision Time

So after we take a look at the option chain for the stock we are interested in, we need to decide what kind of trade we are putting on. We're going to continue assuming that we believe the stock is going to go up. So for our examples we will focus solely on buying calls. Instead of focusing on GOOG, we think it's better to use a generic example.

Let's say that stock ABC went down two dollars yesterday from $30 to $28, a 6.6% drop. We still like ABC, and the news that caused the drop seemed unimportant to us—we see this as an extreme overreaction to a news event. We're going to fade trade this move, looking for it to retrace back to $30 in the next couple of days.

In general we've got three choices. We can either buy a call that is in-the-money, at-the-money, or out-of-the-money.

In-the-Money Call

First then, is buying an in-the-money call. What this means for a call option is that the option's strike price is below the stock price. The further in-the-money the option is the higher the delta. In other words the correlation between the price of the stock and the price of the option is higher the more in-the-money the option is. Eventually an option is far enough in-the-money that a $1 change in the price of the stock means a $1 change in the price of the call option. At that point the delta is 1.

Below is a table showing Hewlett-Packard options with expiration in one month and a current price of $17.21. You can see that the $15 strike price has a delta of 1. If the stock price were to go up $1.00 tomorrow the $16 calls would increase by $.86 while the $15 calls would increase by $1.00.

Option Price	Strike Price	Delta
2.26	15	1
1.35	16	0.86
0.63	17	0.6
0.22	18	0.3
0.09	19	0.13
0.03	20	0.06

[fig 12.10]

An example of a time you would buy an in-the-money option would be after a big price drop that you consider a market overreaction to a news event. You are expecting the stock to return to pre-news levels in the short-term.

ABC stock just dropped from $30 to $28 based on some news about a patent settlement. You feel that the news wasn't that important and that this is still a good company. You anticipate that it will quickly retrace to $30. In this instance a good strategy might be to look at the $25 call options with an expiration date a couple of months out. Let's say the price on these is $4. These options would probably have a delta of around .80, meaning that for every dollar that the stock goes up the option's price would increase by eighty cents.

The benefits of this approach are that, one, your cash outlay is much reduced buying a call ($400) versus buying 100 shares of stock ($2,800). And two, that your downside risk is limited. If some shocking news came out the next day that caused the stock to crash to twenty dollars you would lose much less than if you had owned the stock outright.

If the stock jumps back to $30 two days later you'd have made $2 per share if you had bought the stock outright. A 7% profit.

If the delta on the option was .80 and the stock went up $2 the option would've theoretically increased in value by $1.60, a 40% profit. And there is that leverage *again*. Of course as we've explained, leverage is a two way street; take a look at what happens if the stock price goes down.

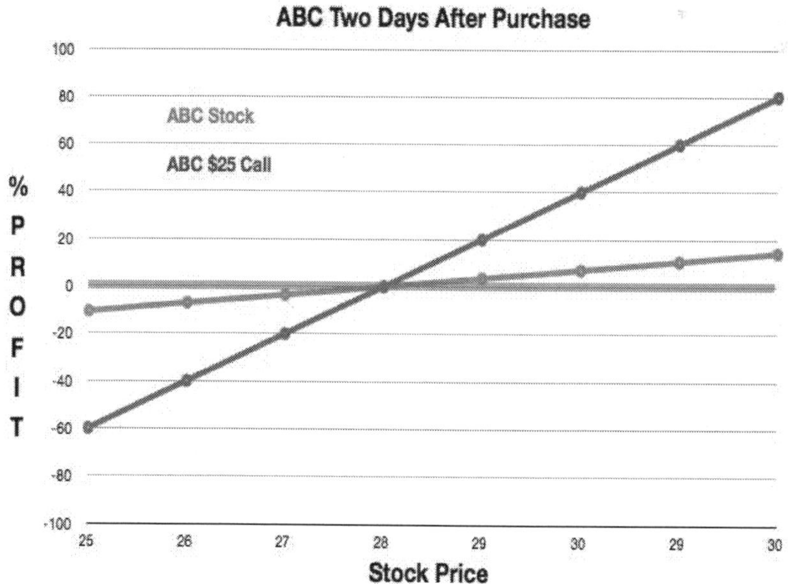

[fig 12.11]

At-the-Money Call

Buying an at-the-money call means you are buying an option with a strike price equal to, or at least pretty darn close to, the current stock price. This is often considered a beginner's approach to buying naked call options because the delta will be right around .50, meaning it's neither the most high risk nor the most high reward play. It's right there in the middle and doesn't require a lot of analysis. It will make money if the stock price goes up and it will become worthless at expiration if the stock price goes down. Simple as that.

In the above example buying an at-the-money call would've meant buying the $28 strike price. Let's assume the delta was .50. In this case the option would've increased in value by $1.00 when the stock went back up to $30. If the option had cost $2 you'd have made a 50% profit. A tidy return, no doubt. Especially compared to that measly 7% owning the stock would have netted you.

Out-of-the-Money Call

These are the riskiest of all options because it would take a large price move for the options to become in-the-money at expiration. For this reason out-of-the-money options are often used by veteran traders looking for a dramatic rise in a stock's price in a short period of time.

Perhaps a drug company not known for public announcements suddenly says it will be holding a press conference after the close of the market. Why? A breakthrough? We don't know, but a trader who has been following this company might view it as an opportunity and decide to buy out-of-the-money calls before the mystery news is announced.

In this case let's say ABC stock is currently trading at $50. A trader looking for a big announcement tonight would likely look at options with an expiration of just a month away. In this case the $60 calls might be trading for only $.15. That's a total outlay of just $15 per call. They've got a delta of only .07, meaning that for every dollar the stock goes up the price of the option will go up seven cents. Remember that as the price of the stock climbs the delta will climb along with it so that at $60 it will be around .50 delta.

Now let's say the company comes out and announces that it has developed a drug that can cure acne overnight. The next morning the stock opens at $70. The option is now closer to in-the-money and has a delta much closer to 1.00. The option's value this morning is $11. This represents a whopping 7300% gain.

Long Shots

It's easy for the beginning trader to look at that number and think, "Well I'll just buy out-of-the-money calls. Even if I have fifty losers all I need is one big winner." Seems simple enough doesn't it? Veteran traders can only shake their heads at this reasoning. Traders who employ this method will more likely see themselves with a hundred losers, ten moderate winners, and zero home-runs. Over time they will lose all their money. They will just do it slowly.

Death by starvation.

Even the big winner in the example above takes for granted that you are the first person to recognize the potential this news event holds. In reality lots of others would've already seen the opportunity and the price of the options would've skyrocketed. Granted, even at a dollar the options would've ended up being a bargain. On the flip side, and probably more likely, the company could've just as easily held the press conference to announce that one of their drugs had actually been causing vast numbers of people to become ill. Thus your options are worthless.

Trading on Earnings

A popular way to utilize out-of-the-money options is in anticipation of a company's earnings report. Every quarter companies report their earnings which are quickly compared to estimates that the company as well as analysts had prepared in advance. A company who substantially beats earnings can see significant price jumps. Of course the opposite can also be true.

In the case of earnings, let's say you really like this company and feel as if everywhere you turn these days you see their products. Maybe you are traveling overseas and see that demand among the young kids for their products is absolutely crazy. You think that maybe the overseas markets have been overlooked by the analysts who have historically been focused on the company's domestic growth.

But you are leery. You feel good about it, but in truth you have no hard and fast numbers to plug in. You decide you want to participate in an earnings play, but not commit a lot of dollar risk to the proposition. Out-of-the-money calls give you that opportunity. In the case of a big beat on earnings and a corresponding big run-up in the company stock price you will be there to participate.

Just like in the example above you buy calls with a strike price at least a couple of strikes out-of-the-money with a low delta value. If the stock price spikes the delta will spike as well as the option becomes closer to being in-the-money. And while you won't earn nearly as much as you'd have with an in or at-the-money call option you also won't have risked nearly as much on a dollar basis.

Selling Your Options

The money isn't made on a winner and the loss isn't taken on a loser until you sell. Until that day it's all just "paper money," with paper meaning your P&L (profit and loss) statement. Selling correctly is what sets a profitable trader apart from an unprofitable one. Selling is key!

We've talked a lot about what your options *would* be worth at expiration. We do this because it's the simplest way to give examples and make them understandable. In truth however, traders rarely hold their options until expiration. We can't remember more than a couple situations in which we held in-the-money options at expiration.

Estimates range, but the best numbers we could find on the subject suggest that forty-eight percent of options are bought and sold to close before expiration. Thirty-five percent expire worthless. These are often the far out-of-the-money calls that were bought for pennies in the hopes of some big piece of market moving news that never came. When trading commissions are figured in it is often cheaper to simply let the options expire worthless than to try and sell them for a penny or two. The remaining seventeen percent are exercised, meaning they are in-the-money.

The reasons for this are many, but basically for us it comes down to this: we bought these calls for a particular (i.e. specific) reason looking for a very particular move in the underlying stock. If the move we were looking for happens we take our profits—we sell, sell, sell! We don't simply gamble on the future direction of the stock continuing upwards. That's called investing, and what we are doing here is trading. "Seeing what happens," has no place in an options strategy.

On the other hand, if the move we were looking for doesn't happen we sell the call for a loss. This is the most crucial aspect of risk management. We bought this call for a very specific reason and for a very specific period of time. If we do not get that move in the stock that we had anticipated, that's our signal to get out. To do otherwise is to transform your trading account into a gambling account. You no longer have any specific reason to think the stock is going to go up sharply, you are simply hoping against hope. The options trader who does this will soon have no money. Veteran traders all know how to take a loss, and rookie traders who don't will never become veterans.

Trading options and trading stocks are completely different activities—and you cannot trade an option like you might a stock. A stock that doesn't do <u>what</u> you think it will do and <u>when</u> you think it will do it may mean that the opportunity hasn't yet arrived—you may need to hold it to get your profit (if there is reason to believe the move is still coming). An option, on the other hand has a time limit, so if the underlying stock doesn't do <u>what</u> you think it will do <u>when</u> you think it will do it, you must exit your position—there are no exceptions to this fact.

The real advantage to closing your option positions before expiration, however, comes in thwarting the time decay factor. We've touched briefly on this before, but we will try to explain it a little more here.

When you purchase an option, you pay a premium for it. This premium, or price, reflects not only the intrinsic value (stock price - strike price) of the option but the extrinsic value (option price - intrinsic value).

For example, ABC stock is trading at $10. You want to buy the $12 call expiring in one month in the belief that a big price spike is coming. The intrinsic value of the call is zero. Right? Stock price minus strike price equals negative two, i.e. zero.

But you can't buy a $12 call for nothing. Who would sell you the right to buy the stock at $12 at a later date for $0? Nobody. The seller is going to accept the risk that the stock will go up and that the $12 call will have value at expiration. In order to accept that risk, he is going to require you to pay him $1. So in this case the extrinsic value of the call is $1.

Now what if three weeks from now, with only five trading days until expiration, the stock is still trading for $10? Does that $12 call still have $1 in extrinsic value? No freaking way, right? The chance of it going up that much over a shorter period of time is much less. Think of it in simple terms: with one month to go it seemed somewhat likely that the stock would move up a couple of dollars. But with only one week left it seems less likely that it will move that much. The call in this example is now worth just $.30.

So what happened to that $.70? Time decay. As an option gets closer to expiration it's extrinsic value, or time value, declines—because the probability of the option being profitable is reduced. So where did that money go? Well, in a way, it evaporated since the option hasn't reached expiration; but if the option reaches expiration worthless, that time decay money went into the pocket of the guy who sold the option to you in the first place. Selling options can be very lucrative, but the risks are very, very high. Believe us, there is a whole set of trading strategies people use in selling way, way, way out-of-the-money options—but we aren't going to even touch that in this book.

Every day that you hold your option, it loses some little bit of value. If you've already experienced the stock move you were looking for—or even if it didn't happen in the time period you had been anticipating—it behooves you to sell the option and save yourself the time decay.

In the Real World

Is trading options a realistic trading approach for somebody without a hundred thousand dollars plus in their trading account? If everyone agrees that trading options is risky and complicated to understand in the beginning, why are we mentioning this method in the first place?

Well let us give you an example. When Pat started out in the business he went to work as a clerk on the floor of the Minneapolis Grain Exchange. He was making ten bucks an hour and had no savings. What he did have was a pickup truck worth a few thousand dollars.

He sold that truck and opened up his first trading account with $5,000. His first trade was in options; it would be fun to see if he'd saved that trading card. According to the settlement prices that day, he was up a hundred bucks. A graph of his account that first year would show a pretty steady increase. Whether due to his own genius or the help of the smarter traders around him who were always willing to give him their time, knowledge, and honest advice, at the end of the year he was up to $25,000 and had even started pulling out a monthly check.

Pat and his wife went out to Home Depot, bought $1,500 worth of lumber with cash from that account and walked out feeling as if they had just robbed a bank. He was officially a trader, and by god he could afford the finer things in life; fancy things—like lumber that cost $1,500! They were feeling pretty flush for a couple of twenty-five year olds. Could life get any better? Well of course it could. He still had to build the deck on the house with his own two hands. *Better yet* would have been being able to afford to hire somebody who knew what he was doing.

Anyway, options are a very real trading tool that for somebody with at least a basic understanding of the risks, as well as a risk management strategy in place—one that they will actually stick to—can be used to maximize a small trading account.

It's all about the leverage that options give you. Percentage gains and losses are indeed magnified with naked options; but one thing that options give you that straight stock buying doesn't is a known, quantifiable, loss limit. By buying options you can never lose more than you originally paid.

Advanced Options Techniques

Up to now we've talked solely of the most basic option trade there is, the naked call. It's the most simple to understand for the beginner because in essence it's nothing more than replacing the purchase of stock with the purchase of the call. You are long.

It's also a great way to get your toes wet. Now you've made your first few options trades, feel more comfortable with some of the lingo, know the ins and outs of an option chain, and how to navigate your trading platform to find the necessary greeks. You're on your way to becoming an option trader. Congrats.

So let's up the ante a little bit. We'll throw a few slightly more advanced strategies at you and let you ponder the many ways you might find to use them.

Naked Puts

All right, there really is nothing too advanced about trading naked puts—they are basically just the opposite of a call after all. By buying a put you are buying the right to **sell** the stock at a certain price on a certain date. You are essentially shorting the stock. You do this for one of two reasons. One, you think the stock is rubbish. Two, you own the stock already but want to purchase some protection to the downside. Insurance, if you will.

Earlier we talked about buying naked calls. We did this in order to use the leverage of options to get long a company. Naked calls can be used effectively in our fade trading strategy when we are looking for a quick retracement on a stock that has been beaten down.

While naked puts can be used in the same way, though opposite, we prefer to use them a little differently. The reason is that we haven't found it to be as easy to fade trade a crappy stock that just happened to pop higher on inconsequential news. The slight variation we make to our fade trade strategy for naked puts and stocks we hate is to buy puts when a stock has had a bit of terrible news but hasn't really reacted to it.

We tend to use naked puts more often with our swing strategy. Just as we like to follow stocks that we love, we also tend to follow stocks that we hate. And when those stocks start trading in a downward trend and we can't discern any reason for that trend to come to a stop, we buy naked puts.

A prime example of this was the big BP Gulf of Mexico oil spill. On April 20, 2010 the oil drilling platform *Deepwater Horizon* exploded. It was a horrific accident that killed eleven men and sent oil flowing freely into the ocean. For a month BP, the oil company who owned the rig, said the leak was "only" 1,000 barrels a day. Then it was 5,000, but nobody really trusted that the company which was leaking oil into the ocean was telling us the real number.

On May 20, BP's containment system is drawing off 5,000 barrels per day, but we can all see from the underwater footage that that isn't even a small percentage of the total leak. Experts come out that night and estimate the spill between 20,000 and 100,000 barrels per day. The next day BP stock continues trading near the previous closing price—around $44.

And this is when Pat finally thought, "Well, this stock sure isn't going to go up any time soon. It may not go down like I want it to, but it definitely is not going up." Pat bought a bunch of $40 puts expiring in July for $1.57 and sold them within the next couple weeks for between $4.50 and $8.00 as the steady downward trend continued unabated with daily news briefings just adding fuel to the fire.

Vertical Call Spreads

Sometimes you find yourself bullish a stock, but you just can't find either the money or the commitment to simply get long. Vertical call spreads can be a good answer. They are less capital intensive and less risky than being long the stock or the naked calls.

A **bull call spread** as shown in fig 12.12 contains two calls, one long and one short, with the same expiration date. The strike price of the long call is lower than the strike price of the short call, which means that you will be *paying* a premium for it. The purpose of selling the short call is to decrease the overall cost of the long call option. The result of selling that option however is that you limit the upside profit potential of the long call.

You might use a vertical call spread when you feel that there is upside potential to a stock but that it isn't in for a real big run higher. Let's say ABC is trading at $45 and you think for whatever reason that it has the potential to rally ten dollars. You might look at buying the $50 call and selling the $55 call. The price of the $50 call is $7.00, but you are reducing that outlay by selling the $55 call for $5.00, for a total premium paid of $2.

By selling that $55 call you have decreased the cost of the $50 call but you have also put a cap on its potential. Now instead of the $50 call having unlimited upside potential, its upside is $5. Actually, the $50 call still has unlimited upside potential, it is capped only by the $55 call which begins losing an amount equal to the gains when the stock reaches $55—the two cancel each other out at that point. Your maximum potential profit is $3, the difference between the two strike prices, $55 and $50, minus the $2 premium you paid for the spread.

Maximum Profit = (Difference Between Strikes - Premium Paid for Spread)

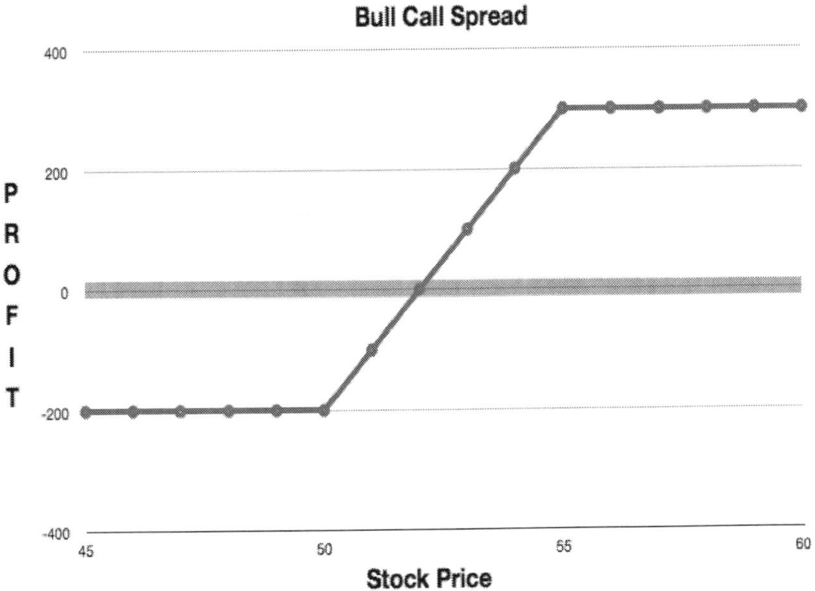

[fig 12.12]

Note: This spread can be reversed if you believe the stock is not going to move or is going down. As shown in fig 12.13 this is called a **bear call spread**. In this case instead of paying $2 for the spread you would be the person collecting the $2 for it. That would be your maximum gain on the position. Your maximum loss would be $3, the difference between the strike prices minus the premium received.

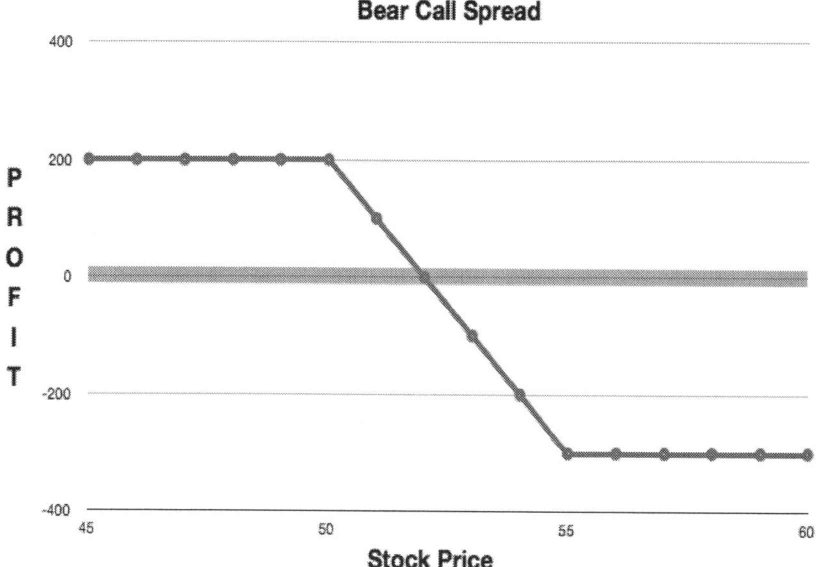

[fig 12.13]

Vertical Put Spreads

When you are bearish a stock but want to limit both your risk exposure to an upside move as well as the total cash outlay needed to initiate a short position, a bear put spread is a good answer.

A **bear put spread**, as shown in fig 12.14 consists of two puts, one long and one short, with the same expiration date. The strike price of the long put is higher than the strike price of the short put, which means that you will be *paying* a premium for it. The purpose of selling the short put is to decrease the overall cost of the long put option. The result of selling that put option however is that you limit the upside profit potential of that put.

Sound a lot like a vertical call spread? That's because it's exactly the opposite. Instead of calls you are using puts. Instead of upside potential you are looking for downside potential.

If stock ABC were trading for $45 and you felt it was due for a ten dollar break you could consider the bear put spread. In this case you might look at buying the $40 put and selling the $35 put with an expiration somewhere beyond the time frame you believe the price break will occur. The $40 put is trading for $7, while the $35 put is trading for $5, so that your total premium paid is $2.

If you had just paid $7 for the $40 put, your positions profit potential would only be limited by the stock going all the way to zero. By selling the $35 put you limit the profit potential to $3, the difference between the two strikes of

$5 minus the premium paid of $2. Vertical spreads require careful consideration for this reason. You have to weigh the potential profits, the costs, and weigh them against exactly what you expect the market to do. It might seem silly to limit your potential profit, but if there is no reason to expect a move below $35, then there is no reason for you *not* to sell that $35 put.

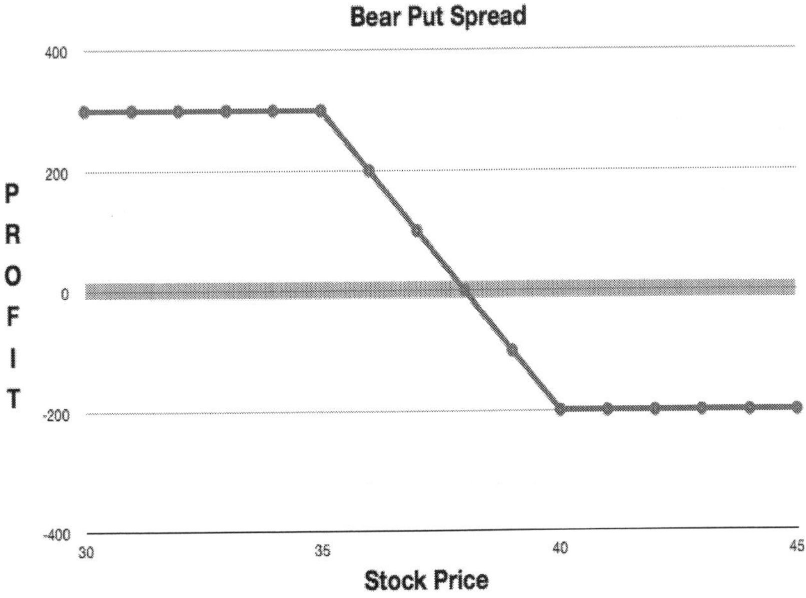

[fig 12.14]

Note: The reverse of this is a **bull put spread** shown in fig 12.15. In this case you would collect the $2 premium by selling the higher strike price and buying the lower strike.

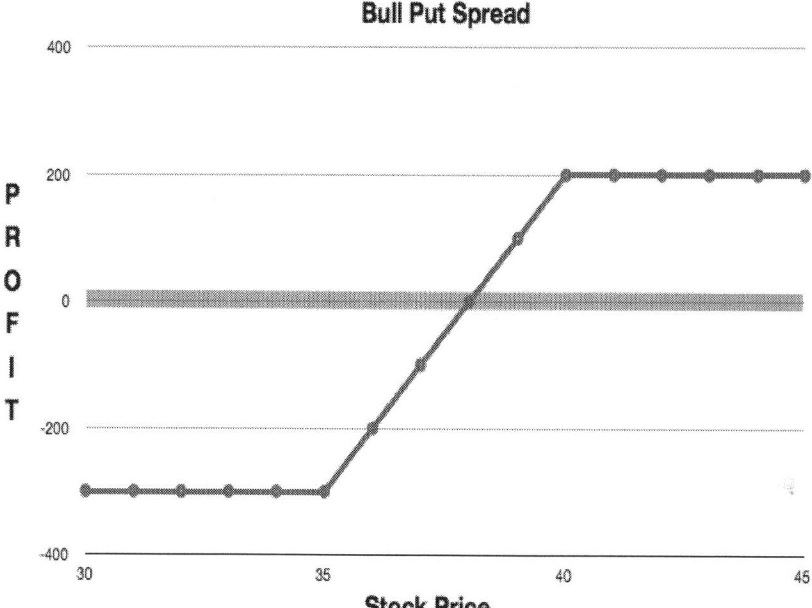

[fig 12.15]

Covered Calls
A covered call is the act of selling one call option for every 100 shares (though this amount can vary, often depending on the delta of the option) of a company's stock that you own. It allows you to collect premium on an option without incurring additional risk.

If it sounds too good to be true that's because it is. While you may not be incurring additional risk, you are limiting your potential profits.

How? Well, you own 100 shares of stock, meaning that your upside profit potential is unlimited. You then sell a call option with a strike price above the current stock price. If the stock then goes down you will lose money on the stock but offset some of those losses with the premium collected from the sale of the call option. If the stock goes up you will make money on those 100 shares of stock—as well as the premium collected on the option. When the strike price of the option is reached you are no longer making or losing money, the position goes flat, and you've capped your profits.

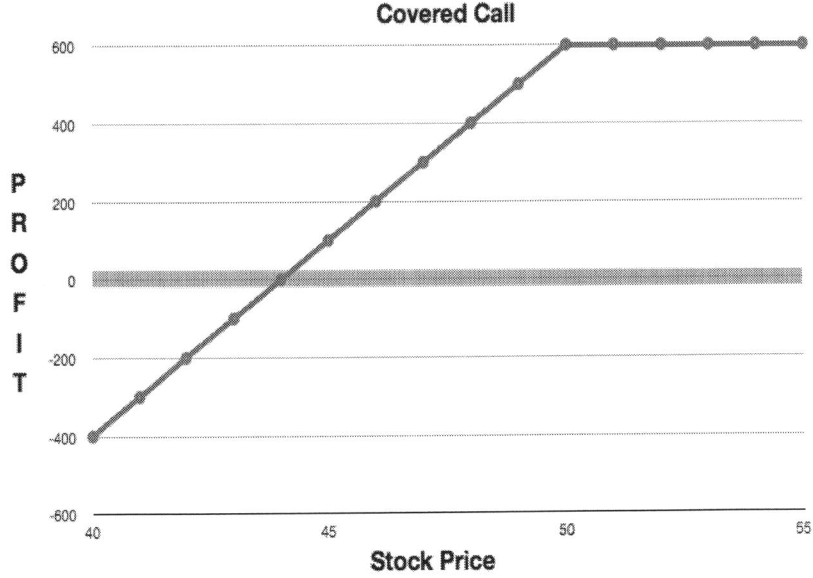

[fig 12.16]

This is an especially good investment strategy for those who already own a stock and are looking to set an exit strategy. Let's say that you own ABC stock from $45 and you are looking for the stock to eventually increase to $50. That's your target price for the stock. In this case you could sell the $50 call, let's say for $1, and not be concerned with limiting your upside because your plan was always to sell the stock at $50 anyway. If the stock increases above $50 by expiration the call will be assigned to you, effectively canceling out your long stock position.

Covered calls are more of an investment strategy than they are a trading strategy because they require you to own a company's stock for a period of time at least as long as the life of the option.

Strangle

The strangle is used for those times when you just can't make up your mind. You know something big is going to happen, you just don't know what. Maybe a company is in a heated court battle over patents and you expect that whatever way the verdict goes, the stock is going to react in a big way.

With a **long strangle** you are buying a put option and a call option with the same expiration. For example, XYZ is currently trading at $45. Sometime in the next month you are expecting a big move based on whether the company's new drug gets FDA approval or not. You obviously have no way of knowing the outcome, so you play it to profit from a move either way. You buy the $40 put for $1 and buy the $50 call for $1. If at expiration the stock is still in between those two strike prices you will lose the entire premium paid for both options. If the stock price is above the call or below the put by more than the premium paid you will have made money.

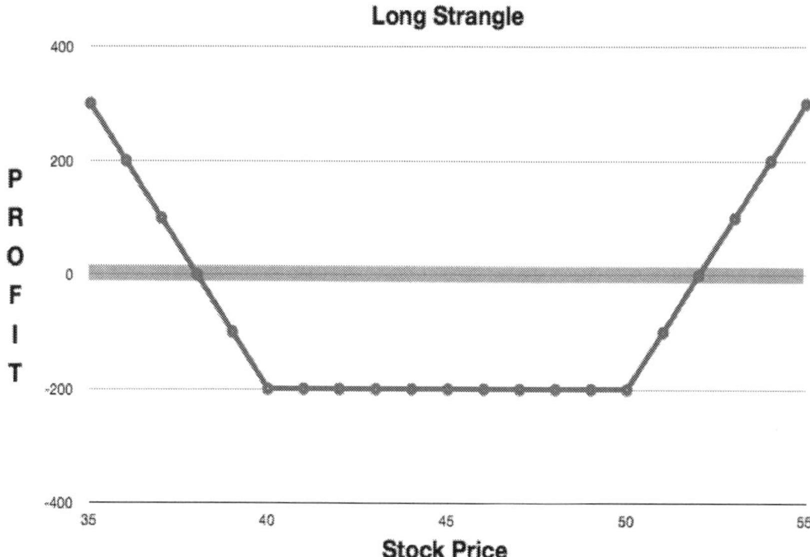

[fig 12.17]

The biggest risk in owning a strangle is that nothing happens. If the FDA's announcement comes out but for some reason the stock simply doesn't burst to the upside or downside as you anticipated, instead it just sits there near unchanged—you have got a problem. If this were to happen, you could anticipate a big drop in implied volatility, which would have a very negative effect on the value of both of your options. Time decay also presents a problem with this scenario, since you own two options, both of which are losing time value with every day that goes by.

Straddle

Another very similar strategy is the **long straddle**. In this case you once again are buying both a put and a call with the same expiration date, the difference is that they both have the same strike price. When doing this you assume that the market is going to make a significant move away from that strike price.

Using the XYZ example from above, with the stock at $45 you would buy a $45 call for $3 and a $45 put for $3. This method has a much higher initial premium outlay than a strangle; but just like a strangle, you are buying this because you expect either a big price move or a great deal of volatility.

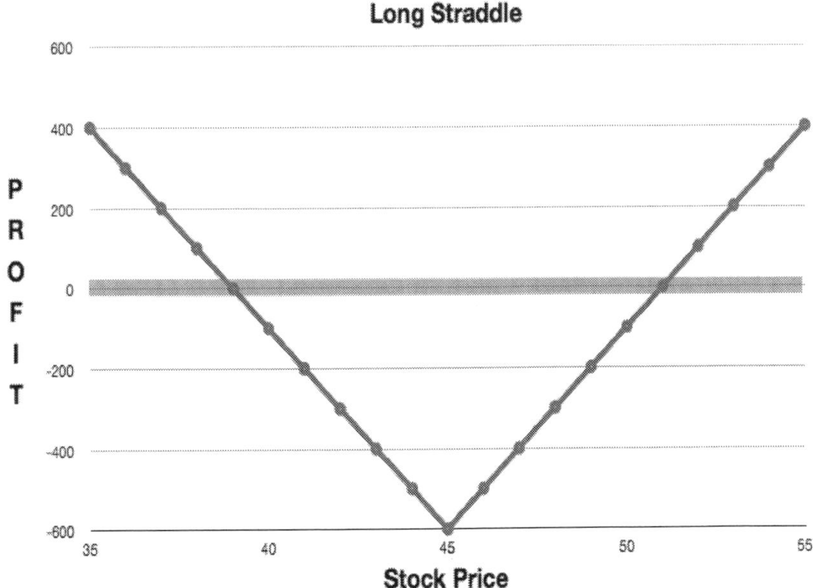

[fig 12.18]

With a straddle, you profit as soon as the stock moves up or down away from the strike price by more than the total premium you paid for both options. You paid $6 total for the $45 straddle, so when the stock price went to $55 at expiration, you'd have made $4. Same if the stock went down to $35. If the stock were only to go to $47, you'd have lost $4 ($6 total premium paid - $2 value of the $45 call at expiration). If the stock had gone down $2, you'd still have lost $4, the difference being that the put would now be the option worth $2.

LEAPS

Long-Term Equity Anticipation Securities. That's a fancy name for an option that expires a year, two, or even further in the future. These options can legitimately be considered investments, as they are generally purchased for long-term holding—not for short-term trades. They are a great way to give yourself exposure to a stock for the long-term without tying up a ton of capital in your trading account.

LEAPS aren't generally used for advanced options positions; more commonly they are used to take a specific position in a stock, such as long calls or long puts. The exception to that would be call and put spreads which they can be used effectively for.

The reason they aren't used for active trading or for more volume intensive positions (butterflies for example) is that there is relatively low volume in them. Low volume leads to large bid/ask spreads—meaning you are going to pay to get in this position and you are going to pay to get out. To mitigate that you need to let the position "work" by using the time that it's giving you.

Endless Options

We've covered a lot of ground, and yet we've hardly scratched the surface of what you can do with options. The strategies are literally endless. There are still butterflies, condors, ratio spreads, calendar spreads, and many more. As you become more comfortable with options and understand how stock price and the greeks affect them you will find more and more ways to use them to your advantage. You've now got the tools at your disposal and hopefully no longer think of options as black magic or voodoo.

Market Timing

Have you ever had a conversation that included, "If I had held onto that stock in XYZ back when I owned it at $10 I'd have that brand new boat, because now it's trading at $750!" Of course you have; we all have.

Yeah, you'd have made a ton of cash if you had held that stock through the ups and downs, the innovations, the new competition, the weak sales, the last four CEOs, two market crashes and uncountable market corrections, dozens of earnings reports, that accounting scandal, market-shaking new products, and the uncountable up and down tics in stock price. Yeah, sure you'd have done that—and now you would be rich.

But you don't apply that same logic to the rest of your portfolio, do you? How about the ten stocks that crashed and burned. You'd have held them, too. And what about that stock that did almost nothing over the last eight years—you would still own that little prize. How about that one you bought at $5 before it soared to $220, then closed below $1 and got delisted from the exchange. You owned it from birth to death, and never sold at the right time.

Yeah-right, that's not how it works, and we all know it. We call this argument about *what might have been,* "selective potential past performance," or SPPP. See, you can come to whatever conclusion you want to about the return or loss you might have seen had you been in or out at this time rather than that, or this price or that. It's great material for the war stories you tell other traders.

But entire investing schools of thought are founded on SPPP. The same statistical arguments are made by investing professionals: they use backward analysis and focus on what would've happened IF you timed the market randomly, or missed the biggest moves one way or another or if you had been on the wrong side of moves both up and down. And they come to the only conclusion that they can—that timing the market leads to lower returns, and a better strategy is a diversified, managed portfolio—and yes, it just so happens they have one that suits your needs...and the fees are really low...

Beware of finance professionals who use selective potential past performance to sell you on mutual funds or other buy-and-hold strategies.

Reality

Don't try to time the market! You can't know! You will underperform! Buy and hold! Depending on what statistics you look at, the "experts" are either really right or really wrong—but their argument depends on what particular time scale they are talking about, and whether we are talking about trading or investing, which are completely different activities. Statistics are a great tool for proving whatever it is you want to believe.

For us, and for a lot of "trader/investors," the line between investing and trading is blurry, and we tend to move in and out of positions based on market conditions and opportunities, not necessarily a certain time period. So statically, we are in very muddy waters.

As a trader—and not just a long-term investor—in *real life* you aren't selling all your equities and going to an all cash portfolio while the market is rocketing upward. In reality, you might be moving to cash when the market has stalled out or when nine out of ten news stories are negative but the market is still hanging in there. You are selling individual stocks when you perceive something strongly negative has occurred or is about to occur. You are timing the market (or trying to time the market) for a plethora of reasons, all of them legitimate to you, none of them random like they are in the studies.

So sure, as a trader you can and will be wrong about individual stocks, but as an investor with a longer time horizon can you be wrong during ten of the biggest broad market moves as these studies would have you believe? Or even five of the ten? If you are paying attention and using your own judgement, you'll be much less likely to miss those big moves and big opportunities—unless, of course, you truly are an imbecile. We're kidding. We all miss those big moves from time to time.

So the experts/brokers who tell you to *buy and hold* a mutual fund because you can't time the market over long periods of time...what do these guys do for a living? Do they simply buy a portfolio of strong stocks and sit on them until you ask to take your money out at retirement? Of course not. They trade! And they trade a lot. Their business is run on commissions; and commissions are not generated by using the long-term buy and hold strategies that they all publicly suggest.

If all of these money managers believe that timing the market is a losing proposition, why are they all doing it? And why, if *they* are doing it, can't *you*? The answer, of course is that you can. And probably better than they can because you have no investors to answer to other than yourself; you have no commission quotas to reach, you have no reason to make something happen in a market where nothing is happening.

An Example

Let's use something that's fresh in everyone's minds: the financial crisis of 2008 and early 2009. It's pretty plain to see where a buy and hold strategy would've left you. If you had done nothing but sit on your hands and turn off the news, it would've taken three years to recoup the losses suffered in the market in that year and a half—at a minimum. If you were weighted in financials or auto, you may still be waiting.

But what if you had decided to trust what you were seeing, and made decisions based on what you perceived as real vs. what was being hyped? What would've happened then?

Here's where we toot our own horns a bit. For us, this financial collapse was relatively easy to spot, and it represented the biggest money making opportunity we have ever been a part of.

In our opinion, the writing was clearly on the wall by the end of 2007, several months before any real damage was done. It was crystal clear that the foreclosure crisis and resulting real estate price crash was real and not imagined, so we asked: who is exposed to this risk? Banks. Who else? Anyone holding mortgage debt. Who is that? Everyone: the entire economy.

Quick Summary
The DOW topped 14,000 in October 2007. Not long after, when fourth quarter GDP came out at -.2%, foreclosure rates started skyrocketing from out of nowhere on a market-by-market basis and home prices were crashing here and there—homes weren't just losing value, they were going under. These were clear signals that big things were about to happen. What exactly? Like you, we didn't know for sure, but knew with absolute certainty that it wasn't going to be good.

[fig 13.1]

We both independently (we hadn't reached the portfolio sharing point of our friendship yet) went to nearly all cash portfolios: Nick at the end of 2007 while Pat scaled out in the first months of 2008. What happened to the DOW next? Punished, but not at first, and the details hold some really valuable lessons about "timing the market."

As the bad news kept coming and coming through the spring of 2008, the market slowly edged up and down, lingering at DOW 12,000 or thereabouts. Unemployment numbers steadily got worse, and there was tons of gloom and doom all over the news. There was also broad-based denial and questions about whether "it could all be as bad as it looks" lingered—after all, no one knew what the future held.

Reality finally set in at the end of the summer. On September 29th the Dow fell 777 points. By November 2008, the DJIA was down to near 7,500, and it made a final plunge to 6,500 by March 2009. The market had lost more than half its value in 17 months.

Post-Mortem

Did we pick the top and time the market perfectly? No. Nick was maybe a month late at DOW 13,800 and Pat maybe a month or two later than that at DOW 13,000. At the time, did we feel like we had been premature as the market seemed to ignore the dire numbers coming out that spring? Absolutely—of course we wondered (how could we know for sure?), but we stuck with our independent opinion that the underpinnings of the economy were at tremendous risk. Did we time the bottom of the market and move back in at the perfect time as the recovery began over the next several months? No, we slowly and tentatively bought very selectively and we missed the bottom. More on that a little later.

You be the judge: did we time the market?

Why were people so blind?

Why didn't more people see this coming? And how many saw it coming but still just sat on their hands doing nothing? The signs actually started much earlier than the market took note: by the second half of 2007, oil prices were rocketing upwards, housing values weren't falling nationwide, but in select "hot" markets, they were crashing, and foreclosures were climbing quickly in those same areas. Yet the stock market was screaming higher and higher and higher. Let's revisit some facts mentioned above that were very widely reported by every news outlet:

- The market peaked around 14,000 in October 2007.
- The DOW hovered then sagged through the 12,000s through spring 2008.
- Home prices cratered market by market. Foreclosures climbed.
- Oil prices by July were over $140 a barrel, and gas had reached four dollars a gallon.

- By August unemployment was at 6.1 while a year earlier it had been 4.6.
- Yet, by the beginning of September the Dow was still above 11,500 and at worst we were seeing a trending bear market—no crash in sight...

By this time, economic indicators were ugly by anyone's standards; and yet, the stock market just lingered there at 11,500 as if waiting for a push. It got that push on September 15th of 2008, when Lehman Brothers, a bank that had traded as high as $80 a share a year earlier, filed for bankruptcy. Warning signals should have been sounding in every investor's and trader's ears. Clang! Clang! Clang! Alarm bells were ringing, but most chose to continue ignoring them.

Amazingly, the market barely budged when Lehman went belly-up. It would take two weeks' worth of horrendous news from the other megabanks and insurers around the world for the market to finally admit defeat when the House of Representatives rejected a $700B bailout plan from the United States government. On that day, September 29, 2008, the DOW dropped 777 points, 500 points of which happened in about 20 minutes. By November the market would be dipping into the 7,000s, and by that next March, we were down to DOW 6,500. Ouch!

Drinking the Kool-Aid?

So most market participants waited through months and months of dire economic reports until there was a clear catalyst and "proof" that the economy was (at least temporarily) in deep doo-doo. In retrospect, it seems so easy to see, doesn't it? There were signs all over the place that big things were afoot, and those signs appeared a full year in advance of the penultimate "crash." Why was it so hard to acknowledge when it was right in your face? Part of the reason is because of what has been preached to so many for so long:

- "Buy and hold, everything is going to be all right."
- "If you get out now you'll lock in your losses."
- "If you sell now, you will miss the next big rally that must surely be right around the corner."
- "You can't time the market."

Was everyone just drinking the Kool-Aid? Hoping for a miracle? Pretending it wasn't actually happening? In total denial? Maybe, partially, but we don't think that's the whole story.

Blind to the Impossible

There is a legend or myth or story or whatever you want to call it about the native Mayan people living on the Yucatan Peninsula (near Tulum, Mexico) when the Spanish Conquistadors arrived in the early 1500s. The Mayans were farmers and traders; they could be violent, but picking fights with each other wasn't high on the agenda—they were mostly about keeping the peace. The Spanish had one thing on their mind: gold. Well actually, two things: they also wanted silver. And they weren't above killin'-a-few-'folk to get it.

When the Europeans first pulled up to the coast in their massive ships, they anchored well offshore because they had to make sure it was safe further in and not so shallow as to run aground and poke holes in their ships. When they saw the Mayan settlements perched above the beach landing areas, they knew that any resistance would have the upper hand and they'd be vulnerable if the locals fought back. So the Spanish "explorers" just hung out and waited in the deep water farther out to sea and observed for a while.

Meanwhile, the Mayans didn't realize that the "little" boats anchored out from their stretch of coast weren't the small trading vessels that usually visited but actually huge galleons. So they ignored them.

It wasn't until the Spanish finally rowed ashore in their longboats that the Mayans realized that the foreign ships were actually really, really big, and only seemed small because they were far away. They had never seen ships that size, and their inexperience led to disbelief as well as assumptions about what they were actually seeing.

By the time the longboats arrived it was too late. Even though they resisted, the small-statured Mayans were easily handled by the much larger and better armed Europeans. There is a theory that given their cliff-front perch, had the Mayans realized the threat they were under, they would've taken better steps to protect themselves and would probably have thwarted a landing.

Getting to the Point...

Like the small vessels the Mayans commonly saw anchored off their coast, the market in 2008/2009 was flooded in the usual doom and gloom news stories about higher commodities prices, lower home sales, and higher unemployment. However the market simply couldn't perceive the galleons just offshore—it just couldn't see the dramatic threat to the credit markets that mortgage backed securities and credit default swaps had become. The threat of widespread default was so immense a problem that disbelief removed it from the realm of possibility.

We think that this disbelief and resulting blindness is probably the reason why so many investors ignored clear evidence, signals, and indicators like we saw before the crash of 2008/2009.

The lesson, we think, is pretty clear: media noise is now so loud that you have to rely on things you see with your own eyes and learn to trust yourself.

Our Own Tipping Points

For Pat, there were two main points that helped make the decision to go to a cash portfolio in 2008. One, at the time all of this was going on, he and his wife were traveling from Alaska to Argentina in their 1958 VW bus. While not exactly a gas hog he was still feeling the pinch when having to drop a hundred dollar bill at every fill up along the way. Innocuous indicator, perhaps, but when you are paying $7 a gallon for gas in a state with the richest oil reserves in the U.S. (Alaska), it's not a stretch to conclude that fuel costs will have dramatic effects on any industry relying on transport.

Secondly, at this exact same time Pat's mother was dealing with an investment property that she had somehow managed to get mixed up in with a shady partner. They had originally intended to list the property for $950,000. By the time the work was completed the listing had dropped all the way to $700,000. Within a couple more months, with not a single interested party showing up, they were listing the home for $590,000. In the end it would sell for $450,000. A substantial loss to all involved. Clearly the real estate market was not what it once was.

Nick's story was similar—the indicators didn't come from the news; they came from his own firsthand experience. His company ReFlight produced a cockpit recorder for aviation test flight programs. Sales were climbing through early 2007, then within two months sales had dropped by more than 50% and the largest customers had to delay their capital expenditures without any explanation. They also started asking for 60- and 90-day purchase orders, which basically meant that Nick would have to extend credit to these big companies in order to close sales.

Then one day Adam Aircraft, his largest customer stopped answering their phones on day 29 of a 30 day purchase order. Adam Aircraft filed for Chapter 7 bankruptcy—literally closed the doors and turned off the phones (which is different than a Chapter 11 restructuring) shortly thereafter. Nick was left holding the bag and took a huge loss on product he had sold and shipped but had never been paid for.

One of Nick's neighbors was a former CEO of two major aerospace companies. At the time he was heading up a single-seat personal jet project which was basically a mini-fighter jet at a $1.1M price point to be marketed to the boys with the biggest toys. Their market was drying up, however, as presale deposits were falling short of expectations. They eventually sold the program to the Israeli Military without ever making it to FAA certification.

Something big was going on, and Nick knew it.

At the same time, he noticed that there appeared to be a new home on the market in his neighborhood every day. Seeing that other housing markets around the country were imploding and prices were cratering, Nick decided the real estate tide was turning for the Colorado Front Range. He and his wife listed their house in June of 2007. Without an offer in 60 days, they got aggressive and dropped the asking price by $100,000, selling in September (still at a significant 14-month profit). By the time the moving van was pulling away, every single house on his cul-de-sac was on the market (many of which ended up in foreclosure over the next year). Nick and his wife got out by the hairs on their chinny chin chins.

Waiting to Believe What You See

Without ever listening to the talking heads or analysts or "experts," we both could clearly see the fundamental issue confronting the economy: credit was drying up, and the rate at which this was happening was incredible. Our reasoning and thought processes was very simple: if people and companies can't borrow to buy, asset values in every class were about to drop. And that included the stock market. It was clear as day.

These are exactly the types of things that we all can see happening around us and are the types of catalysts that we need to react to. None of us can see the inner workings of Lehman Brothers or OPEC; but instead of worrying about what we can't see, we need to focus on what we can, and act accordingly.

When you see a cause, and realize that it's a fundamental factor in a market, a sector, an industry, or a company, understand that there will be real effects. There is absolutely no need to wait for someone else, be it a financial advisor or the news media, to tell you that what you are seeing is real. Trust yourself ahead of everyone else.

If Bearish - Where is the Upside?

What we find most amazing about the financial crash of 2008 was the two week period of time after Lehman filed for bankruptcy when the market did almost nothing. This was a period of extremely negative news about the overall economy, followed closely by a lot more really, really, really bad news about banking—and not just a credit crisis, but a solvency crisis. None of this was being "leaked out" here and there—this was major headline material for every news outlet for months and months; this was no secret.

Even if you didn't understand everything you were hearing at the time, what, if any reasoning was there for staying in this market? *Where was the upside?* How high could the market have gone, and how big an opportunity would we be missing if we were sitting in cash?

At that single moment in time when one of the biggest banks in the world completely failed, could *anyone* have believed that taking their money out of the market was going to result in missing a big move *to the upside*? At that moment, even if you were feeling extremely optimistic about a positive outcome (and how could you have?), how could you have predicted anything but a slow grind higher? How could you have envisioned an explosive, all-encompassing upward move that you'd have missed by converting to cash? Given the depth and breadth of the banking and credit crisis, how could anyone have thought that converting to cash meant missing an opportunity? This one was obvious.

So when the news is bad and the fear is high, and you are trying to decide whether you are making the wrong decision by standing on the sidelines, ask yourself, "If I am wrong, what upside might I miss?—How high could this go while I am out of position?"

If Bullish - Where is the Downside?

The opposite is a good guide to use as well. When the bulls are running and everyone thinks the sky is the limit for the market or a sector or even an individual stock, ask yourself what is the worst that could happen if you went along for the ride. Even when you yourself are bullish, you agree with the positive sentiment, and the "price target" of $800 on a stock currently trading at $700 seems reasonable, stop for a moment and think about how big your downside might be if you and everyone else is wrong.

How much do you think you could lose? If you are looking at a company you feel confident is headed from $700 to $800, how much downside is there? Do you think that this stock could give back $10–20, but certainly not $50? Well, then you have a trade in front of you that has $20 of downside if you are wrong, but $100 of upside if you are right.

You will never be able to predict the future, but you sure can formulate what is *possible.*

Jumping Back In

So when we left off with our summary of the 2008 financial crisis, we hinted that it carried into 2009 as well. And it did. It was March 2009 before the market actually bottomed out. And what happened between the massive sell-off that began at the end of September and concluded in March? The market bounced between 7500 and 9500. How in the world could you spot the right time to get back in amongst the turmoil?

The answer is that you couldn't have.

We didn't "jump" back in at all. We moved back in very tentatively and took losses when we tried to get back in at DOW 10,000, again at DOW 8,000, and finally again after the DOW touched 6,500. By the time the DJIA was climbing through 7,500 on its way back up to 12,000 and 13,000, Pat was fully invested in stocks and capitalizing on the largest broad-market rally of our adult lives. Nick was much more conservative, taking his time to get back in until the market was consistently above DOW 9,000 in June of 2009. Even then, Nick maintained a significant cash position.

AT THE END OF THE DAY...

So you can see that our market timing wasn't perfect. We didn't sell the high or buy the low, but we still managed to stave off four or five thousand Dow points worth of pain and misery. By November of 2009, the market was back above ten thousand, at which point even the worst of our buys were winners while the stocks we bought near the bottom were all performing wonders for the bottom line.

Unmatched in Our Lifetimes

This was a two-year period unlike any other we'd ever been a part of; and we use it here to illustrate our thoughts about market timing, because it was so dramatic and obvious, and also because unless you lived (literally) under a rock for that period, you probably have some experience with what happened.

While all this was going on, did we sit around waiting for the end of the world or worrying we had made the wrong calls? Nope, we kept eyes and ears on what was going on, but continued to live our lives. After he was back into stocks, Pat hardly traded at all during the market recovery, as the entire period fit right in with an epic two-year journey that he and his wife set out on in their '58 VW bus. And yet it was the single most profitable year he's ever had in the markets.

Nick sold a little closer to the highs but waited in the wings until the risks looked a little lower and bought back into the recovery later. Once he was long on his favorites, he and his wife purchased another sailboat and headed off for a new adventure in the Pacific NW. June 2009 to January 2011 was spent sailing around, writing his first book and very occasionally trading.

Notice that throughout this book we make it clear that we are traders, not investors, and yet during this time period we both became investors. It was simply too easy. The market just climbed and climbed. There was no reason to cut winners short. And the fact of the matter is, during that time, they were all winners.

By early to mid 2011, it was time to get more selective as most of our "sure things" had made it back to pre-crash levels. So we started trading more actively...or more appropriately, "slacktively," a few times a month.

If the last few paragraphs don't prove just how dedicated we are to *living on the margin*, nothing will: Christ, we could've been living like kings and queens over that same period of time, but instead we were doing things like driving through the Andes Mountains in a fifty-year-old VW bus with a 1600cc engine trying to propel it up and over 14,000 foot mountain passes. All the while searching for suitably abandoned looking dirt roads on which to camp.

And instead of sipping lattes and sitting in front of a computer, we were doing things like exploring new anchorages on a new-to-us sailboat in the San Juans and Canadian Gulf Islands, eating fresh caught crab and wild blackberries.

Global financial crisis? How about biggest opportunity to slack, ever. We had driven right over the margin and into the abyss, all the while managing our own finances and having crazy adventures of our own making. True, we were managing our finances by doing basically nothing a vast majority of the time; but that's part and parcel of being a trader.

We are always on the lookout for opportunities, and when there are no opportunities we are content to wait for them. You can't simply make market opportunities appear out of thin air because you want them to. If that's "timing the market," then we say it's a better idea than throwing up your hands and accepting whatever comes your way.

Investor Psychology

"Why in the world did I just buy those options?"
"I am such a fucking idiot."
"I've got to get out of this position."

In about two hours I (Nick) had lost just under $500, reaching the maximum intraday loss I'd set on the position, which I typically keep at about 15%. Rules are rules, I told myself, so I gotta sell.

And sell, I did.

Two hours later, the stock recovered, and so would my position had I not sold. If I had held those calls until the next trading session I'd have made close to $3,000 as the stock rallied. Instead, a $500 hit.

That's a lot of money to lose and to leave on the table; it doesn't matter whether you have a thousand or a million in the bank, that stings. And when you are depending on that trade to pay for your food this month, that kind of loss takes on a whole new gravity. Living on the margin means you are putting your adventure on the line with every trade. Lose too much too often, and it's back to work sooner than you'd like.

"Don't sweat it—this is part of the game," I told myself. Then five seconds later...

"Fuck! I am such a fucking idiot! Buy high and sell low. Great fucking plan Nick! Fuck, fuck, fuck!" (Please excuse the harsh language, but in this instance none of us are saying *fudge*.)

The Game Within

No one is harder on a trader than the trader himself. An independent trader is fighting two battles at any one time: one battle is with the market, that anonymous *other guy* tooth and nail. The other battle, the one you wage day in and day out no matter what the market is doing is with *yourself*; with that part of you who hates to lose more than anything in the world.

That anonymous other guy? You'll never be able to guess what he is going to do 100% of the time, but the battle with yourself—that's something you can control. In fact as a trader, you are the only thing you can control. The market will do what it does.

Risk and Loss

If you are willing to say goodbye to the workaday world for a life of uncertainty on the high seas in a small boat, or in a camper touring the arctic tundra, or on an enduro motorcycle riding across the Australian Outback, we can all agree that you are probably less risk averse than your average desk jockey. You understand that risks are worth taking; that there are no big rewards without putting it on the line here and there. You understand risk better than most people, but tell us Mr. Big Time Adventurer, how do you feel about loss?

We're going to guess that you hate to lose. Maybe more than anything in this world. Are we right?

Loss Aversion

Fear of loss, or loss aversion is not the same as risk aversion. As ready as we are to sail off through a dark and stormy night with the slightest chance of sinking and dying in the process, we can tell you that we HATE to lose. We take that back, we DESPISE losing. There is absolutely nothing worse than leaving the poker table with less than you showed up with. Losing sucks. Losers suck.

Here is the important part—the most important thing to understand from this chapter: hating to lose is the Achilles heel of anyone attempting to profit from the stock market. Here's why: you hate losing more than you like winning. We are going to say that again for emphasis:

You hate losing more than you like winning.

This isn't our opinion. This is a psychological fact born out of years of research. Here is what that means: people are more loss averse than they are reward driven. This one fact, that people hate losing more than they like winning, is the single biggest reason that traders lose money in the market. How does that work?

People routinely make reasoned, substantiated decisions in an attempt to gain a reward, but they make quick, unsubstantiate decisions in order to avoid a loss.

This isn't anecdotal evidence from a couple of hacks (though we are indeed hacks)—this is a fact which has been tested and corroborated in laboratories for years, starting back in the 1970s. The conclusions are always the same:

People hate losing so much that in absence of certainty, they will make irrational, unsubstantiated, and unreasonable decisions to try to avoid loss.

We know what you are thinking: people lose money in the market because they aren't as smart as the guy who wins. Sure, that's absolutely true as well; information, experience, and skill are a big part of doing anything successfully, but there is a secret sauce that makes one trader more successful than another: the person who wins has a vision and a plan, and the emotional discipline to follow that plan for as long as the trade behaves as expected, or within tolerances.

This goes back to the old saying, "Plan the trade and trade the plan." Simply put, this means having a strategy; a set of guidelines and rules that you follow, then following those guidelines even when every cell in your body tells you that your initial assumptions were wrong (unless there is substantiated evidence to believe otherwise). Your assumptions will be wrong and you will lose sometimes, but by being consistent, you will win more than lose and you will profit from it.

Losing Before You Buy

I (Nick) still look at how I handled that trade with disgust. It wasn't the market that cost me $500, it was me. I was toast before I ever bought those contracts. How did I end up losing before I even bought?

I didn't want to win bad enough. What does that mean? Of course you want to win; that's the name of the game. Nope, I didn't want to win bad enough. How do I know that now in hindsight? Because I bought those calls with no substantiated information and with no plan or expectation for how the stock would behave. I went in blind making a series of bad assumptions—I relied on gut instinct.

Going with your gut will cost you a lot of money.

We'll tell you a little bit more about this particular trade. In the spring of 2012, AAPL (Apple Incorporated) was the most talked about stock anywhere, next to the impending (at that time) Facebook IPO. AAPL had more or less soared over the previous five years, with compounding growth, impressive earnings, tons of cash in the bank and good sales trends. AAPL was a clear winner over the short and the long term. We both owned (and probably do own today) AAPL stock. Anyway, Pat had just made a bunch of money on May calls when the stock surprised everyone, jumping from 570 to 605 in an afternoon. Nick missed out. He was out surfing at the time.

Even if Nick had been around a computer, he wouldn't have traded the stock in the same way Pat did. In fact, his thinking on the stock at the time was: AAPL is all played out *right now.* He was so certain that he put it into an email to Pat. *"AAPL is now a value stock—akin to MSFT or GE that will turn in consistently good earnings and growth."* To Nick, AAPL looked like a good portfolio stock, but for fading and swing trades, this one was not worth his time. He also didn't like that everyone else seemed to like AAPL so much—the consensus was that AAPL just couldn't lose. (In our experience, when everyone and their brother is blogging about how fantastic a stock it is, that's when it tends to fall.)

After the stock jumped higher making Pat a ton of cash, it turned out that Nick was pretty much right in the short term: after AAPL rose to near $620 with a market cap of $500B, it started a slow slide through the first three weeks of May—first down to 600, then to 580 for a week or so, then hovering in the mid–570 range for another week or so. Just a slow fade...until the morning in question.

*I (Nick) woke early to take a quick pre-market look at a couple of positions and contemplate what moves I could make given that the FB (Facebook) IPO was the next day, May 18, 2012. I had no interest or intention of buying FB itself, but figured that whatever it did, a few other stocks might go along for the ride. Perhaps LNKD (LinkedIn) or that piece of sh*t GRPN (Groupon). But my attention was diverted—when what do I see on my watchlist?*

AAPL down to $545. Wow, that's cheap...that can't last. But it did: AAPL to $540...$538. "Time to make some easy money."

I hadn't for a minute considered why or how AAPL might be moving lower—in fact I hadn't really had it on my news radar for a few weeks, so I took a glance around. No news on AAPL. The market was broadly lower, so I thought, "This has got to be part of the broader market move. It will probably bounce tomorrow when everyone realizes that they are oversold."

Quickly, while the stock was trading at a relatively stable 539, Nick bought the cheapest midterm calls that he expected could be in-the-money or close to it within the exercise period: he bought June 565 calls at $9.10. Just two contracts (each contract is for 100 stock, so the order was $1,820) though...no need to put more than a couple grand into play. If the stock went back to where it was the day before, he'd make an easy grand or more selling the options. Not bad for ten minutes work! We are talking AAPL! This thing is rock solid—a company that we believe in!

But AAPL didn't stop sliding. Two hours later, the June 565 call options were selling at $6.70. A loss of 27%...or almost $500 on the two contracts. He knew to expect to be underwater on these calls in the near term, but a day or two later, it had to rebound. We are talking about AAPL! Rock solid!

Only then did I (Nick) start to dig a little deeper to find why such a high quality company was sliding on NO industry news or company announcements of any kind. Here and there, I found small notes about hedge fund managers needing to liquidate tech positions to buy into the Facebook IPO. This wasn't company news, and it was hardly even sector news, but it was news, and whether that was the reason for the liquidation or not, it was happening, and others were piling on.

This is where I made my big mistake...and this is always the same mistake when looking back on a bad trade: I got scared. Only 29 days left until the contracts expire, and each day they depreciate just a little bit because of time decay. My mind started racing: What if I'm wrong about this turkey and FB really does pop, and drains further money out of AAPL? Do other traders share the same sentiment about AAPL being a value play now? The price might not recover in time and I will be stuck with a bigger loss than I have now. Also, I'm already below my normal 15% loss tolerance.

I gotta sell.

So he sold.

Here is the post-mortem on this trade: Nick very reasonably started to question the premise and expectations under which he bought the options in the first place. These were the exact discussions he should've had with himself before he made the purchase, but didn't. Had he taken the time to question those premises and expectations before buying, he'd have noted:

- 29 days left on the contract is plenty for AAPL. In most circumstances, Nick will trade AAPL options up until four or five days before expiration. Why was he so nervous about time decay when there was so much potential upside?

- Nick (both of us really) had never believed the FB IPO hype, so why all of a sudden would he think a FB pop would drag a lagging AAPL stock lower? He had never once considered buying FB. His guesstimated closing price within a day or two would be at or around $40—so why would he think that the opposite performance would drag AAPL down? *(As it turned out, the FB IPO was littered with problems and the stock fell from $38 to $30 or so in three sessions before falling into the teens a couple months later.)*

- He had decided in the month prior (April) that AAPL was now a value play instead of a growth play—a large drop on a value stock would substantiate HOLDING, not SELLING the options, as it was likely that buyers would come back into the market very quickly. Alternatively, why not just buy and hold more AAPL stock?

The long and the short of it is that Nick became irrational, and traded against his well-established beliefs. In essence, he decided to purchase the call options without deciding ahead of time what he expected to happen with the stock and how long he expected to hold the options.

He made the decision to sell, not based on his pre-purchase sentiment of the stock, but on what he perceived to be others' perceptions. He made two fundamental errors:

1. He bought without a plan.
2. He sold when he realized he hadn't made a plan.

Nick made two emotion-based trades, and got eaten alive. How in the world does something like this happen, even to someone as smart as Nick?

You Will Always be Five Years Old
You are losing NOW. That's why you want to sell NOW. The upside is later, when the stock is oversold and the buyers come back into the market—that's when the stock will go up and you will realize a profit. But at this very second, it's down, and that makes every cell in your body scream to SELL!!!!!!!!

We are all five-year-olds at heart and when all things are equal, now always wins out over later; we want the ice cream right now, not when we get home from the store. We want to retire now and not wait until we are 65. Study after study has shown that people will take $100 now instead of $200 next year. Financially, it makes a lot more sense to wait, but we don't want to.

These same studies have found that those who are better able to hold off on their short-term need bias turn out to be better performers on standardized tests. So as it turns out, the cooler and more calculated you can be about your trades, the better you will perform.

No Parachute!
Stocks always fall a lot faster than they rise. So that means that when a stock or option goes down, it will go down quickly compared to any recovery. There are exceptions, and we try to predict and capitalize on them, but in general, when a trade goes against you, it will be sudden, unforeseen, and it can drive you to a panic sell.

Panic moves are almost never the right moves. So how are we going to deal with the emotional ups and downs of trading? Let's start with understanding risk.

Risk
We hope we have been clear throughout this book: you *will* make losing trades—we guarantee it. If you trade frequently, you will lose frequently.

The same can be said of any adventure you might be contemplating. If you set off around the world on a small boat, you are absolutely positively going to see some bad weather. How much? Depends on the choices you make and the risks you take. Pat and Ali sailed to the right destinations at the right times of year and only saw a handful of truly bad weather days.

Going to set off across continents in an old VW bus? You are going to have mechanical problems. You will get stranded. The paint will get scratched. How much? Depends on the decisions you make and the risks you take. Going to backpack Europe? You are going to get stuck in a train station or lose your camera.

The same goes for trading because if you take risks, losses simply cannot be avoided—it's just as much a part of trading as profits are.

Even the winners lose. They just lose little bits here and there; and when they win, they win big. The goal is to lose less often and to a lesser extent than you win. So to win, you need to take the right risks with the highest probability of paying off. And to lose less, you need to recognize bad risks with low probability of payoff.

Risk, Fear & Worry

One leads to another, which leads to the other. You wake up in the middle of the night and for some reason, you think that your water heater may kill you. There was that story on the news about the family of four found dead of carbon monoxide poisoning—they never saw it coming—poor bastards. And you could be next. So you lie awake, fretting away:

We have an old water heater; it's got that rust stain. Should we install a new one? What if there were an earthquake and it tipped over and caused a gas leak and the house exploded like in the Bourne Identity movie. How much do water heaters cost? What about the pilot light? I didn't see it flickering when I was down there doing laundry yesterday...

The next morning, you wake up not so refreshed, and for a fleeting moment you think about going to Home Depot to get some mounting straps and a carbon monoxide detector. But you don't go. Why not?

We tend to think of risk, fear, and worry together—somehow inseparable—but that's not the case.

Risks are real. Water heaters do kill people. That's not fiction—that's real life. Boats do sink. Planes do crash. Thieves and pirates do kill travelers. If you drop everything to head off for an adventure, you do risk not being able to go back to your career. Risks exist in a world outside of your own creation. Risks are real.

Fear is a reaction to risk, but unlike risks, which are real and exist in the outside world, fear is on the inside and fear needs a fearer. Fear is very subjective and personal—one person looks at the real risk of dying in a plane crash and says, "I don't want to spend three days driving to Boston, so I am comfortable boarding this plane." Someone else looks at that very same risk and says, "I'd rather walk to Boston than get on that plane." Fear depends on you. The statistics don't care which one of you boards that plane; you both have the same chance of dying in a crash. Fear is a reaction to risk.

Worry is the brain's continual analysis of risks. It's your mind trying to solve the problem defined by the imagined risk. Worry is wondering if you are close enough to the exit row to get out when the plane crashes. Worry is guessing whether the water heater should be strapped to the foundation. Worry is imagining how to eliminate or mitigate risks.

The thing you need to get your head around is that the actual risk is outside of you, and often completely independent of any control you might think you have over it. The plane is going to crash or not crash, regardless of where you sit. The earthquake is going to happen or not happen, regardless of whether you replace the water heater.

When faced with a problem that involves risk, people commonly make two errors:

1. Mistake fear for risk, and
2. Worry too much about mitigating fear and not enough about mitigating real risks.

With this clarification, you can see that there are only two things to do about the water heater: identify whether the risk is real, and if necessary employ your brain (worry) to mitigate that risk. Worry, also known as *diligence* is not a bad thing in and of itself. That's your brain taking care of you. Fear, on the other hand is completely unnecessary and a waste of time and energy. In most cases, you can skip right over fear and head straight to worry.

What is Risk, Really?

According to the dictionary, risk is, "A probability or threat of negative occurrence (damage, injury, liability, or loss) caused by external or internal vulnerabilities that may be neutralized through pre-emptive action." So from this definition, we know:

1. Risk is caused by vulnerabilities.
2. Risk is something you can prepare for.

The mistake most people make is in not thoroughly understanding #1, and often overestimating their vulnerabilities. Then because they don't understand their vulnerabilities, they overestimate their ability to do #2 and go way too far trying to prepare for the risk that they do perceive. Overkill times two!

It sounds silly, but people make decisions every day that they think limit risks but actually don't; or on the flip side, they take risks that they don't know they are taking.

Confusing Risks and Fear

Take a would-be adventurer on a capable cruising sailboat. The mighty captain buys a boat to brave the oceans for thrill and adventure and travel. He writes that check with visions of distant coral atolls and crystal clear blue water. He outfits his vessel so he could easily sail around the world nonstop. Does he go? Does he head offshore for a multi-day and multi-week passage to go find paradise? No, he decides that it's safer to coastal cruise, or day-sail within sight of land.

People make the same mistakes over and over again: when they can't understand a risk, they focus exclusively on their fear. For example: Which is more dangerous? Coastal cruising or trans-oceanic passage making?

Statistically, coastal cruising (traveling within sight of land) is actually a lot more dangerous than crossing oceans. It's collisions with hard things like land that sink boats, not sea monsters or bad weather in the middle of the ocean. The perception of risk is the opposite of reality.

Human beings are irrational. The sailor fears being out of sight of land because that's what he is accustomed to and where he thinks help is more accessible, so he'll take the higher risk of sailing close to shore to allay his fears instead of truly mitigating the real risks by sailing farther away from land.

Greed = Fear

There are all sorts of "fear vs. greed" indexes used by the financial media to try and gauge how investors are feeling about the market. They report these things as though fear is the opposite of greed; as though bearish means fearful and bullish means greedy. That is at the very least overly simplistic, but more likely just total BS. In our opinions, fear and greed are the exact same thing, except that greed is dressed up a little bit:

Greed is the fear of missed opportunity.

Why is it so hard to sell a stock that continues to climb? Because you fear that if it keeps going up you will miss out on profit. You have a hard time selling that winner because you are greedy.

Why do people take more food at the buffet table than they should? Can't miss an opportunity to "take advantage" and get their money's worth.

Let's take this a step further; why are people so fat in the U.S.? Fear and collective unconscious anxiety, we say! Fear of what? Fear that if they don't take advantage of that whole bag of cookies in one sitting, that they'll starve to death when the unknowable bad thing happens.

Greed in the Market

When you are making decisions based on your fear of missing an opportunity to make money, you are being greedy. Hey, being greedy is NOT necessarily a bad thing—you don't want to miss opportunities. But getting TOO greedy will cloud judgement; you will lose objectivity, and that can work directly against what you are trying to accomplish.

"Greed is good."
– Gordon Gekko, *Wall Street*

The market—those nameless, faceless "others" who are out there trying to make money just like you are—they are greedy too. In fact the greedier they are the greedier they get. We use this to ride momentum and profit, however there are occasions, specifically around large company events—like product announcements and earnings calls, where an overly-greedy market can go against you if you are being just as greedy as they are.

Here is an example: a recent earnings report (July 2012) from AAPL. Apple is a monster company with incredible growth, great fundamentals, and a pile of cash. There isn't a lot to not like about Apple, and they are one of the most talked about and praised companies of the last ten years. AAPL is a rock star and everyone knows it. In recent memory, they seem to do no wrong.

By July 2012, Apple had beaten their earnings projections five of the last six quarters, and beat consensus Wall Street estimates by big margins. Each time, the bulls won big as the stock jumped higher after the quarterly announcement. So with the upcoming report, it wasn't a question of whether the stock would go higher, but by how much.

Everyone, it seemed, thought they were doing the safe thing, including your two distinguished authors. We bought 90-day (September) call options way out-of-the-money (a long shot). The day after our initial purchase, our options went down about a buck. Paper loss...no biggie...and in fact an opportunity to...buy more Sept 700 calls...which we did. The day before earnings, our options went down another buck...no biggie...and in fact an opportunity to... you guessed it: buy more calls. We did just that.

Apple's earnings came in way short of expectations—one of their biggest disappointments in recent memory. The stock dropped 30 points, and our options were decimated. We each lost several thousand dollars. What did we do wrong?

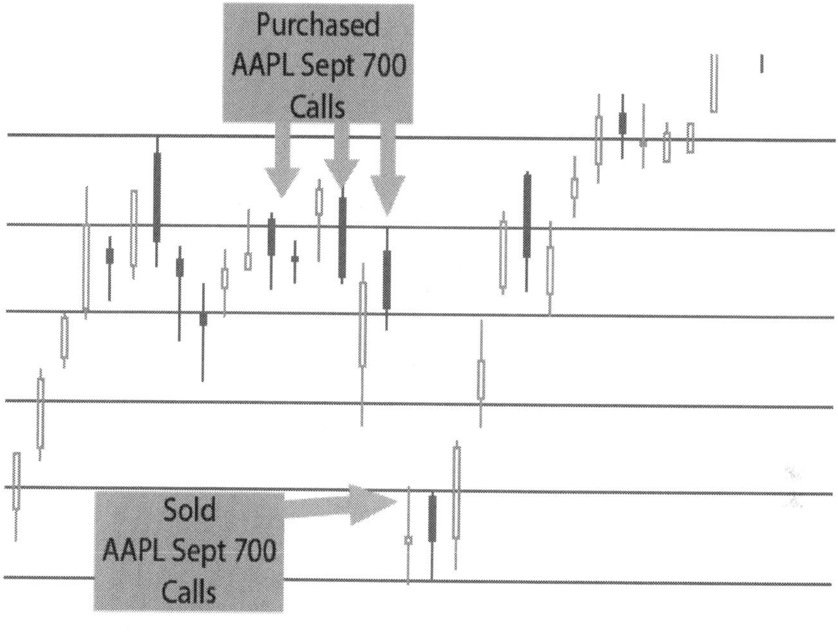

[fig 14.1]

Instead of focusing on the risks, we let our fear of missing out (greed) drive our decision. Here are the risks that we couldn't see:

- Consensus before the announcement was that AAPL always beats expectations. This meant that the beat had to be very dramatic to move a long-shot position such as we took.

- Options traders were buying calls (bullish) six times as often as they were buying puts (bearish). We were following the herd, and that's a bad idea when the risk is 50–50.

- Apple had lowered quarterly guidance and done it late in the quarter, but other than that there was no other information we could use to predict AAPL's earnings. We were making a 50–50 bet, which is basically just gambling—there was no real skill that we could apply.

We want to take **big** risks, but we also want to take **smart** risks. Greed and fear drive markets. It is best to know when they have hold of your psychology.

Riding the Wave of Greed

The thing with this bad Apple trade that really got to Pat was that just the previous quarter he had made a killing on another favorite company of his, IMAX, making a very similar play. (We know it seems like we talk a lot about AAPL and IMAX. We go through cycles like these often, focusing intently on one or two or three stocks for months at a time until something changes, the stock's momentum peters out, and another stock suddenly pops up on our radar. These two happened to be our most popular in the six months or so leading up to the writing of this book.)

For about a month Pat watched as IMAX trended lower on news of little importance. There didn't seem to be too much behind the move down from a price of $26.50 to near $22. The day after a particularly severe 6% bashing of the stock Pat had had enough and backed up the truck on what he felt were underpriced $27 calls. The trade didn't fit perfectly with our fade rules, but the RSI was indeed under 30 and the price was hovering just above the 3rd BB. It was a judgement call on a stock that he'd been following closely for a long time.

IMAX had what appeared to be a good quarter and this seemed like a good way to play the earnings report two weeks away. The very next day the stock was up 4%. The following week it trended sideways, up a little then down a little, and then boom, up 3%, then 4%, and the day before earnings another 2%.

He'd bought those $27 calls in order to try and profit off of what he expected to be good earnings; but with the earnings call due out the very next day he sold the whole batch. All those calls he'd bought were up 120%. Great!

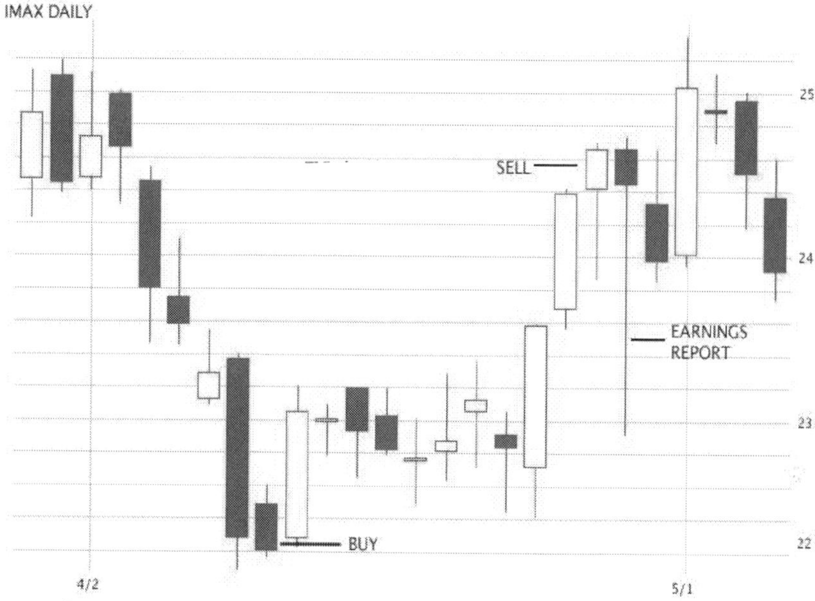

[fig 14.2]

But why sell if he expected good earnings? Because, as we said, we want to take big risks, but we also want to take smart risks. Remember that before he bought anything and opened a position, Pat was looking for a big move on earnings day. Even though he had not been expecting a nearly eleven percent run up in the stock price *before* earnings, he had already taken a big risk on the opening of the position–he had already ridden the wave of greed sweeping through the market for IMAX. He had already made a large profit on that wave, and to hold those calls and continue to risk those profits into an "unknown" event, the earnings report, would not be a smart risk.

As it turns out he played it perfectly. The report came out negative, and the stock dropped as much as seven percent—at which point his gains would've been completely wiped out.

The moral of this story? When the market is being fueled by greed and speculation, there is nothing wrong with riding the wave. However, remember that everyone else is playing the same game that you are. Be the first out the door when you see any reason the greed bubble might pop. Lead, don't follow.

Risky Business is Good!

Those beautiful South Pacific atolls wouldn't be quite so spectacular if everyone with a ski boat could get there from LA in a couple of hours. What fun would it be to drive across continents if everyone with a driver's license and a car was doing it? It turns out that it would be impossible to have great adventures or to make money in the stock market without risk.

Only those who risk going too far
can possibly find out how far one can go.
– T.S. Eliot

If you want to live a bigger life than you do now, you need to take a different view of risk. Risk is not something to be feared; it's something to be understood and embraced. Most people focus inordinately on reducing risks; but without risk, there literally is no reward.

The Risk Equation

First off, what is it that you are trying to protect from a particular risk? Is it your wife, your children, your money, your boat, your life, etc.? Let's call this thing you are trying to protect an *asset*. An asset isn't strictly property of some sort, it's anything that you *value*; it's something you wouldn't want to lose or have damaged. *Assets* are everything in your life you try to protect.

A *threat* is anything that can hurt or damage an asset. An iceberg is a threat to a small boat. A nail is a threat to your car tire. A thief is a threat to your diamond earrings. So a threat is literally anything or any occurrence that will diminish, decrease, or in any way lessen or cause loss to something that you value.

The ice in the iceberg isn't a bad thing in and of itself of course; it is great for keeping your drink cold. The nail in your tire could just as easily be used to build a house. The thief? Well, he doesn't have much of a chance to steal your earrings if they are kept in a bank vault.

Threats depend on *vulnerabilities.* The iceberg is only a threat if it can exploit vulnerability in a boat's hull. The nail can only flatten your tire if the tire is thin and soft enough. The thief can only steal your earrings if he is able to break into your house. Vulnerabilities are weaknesses or gaps in any protocol or measure or thing or substance that can be exploited by threats on an asset, so threats and vulnerabilities go together like butts and underwear.

You can see that risk is dependent on assets, threats, and vulnerabilities. You can put all these things together with a neat little equation:

Risk = Asset x Threat x Vulnerability

No need to get hung up on the mathematics here—that's not the point of this exercise. What you should understand is that risk changes if you add or subtract from any of the above components on the right-hand side of the equation. Hold any two of those three variables (asset, threat, vulnerability) constant and you can see some basic relationships between them and risk. Here are some examples that illustrate how the different components of the risk equation work in the real world:

- **Asset**. There is a ten times greater financial risk driving a $100,000 Porsche 911 than in driving a $10,000 Toyota Camry.

- **Threat**. There is greater risk leaving a Porsche parked in a bad neighborhood than the Camry.
- **Vulnerability**. There is greater risk driving the Toyota around a corner at high speed than taking the same corner at the same speed in a Porsche.

Limiting Risk

Neuropsychologist Rick Hanson sums it up best: "To keep our ancestors alive, Mother Nature evolved a brain that routinely tricked them into making three mistakes: overestimating threats, underestimating opportunities, and underestimating resources (for dealing with threats and fulfilling opportunities)."

When it comes to risk, most people only focus on threats and vulnerabilities, because those are the things they feel they are most in control of. This makes sense: you can't control which house the thief will rob. You can't see and avoid every nail on the road. If you sail in the Arctic, you can't assume you will see and avoid every piece of ice. So in an effort to control risk, people lock their doors, buy tires that don't lose air when punctured, and they don't sail in the high latitudes where there might be sea-ice.

People control what they think they can control because the risk equation teaches them over and over that:

- The smaller or lesser the asset, the lower the risk. If you put fewer assets into any situation, you have less risk.
- The smaller the threat, the lower the risk. If you avoid threats, you have less risk.
- The lesser the vulnerability, the lower the risk. If you eliminate vulnerabilities, you eliminate risk.

There is nothing wrong at all with risking fewer assets and diminishing threats and vulnerabilities. It makes perfect sense, but there is a downside—people often don't take enough risks or they take the wrong risks, and in doing so, they miss opportunities.

Stupid Risks

These are risks in which you know from the very beginning that the outcome is likely not going to be in your favor. The average American household spends close to $1,000 per year on lottery tickets. In Singapore, the average household spends $4,000. *Four thousand!* The chance of actually hitting the lotto is incredibly small. Let's look at the risk equation for lottery tickets: the asset is small, perhaps a dollar or two, but the threat of loss through the vulnerability of incredibly long odds is nearly 100%. So from the risk equation, even if the asset is very small, the actual risk is incredibly high.

Dangerous Risks

These are risks in which the outcome can have catastrophic impacts. Skydiving is an activity in which the statistical risk is very low—in fact there are only 21 fatalities per 3,000,000 jumps, or 0.0007% of the time. Compared to the automobile accident fatality rate of 0.0167% (based on driving 10,000 miles), you are 24 times more likely to die in a car crash than jumping out of a plane. However, from the risk equation, we see that while the threat is very, very low, the vulnerability is very, very high, and the asset (your life) is about as high as you can get.

Based on our risk equation, the total risk in skydiving is very low, so the question becomes: Is the risk worth the reward? One person's answer is going to be different than the next, but statistics are a useful tool in making that decision.

Proportional Risk

Let's use our 9th grade calculus for the first time in a few years and play with the risk equation a little bit. Try not to get hung up on the mathematics here, but what if we moved the assets to the other side of the equation:

$$\text{Assets} = \text{Risk} \,/\, (\text{Threat} \times \text{Vulnerability})$$

From this equation, if we hold threat and vulnerability constant, we can see that if we increase risk, we see an increase in assets. Since threat and vulnerability are on the bottom now, increasing either of those will decrease assets, and decreasing either of those will increase our assets.

So in an idealized scenario, to maximize our assets, we want to take as much risk as possible while limiting threats and vulnerabilities.

Holding threats and vulnerabilities constant while taking greater risk isn't reality of course. So what we should aim to do is increase our risk while threats and vulnerabilities increase proportionately less. For example, we can risk a trip to the higher latitudes and see more icebergs; but if we do it in a steel-hulled boat we can take on an occasional growler without being harmed. The vulnerability to the threat is increased proportionately less than the risk; and the asset, the thing we value increases—we get to see what others rarely do.

Profiting From Life Risks

Higher risk means higher reward—that's been our experience in the real world, not just in the financial world. We have certainly taken greater risks (top of the equation) by spending our (potentially) greatest professional earnings years out surfing Central American beaches and sailing to undiscovered ports. We have mitigated those greater risks by limiting our vulnerabilities. We've done that by limiting debt, by limiting overhead, by proactively making healthy lifestyle choices, etc. As we spoke about above, limiting vulnerabilities often limits threats at the same time.

Risk in the Market

Trying to make money in the markets trading stocks, derivatives, commodities, etc. is a risky activity. You can and will lose sometimes. This isn't just a disclaimer or a sobering warning—risk is the primary reason that the markets exist in the first place, and it's the only reason we are able to make money trading. We will say it again for emphasis: **markets exist because of risk**. No risk, no market. How and why?

Let's say that you are a corn farmer. You invest your money and your time (labor) planting seed in the spring and fertilizing the crop in the summer, and then finally your investment is paid back when you sell the corn at a market in the fall.

For simplicity's sake, let's say that from seed to market takes six months. During that time, you are risking capital with the hope of being paid back more than you invested, which is profit. Why are you doing this? Is it simply so you can feed your ten children?

Nope. It isn't that simple. If you don't plant your crop, your assets depreciate; your tractor lays idle and starts rusting while you still have to make payments on it. Your taxes will come due and the IRS will seize your farm. You plant those seeds because if you don't try to profit, you *risk* losing assets through depreciation or interest payments or through inflation.

The same happens with any capital asset. If you don't risk the capital by investing in the market, you risk that capital because others are risking theirs.

This is important to understand: by investing in seeds to plant corn or by investing in a stock you hope will go up in value, you both have the same goal: minimize the risk of loss of assets through depreciation or inflation—and hopefully profit.

If there were no risk, there would be no need for the farmer to do anything. Even if he planted his crop but was guaranteed a return regardless of his yield, there would be no need to take the crop to market. He would simply deliver to a predetermined spot and pick up a check.

The Unknowable Future

People fear risk, and some are more risk averse than others, but what do people fear more than risk? Whether or not a risk will actually exploit a vulnerability. That's called ambiguity aversion. People fear not knowing.

> *Fear of risk and fear of not knowing what will happen are not the same thing, but people confuse the two all the time. They get scared of what can't be known instead of focusing on what is known or can be known.*

Your level of *ambiguity aversion* is how comfortable you can be with an unknown and unknowable future—the idea that no matter how prepared and knowledgeable you are, you will never know exactly what is coming next.

Some people are much better able to tolerate an unknowable future than others. It turns out people who don't fret about what they can't know are better able to synthesize what they can know and are better positioned to make good decisions.

Gender Differences

Interestingly, there is a difference between the sexes here. Research has shown that men and women have—on average—very similar aversion to risk, with women slightly more risk averse than men. However, men are much, much less ambiguity averse than women. This means that while both men and women may have similar tolerance to a particular risk, the average man is more comfortable with an unknowable future than the average woman would be.

He and she will see the risk of breaking down by the side of the road in pretty much the same way, however he is going to be more comfortable than she is heading off on that deserted mountain road for an adventure where the outcome is unknowable.

Understanding and being comfortable knowing that you can't know the future makes you better able to handle situations that call for quick, critical decision making.

Know What You Don't Know

You don't know jack, so accept it. In many trades, unless one of you is purely guessing, one party thinks they know something that the other doesn't. You are buying a stock because the seller thinks it has reached its most profitable value while you think it will go higher. He or she believes the opposite of what you believe—so one or the other of you is wrong. Who has the advantage?

Every stock-picking site, broker, investment advisor, etc. will lead you to believe that the advantage goes to the guy (or gal) with the better information. "Of course," you say.

You are wrong, dead wrong. There is no way to know if your information is "better." Why? Because you, like they, aren't in the club. If you were in the club, you wouldn't have gotten the information from the internet, or from your broker who got it from…the internet.

Don't ever pretend you are in the club. If you are reading this book, you are automatically NOT in the club.

As an individual investor, you are a small fish in a big pond—actually more like barely an amoeba in an entire ocean. Tremendously powerful entities controlling billions of dollars hold the real power to move the market in one direction or another. They share their plans with other large entities, not the public, and definitely not with you.

Remember that you are not an insider. With the understanding that you have NO informational advantage over anyone else in the market, you can begin to make decisions based on your experience with behavioral and market psychology patterns instead.

Focus on What You Can Control

True adventure will force you to recognize you aren't in control, and once you accept what's out of your hands or left to chance, you'll have more cognitive time and energy to focus on what you can control.

You will never be able to avoid the whale that just happens to breach when you cross its path in your little boat. Avoiding that potential collision is impossible, so don't worry about it.

Instead of burning energy on something you will never be able to predict, just relax, get good rest, and keep your wits about you. That way, if you do hit a whale and spring a leak, you will be able to deal with making a repair a lot better.

In the market, be aware that a large player like a hedge fund may decide to dump a bunch of stock a few minutes before or a few minutes after you decide to buy, driving the price down. The reason for the price drop has nothing to do with the company itself or its "fundamentals." Perhaps the manager needed the liquidity to purchase an IPO, or perhaps they needed to lock in their profit or loss on that particular security. You will never know why or how; but it will happen, and it can go either for or against your position.

Better to be ready to capitalize or stop a loss on an unexpected move than to worry about trying to predict the unpredictable. This might be a perfect opportunity to "double down" on a position instead of running for the door. Or maybe not.

MARKET PSYCHOLOGY

No doubt about it—your greatest opponent in the market stares at you in the mirror every day; but to really win big, you need to understand the market's psychology, too. Like crossing an ocean in a small boat, it sure helps to know which way the wind and current usually run, and when they are running differently than they usually do.

Classic Market Theory is BS

One common trading misconception is that the price of a security is directly tied to the underlying value of that company being traded. It's not—there is no direct link from one to the other. It's true that ownership, liquidity, and debt are being bought and sold through equities and derivatives; but a much more subtle and complex game of marketing and selling investment products is taking place.

Selling the Promise of Wealth

Technically, dividend payments are the only income you can derive directly from stock ownership. Let's face it though, unless you have a very high net worth and large investment portfolio, very few investors are living off those $3 quarterly dividends. Instead, it's all about making money as prices go up and down—as money enters and leaves. When money on the whole is entering the market without new shares issued, demand goes up and prices go up. When money on the whole is leaving the market, demand drops and so do prices.

When it comes to investing, you have to remember that someone out there is spending millions of dollars to market their financial instruments to you and to the rest of the market. No matter what it is: stocks, bonds, ETFs, futures, precious metals, currencies, mutual funds, etc., etc. —they are all offering their product and telling you that it has the power to make you wealthy. The message is clear: if you buy what they have, you can profit.

Bloggers, "analysts" (whatever that means), financial news shows, fund managers, market makers, and even the exchanges themselves—they are all dependent on *generating demand* for their products to keep prices up. There is a very good reason why there are disclaimers in the tiny font at the bottom of the TV screen or at the end of the analysis. It is because everyone involved is marketing products that they are promising will make you money, even though there is real risk you will lose it.

Real Value

There are good companies with bad stocks and bad companies with good stocks. The two are separate. As we talked about in previous chapters, the market is very good at finding "perceived value," but the real value in the market is completely nebulous and conceptual. *Real* value is such an esoteric idea that it's better to let it go completely.

In a way, that makes trading a much more simple process—you are no longer looking to buy shares of companies whose "fundamentals" are sound and well understood. Instead you are looking to buy (sell) shares or options in companies whose stock price you think will go up (down). There is a big difference. Stop thinking of the market as a rational forum where the best company wins, therefore its stock goes up.

It is much more of a popularity contest: everyone votes for the pretty girl until she gets a zit, then they leave her for another. This process is happening continuously, so always be looking for the nerdy girl in the corner who will take off her glasses to reveal she is a knockout. That's where the real money is to be made.

All you care about is that stock price and what you think everyone else thinks about that stock price. That's the only thing that matters.

REASONS YOU WILL LOSE

We don't want to make this chapter too negative, but because controlling fear and understanding loss aversion are so central to being a successful trader, we are going to look at some reasons that people lose in the market.

Control What You Can Control

We aren't religious, and we aren't in Alcoholics Anonymous or any other 12-step program, but there is incredible wisdom in the words of the American theologian, Reinhold Niebuhr:

> *"God, grant me the serenity to accept the things I cannot change, the courage to change the things I can, and the wisdom to know the difference."*

This philosophy can be extremely helpful when it comes to trading; you can't expect the market to rationally price stock or options based on the fundamental performance of the underlying company. You also can't completely predict and understand the irrationality of market participants. You can't control the market. The only thing you can control is yourself.

Greed, Fear, and Uncertainty

At their core, greed and fear are really the same thing. Greed is the fear of missing opportunity. Uncertainty, on the other hand, is a product of living in a universe governed by time; none of us can ever know with absolute certainty what is coming next. So uncertainty drives fear and greed. All three are unshakable facts about being human and being alive.

In our opinion, greed, fear and uncertainty govern 90% of human behavior and basically make the world go round: these emotions make people want kids, go on adventures, buy houses, etc. Financially speaking, these emotions move markets and drive economies. They are as fundamental to life on earth as sand is to a beach. Let's call these three emotions, "the big 3." Good? Bad? Why judge?—how about, they just are.

How Most People Deal With Uncertainty

Most people are control freaks. We subconsciously think that we are like the Wizard in the *Wizard of Oz,* the person behind the curtain who directs everything in our life like a puppeteer.

We go about our day making decisions that we feel will point us in the right direction. Choose the right school, get the right job, buy the right car and the right house and everything will go according to plan. If I point the bow of my ship in the right direction, I will arrive at the destination in a predetermined amount of time.

Of course, life usually doesn't turn out exactly to plan. If (when) we come across an obstacle or really anything unexpected that we feel we can't directly control, we have a tendency to not take part in it. The *risk* of being at the mercy of forces greater than ourselves is too great. We end up seeing uncertainty as something to be avoided at all costs. This is a sad way to live, and as we'll see, it is a less profitable way to invest your money.

Dealing with Changed Circumstances

In any adventure, or more broadly in life itself, something happens one day that shows the control freak that they were never in complete control in the first place. The world conspires against them, and in spite of all their precautions, an accident happens, a job is lost, something breaks, an illness comes on, a storm washes out a road, a sail tears or something is stolen.

It is the control freak, the person who is so worried about something going wrong, or not according to plan, who is least able to handle a new obstacle or a change in plans. Control freaks get agitated and are much less flexible when the unexpected does eventually happen, and they are then less able to make corrective decisions or adjust to new conditions.

We see this in marinas all the time when the starchy white collar husband and wife with the beautiful new boat come and go from a slip. They are in firm control of everything in their lives until that last dock line is let go and the wind and water grab hold of the boat and show them who is in control. The yelling begins, the engines get revved, and if they don't bounce off the dock or another boat, they certainly bounce off each other.

Here is what controlling people do in the face of something unforeseen and unforeseeable:

- Nothing. Shocked by the realization that they weren't pulling the strings after all, they wait for what might come next. In panic and in fear, they sit there watching the stock fall, hoping that it will bounce back. Hoping is not doing. Praying is equally effective.

- Look for a leader. What is everyone else doing here? Check the internet, turn on the news, read the paper.

- Try even harder to control the uncontrollable. Instead of thinking, "Wow, it looks like all of this control freak stuff is really wasted energy," they say, "I knew it, the world is a dangerous place, and I need to get better control of what is going on."

How ironic that people who try hardest to control everything in their lives are the most helpless when something goes wrong. Here are a few examples of the above as they happen in the market.

Doing Nothing

One piece of advice you hear the salty sailors give time and again is, "Reef early...if you are asking yourself if it's time to reef, it's *already* time to reef." If you want to have successful adventures or success in the market, you need to learn that doing nothing is not an option when circumstances change.

How many times have you seen someone stay at a dead-end job in a declining industry with no hope of ever advancing? Having worked in local television for many years, I (Nick) knew quite a few print journalists at newspapers. These were smart, well-informed, articulate people with a finger on the pulse of culture and the economy. By mid-2005, it was clear to everyone involved that the business model for the printed newspaper was pretty much done. Newspaper companies, if not in serious trouble, were about to undergo some drastic changes.

A friend of mine worked as a photographer at the Denver Post for a decade. He had covered trials, crime, city hall, wildfires, sports, etc., and won several awards for his work. He continued working diligently at the Post through furloughs, then layoffs, and then a transition to freelance work. Finally he reached a point where he literally couldn't pay the rent with his diminished compensation. That process took about five years. Now he is living off the last of his savings and going to community college. He hopes to get into tax preparation.

The same thing happens all the time when a stock is in decline. No matter how dismal the outlook, you will see investors stick with their stock all the way to Chapter 11. We'll talk more about why this happens in the next section, but the reason the photographer stays at the job with a very dark future is the same reason as the guy who rides Worldcom all the way to zero. They are hoping and praying for something with no chance of happening. From the outside, it looks idiotic, but from the inside they are blind.

Looking for a Leader

Known as the, "I'm not responsible," syndrome, this can also take the form of:

- "I don't know what's going on, so I'll find someone who does."
- "It's someone else's fault and I want someone to blame if I make the wrong choice."
- "He knows what he is doing, so I will just mimic what he does."

Hiring a specialist is a good idea sometimes. For example, it's a bad idea to try to do your own dental work or represent yourself in court. The same can be said of hanging drywall or installing a transmission in a car. If you are in a situation in which someone else has better tools, more knowledge, and more experience than you do and can do it faster or better than you can, it makes a lot of sense to hire them to do the job so you can focus on what you are good at doing. But you need to understand that no matter who you hire to buffer yourself against bad decision-making, you are always ultimately responsible.

Even when it looks like it's time to call in a specialist or if the work is just a little too nasty or difficult, it can be really tempting to hire someone else to take responsibility for setting things right again. But you have to ask yourself the question: will this expert be at my side every time I need them? And what happens if they aren't there?

I (Nick), do all of my own engine work. Why? Because the engine never breaks down at the dock—it literally hasn't happened once. It breaks down only when we are entering a tight channel, or are becalmed 30 miles offshore. We've lost our engine and/or transmission in inconvenient situations so many times that we can't even count, and the reasons have been numerous: water in the fuel, dirty filters, air in the lines, cables broken, heat exchangers broken, electrical problems, oil leaks, alternator problems, starter problems, etc., etc., etc. When the unexpected happens and there is no one else around to fix it, you have to step up and take care of it yourself.

Old marine diesel engines are the trilobites of the boating world. These things have hardly evolved much from a power-generating standpoint since they were invented. They are not terribly difficult to understand really—if they are getting fuel and air, they will run. The complications when working on them come about because each one is installed and arranged differently to take up as little space as possible in the boat, making different parts extremely difficult to access. So it's not complicated to tighten a belt or check fuel delivery, but getting your arm to bend like a pipe cleaner is a trick we haven't managed to master.

Every time we do engine work, we end up battered, bruised, greasy, and with several lacerations on our fingers, forearms, elbows, shoulders, and usually a couple on the knees as well. We hate engine work. So if there is one service (aside from the toilet) that we would gladly hire out on our boats regardless of cost, it would be engine work. But we have only hired a mechanic a couple of times when we didn't have the specialized tools required.

That's exactly how you should view the markets. You can hire brokers, subscribe to analysts, buy books, and invest in managed funds—but at the end of the day that will not change the fact that you, and only you, are responsible for your gain or loss. Learn to rely on you first, others second. By teaching yourself at least the basics you will be rewarded financially, no matter who you invest with, or what you invest in.

Managed Fund Fallacy

Most people decide before they even begin that trading is better left to the experts, so they put their money in mutual funds or other managed investments. If the value of the fund goes up, that's great, if it goes down, well, at least they weren't responsible for the loss. Instead of taking personal responsibility, it's some nameless, faceless schmuck who lost their money, not them. But realize this: that fund manager gets paid whether you see a return or not. He isn't responsible, you are. Now who's the schmuck?

Even among funds, it's interesting that most fund managers don't want to take responsibility for their decisions either. There are entire hedge funds built on buying the exact same stocks that Warren Buffett does. Obviously, they want their fund's value to increase, and there are incredible pressures to perform, but they don't want to lose their jobs if they don't perform. The turnover in fund management is incredible: 20–30% per year. So what do they do? They do what other fund managers are doing. If the "others" are wrong and they lose money, they might still have a job. If they went out on their own and lost, well, their career is probably over, or at least damaged.

The attitude of "it's someone else's fault" is particularly prevalent in the U.S. We live in a society that routinely removes all personal responsibility from every situation. There are warning labels on everything, laws governing everything, and an authority to answer to in every situation. Slip and fall on the sidewalk? Sue the little old lady who owns the house. Get into trouble on your sailboat out in the middle of the ocean? Set off your EPIRB (emergency beacon) and wait for the helicopter to arrive. Whether it's the courts or insurance companies, we are coddled in so many ways that people think someone should always be there to save their hides or at least take the blame.

Being Over-Informed

Looking for a leader leads to an insatiable appetite for information. Before setting off on a grand adventure, people scrub every cruising or RV'ing or backpacking website that can tell them what to expect, what may happen, what the dangers are. Knowing MORE seems to help people feel more confident, however no one ever stops to think about whether the information is good in the first place. Often, it's highly opinionated and/or just plain wrong. And does that next piece of advice or news or whatever change the fact that you are still responsible for what happens to you?

I (Pat) live in Mexico most of the time these days, whether sailing around with my family on our boat or renting different condos when the heat is too much. At some point while applying for American citizenship for one of my kids, I got stuck on the U.S. Embassy's e-mail list. For three years now, I've been e-mail bombed by the ever-helpful American government with warnings about just how dangerous a place this is that I live in. Yet somehow my family and I are still alive, happy, sun-soaked, and salt-water wrinkled.

Everywhere you look: the computer screen, the TV, the radio, the newspapers, etc., there are endless resources available to learn more. And when was the last time you watched a TV news program and thought, "Gosh, now I feel so much more secure and certain about the world." Media of all types are very good at feeding your insecurities and appealing to your risk aversion. *If I just know a little more about what is happening in the Greek debt crisis, I will be in a better position to understand the market tomorrow.* This is looking for the "other" or a leader to tell you what to do.

Information is not a bad thing, but it can be a double-edged sword—it can help just as easily as it can hurt. You need to be able to watch the news and understand the sentiment of the market. The control freak misses this point completely and looks to the media to ***confirm*** what they believe. They look to the internet to find a blogger who agrees that stock XYZ is poised to pop. They don't look critically at an issue, instead they are looking for a leader that they can agree with.

Making a Move Just to be Proactive

So we've established that when circumstances change and something unforeseen happens, fearful and anxious people (and especially control freaks) tend to do nothing or they look to a leader; but they'll also take action, even when none is warranted, and without any justification or reasoning.

Let's say that your trade in XYZ stock isn't working out. Your research was solid, the stock or option *should* be behaving one way, but it simply isn't. The trade so far has gone against you. You believed XYZ would go up $.30 at the open, and it went down $.80. You scour the internet for information that can corroborate the reason for this move, but there is nothing. What do you do? Cut your losses because circumstances have changed, or double your position because a good buy just got a lot better?

The smart way (the right way) to analyze the situation is to understand that you don't have enough information to analyze the decision here, but the control freak will often make a decision one way or another without any reason at all. Why? Because making a decision, even if it's a bad one, makes them feel like they are in control. The control freak feels that they have to make a move. Perhaps all that's really needed is a little patience, or at worst a stop loss.

COMMON TRADING TRAPS

Even veteran traders make mistakes. If you run into a rough patch of bad trades, you might want to step back and see if you are making any of the following trading mistakes.

Pride of Ownership

The oft-heard "buy and hold" strategy of the long-term investor is all about developing a portfolio that you carry for years, if not decades. For the long-term investor, it can be a little hard to sell that General Motors stock if you've made thousands of dollars on it over the course of your entire working life—even after that stock has dropped from let's say $40 to $19 as it did through 2011.

We are talking about a very slow decline in the face of round after round of negative news, bailouts, etc. There was literally no news on the horizon and no reason to think that the company would ever turn around. Even in the face of these circumstances, lots of people held GM through a 50% drop and it was because of pride of ownership.

We are guilty of this one ourselves. I, (Pat) bought Apple stock in 2009 between $120 and $160 per share. Throughout the next couple of years I traded the stock pretty regularly, but mostly using options. Fast forward to 2012, the stock is trading for $700 and I still held on to some shares. The truth is, I enjoyed clicking my cost basis button on my portfolio and seeing those purchase prices—like looking at pictures of your babies when they are all grown up.

But I didn't need those shares any more—it was silly really—as I was often invested in options positions worth ten times the number of shares I held in the actual stock. I eventually got over my own pride of ownership and sold the stock. I found that after those shares were gone from my portfolio I felt even more free to trade the stock again.

Touchy Feely Syndrome

The same pride of ownership can bite you in the butt when you are a fan of a company's products. Apple, as Pat showed us above, is a perfect example of a company whose stock is supported not just by investors, but by fans of what the company designs and sells. As of this writing, AAPL stock has yet to really let anyone down; but it will happen eventually, and hopefully you sell before the same thing that happened to GM happens to them.

Facebook is an example of a company whose stock has too many fans and not enough business. FB made their IPO in May 2012. Everyone and their brother couldn't wait to own stock in the company. "Everyone uses it, every day!" Speculators all—the retail investors ran for the exits the moment the stock didn't pop. In retrospect, the IPO was overvalued from the beginning and couldn't pop. Fans of the product shouldn't have been fans of the company or its stock.

Like many things in this book there is a sharp dichotomy here. Our strategy is about investing in companies whose products you love and whose business you understand. However, you have to realize that this can be a trap as well, because a good product does not necessarily make a good company, and a good company doesn't make a good stock. You must remain objective.

Fear of the Shoulds

It has been said that looking back on your life, you tend to regret what you didn't do instead of what you did do. Regret sucks—it's probably the worst emotion on the spectrum. It leads to all of the "should haves" in life: I should have taken that job, I should have left my ex-wife sooner, I should have taken a year off in college to have a grand adventure. Should have! Should have! Should have! The only thing worse than the *should haves* (past regrets) is the *shoulds*. (By the way—you need to stop with the shoulds and just do.)

People hang on to losing stocks and losing positions in the market for too long because of the *fear of regret*. They know they *should* sell but instead they continue to hold on because they don't want to realize the loss. It isn't so much that they are holding off for a rebound (that there may be no evidence for), but rather they don't want to translate a paper loss on the stock to a cash loss in their account. After all, just because the stock has gone against you, it isn't a realized loss until you exit that trade.

Celebrity Worship

Owning well-known companies' stock feels safer for some reason. Celebrity stocks are the ones that *everyone* has in their portfolio or everyone seems to be talking about. These are the "value" companies like Microsoft, Apple, Kraft, Johnson & Johnson—the brands with good earnings, and long-term positive growth patterns—in a word: stability. But there are other well-known companies like Facebook, Yahoo, Kodak, Morgan Stanley, which are well-known but volatile.

If these companies feel like a safer bet to you than others, you are not alone. Fund managers love to invest in well-known companies. Why? Because they are a sure thing? Nope. They invest in the popular stocks because if and when they do go down (and all of these companies' stocks do go up and down), they will not be blamed directly. "Tom, I can't believe you invested in Microsoft—you are fired!" That's just not going to happen to Tom the fund manager.

Celebrity stocks are not necessarily bad stocks to own, but it's important to remember that they sometimes carry unreasonable valuations based simply on the fact that they are so widely held. When they do crash, they move lower quickly and then only very slowly recover. No one likes to dance with the popular kid who just crapped their pants on the dance floor in front of the entire school, and that's the problem you run into with celebrity stocks.

Present Extrapolation

We human beings are biased towards "nowcasting," meaning that we tend to expect present conditions, trends, and relationships to continue into the future. When the market is down, we tend to think that it will always be down. And just in case we weren't buying into the bearish psychology of the day, all we have to do is look to everyone else: every blog, newspaper article, and financial news cable channel will confirm that the world is indeed going to end and take your non-cash portfolio with it.

When the market is up, we are biased towards extrapolating bullish conditions into the future as well. Just as in a bearish environment, when the market is up, all external media tends to confirm a belief that it will always be rosy. Of course that's not how the markets work. They go up and down.

Nowcasting makes the market in general very bad non-linear thinkers. When disruptive events change the landscape in a fundamental way, the market tends to lag. Early signals of a downturn or upturn are extremely difficult to spot. Even if you are thinking contrary to the market and looking for an opportunity, be aware that the market has tremendous momentum.

Miss Contrary

The market is dumb…really dumb in fact, however over the short term the market is always right. You might remember the English nursery rhyme:

Mistress Mary, Quite contrary,
How does your garden grow?
With Silver Bells, And Cockle Shells,
And so my garden grows.

Simply trading against the market can look very tempting. For a novice trader, this looks like low-hanging fruit—and often it is. We talked about this at length in the Fade Trade and Short Term Strategies sections. You can make a quick buck in a day or two just by buying when everyone else is selling and selling when everyone else is buying. But be careful not to *always* be contrary because even if the market is really dumb, it is right.

One very common pothole to fall into is when you make some money by making a contrary trade. Your bias is going to become very contrary to the market. In essence, you will tend to see contrarian trades everywhere. Make some money shorting a stock yesterday? You will be especially attuned to seeing other potential shorts in the market. Be aware of the biases you carry!

Overconfidence

Confidence is important for success, but you can very easily go too far. The setup goes something like this: you just know this is the *right* trade, and there is no way in hell that it can go against you, this is a *guaranteed* winner. Actually, this is perhaps the most dangerous trap you can fall into; because it's one of the most difficult to self-identify and it will get you into trouble the fastest.

The moment you decide that you can't lose
is followed closely by the moment that you do lose.

The stock market is brutally sincere when it tells you that it wants to suck every dollar out of you. The guy on the other side of the trade wants your money. He will lead you by the hand into the alley and mug you and take your money. The market is always risky. The trade can always go against you. Nothing says "sucker" like someone who thinks they can't lose.

BIAS

Trading is all about decision-making. Right decision = profit, wrong decision = loss. The really, really, really hard part is making rational, correct decisions over and over again; that's what separates the amateur trader from the successful pro. It isn't luck or insider information. It's clarity; it's being able to see what is *really* happening in the market, and not just what you *want* to see.

Why is this so difficult? Our vision is clouded by previous experiences, as well as inclinations and tendencies, all of which we will broadly call *biases*. There are actually two types: cognitive biases and personal biases.

Cognitive Biases

These predispositions are hardwired into your brain, so you have to be extraordinarily diligent about noticing them. There are about a thousand different types of cognitive bias, so we'll focus only on the ones that are really important to traders. Here are a few that can really mess up your trading:

Anchoring bias is the common human tendency to rely too heavily on one piece of information at the expense of the rest of the data. Let's say that your uncle Fred was mugged in a particular park in your town. You will then have an unavoidable tendency to think that particular park is dangerous, even if there had only been that one instance of crime in the last 50 years. Or let's say that you lost big on a particular tech stock last week. You will have an aversion to making a similar type of trade in that sector today because that stock has become "unpredictable." One piece of data or experience does not a trend make!

Attention bias is where you don't see all the possibilities or you focus on two possible outcomes and forget about the rest. You might focus strictly on whether you think a stock will go up or down, but what if it goes sideways? What will happen to your call or put options if that happens? Most of the time, what you expect to happen doesn't occur exactly the way you forecast it will. It's much better to think of future outcomes as a *range* of possibilities.

Illusory correlation bias. This is when it looks like two things are related when they really aren't. The market loves to trade stocks in related sectors in tandem, and often the actual relationship between companies is shaky at best. It's one thing to see ZNGA (a Facebook game maker) trend identically to FB itself.

However, it's quite another thing to think that BP is trading in tandem with MCD. They may move in the same direction based on the sizes and positions of those companies in the market, but there is no other correlation between the two companies—there is no causal relationship. In fact, British Petroleum and McDonald's have nothing to do with one another.

Ego, or egocentric bias. This is the tendency to think that your *sh*t don't stink*. Let's say that you kill it on a trade on Monday. You are the man (or woman)! You can do no wrong! You should write your own book about trading! When you have made a successful move, it's super easy to think you have the magic touch. You will have a tendency to be just a little less cautious on Tuesday—which can burn you big-time. Egocentric bias is basically taking too much credit for your success. Yes, you made the right decision, but that doesn't make the next one any easier.

Negativity bias. As a trader, negativity bias is mostly a good thing; there really are a lot more opportunities to lose all your money in the market than there are to make a lot of money, so negativity bias is your friend except in one regard: it tends to make you underestimate your resources. It's critical that you remember to look at your portfolio, and particularly your actively traded portfolio as either working or not working. Cash can be an important shelter position; but remember that if you aren't putting capital at risk, you can't get the reward. Negativity bias tends to put traders "on the sidelines" too often.

Self-serving bias. This is where you take credit for your successes but blame the market (or a tipster, or really anyone else) for your failures. This bias easily feeds into egocentric bias, again making you think your sh*t don't stink.

Remember, you are the captain, and the decisions you make are your own. We believe first and foremost in personal responsibility. This starts with taking the blame when you make the wrong call. That is leadership.

Hindsight bias is probably the most common and unavoidable bias in the investing world, and we are not immune. In fact we are guilty of this bias in almost every trading conversation we've ever had: "I owned AAPL stock back when it traded for $22 per share. I'd have retired years ago if I hadn't sold at $27." We've all been there; we all have similar stories. Interesting how obvious AAPL's journey seems now that we can look at it in the rear-view mirror, right? The problem is that memory distorts, and if you were to try to find another AAPL—type company today which was trading at much lower levels, you might have a tendency or bias towards favoring them in the absence of other information. Hindsight makes previous moves look obvious, but it's an error to translate the history of one company to that company or any other company today.

Confirmation bias. People have a tendency or bias towards information that confirms what they already believe. Let's say that you love GE stock. This morning, you read two analysts' reports: one favorable and one not favorable. Which one are you going to tend to trust more? The one that confirms what you already like about the company, or one that slams it?

That's right, only the guy who agrees with you knows what he is talking about. You may weigh the opposing information, but your tendency will be to believe more of what you already believe.

This is a good list to revisit if you feel that you are having a tough time in your trades. If you are analyzing a trade with a "can't lose" attitude, stop to think if you might believe you are on a winning streak—thinking you can't lose means you certainly will. Or if you aren't considering all possible outcomes, or if you are starting to see connections in the market that don't really exist—no need to see a shrink—these biases are built into your brain.

One of the biggest traps you can fall into is thinking that you can override your own biases. It's much better to simply recognize them when you can.

Personal Bias

We all see the world through our own individual lenses. You see a beautiful car, and I see an overrated piece of junk. I like Corona, you like Pacifico. He prefers redheads, she prefers latin hunks, they like chocolate ice cream while the other guys like vanilla. Call it taste, call it preference, call it whatever you want; but at the end of the day, it is *bias*. These are the baseline inclinations towards one thing and away from another that can make rational decision-making nearly impossible.

When it comes to trading, personal biases will make one stock more attractive than another. Your history in that sector, or with that company, or with that type of security will all bear on how you see the opportunity. One trader will see a definite buy, another will see an absolute hold, and a third will see a definite sell.

With personal bias, it's best to just realize when others in the market—be they other traders, managers, or analysts—are bringing their own bias to their position. Are they right? Are they wrong? The market is always right, so if they are on the right side of the trade, they are right.

Avoiding Bias

Just about the only thing you can do to try and avoid your biases is to keep an open, un-opinionated mind about everything in your life. Try not to paint the world in black and white or right and wrong. Be balanced and measured and unemotional about issues; try to see things from the other guys' point of view.

Being Too Smart

You would think that smarter people are less biased. A 2012 study in the *Journal of Personality and Social Psychology* ("Cognitive Sophistication does not Attenuate the Bias Blind Spot") found the exact opposite, especially when it comes to relatively simple problems. Here is a sample question from their research:

> *A bat and ball costs a dollar and ten cents. The bat costs a dollar more than the ball. How much does the ball cost?*

Simple, right? Ten cents. Wrong, it costs five cents. If you got this question wrong, it's because your brain made a couple shortcuts along the way and forgot the simple arithmetic completely. Don't feel too bad though, half the students in the study got this one question wrong, and went to schools like Harvard, Princeton, and MIT. In fact, researchers found that smarter students actually scored slightly lower on this question.

Being smart does give you an advantage in seeing and understanding patterns of behavior in others, however. So while you won't have any better chance of seeing your own biases, being smart does help you identify other people's biases. In the market, this is extremely helpful, especially if you employ a contrarian's trading style.

Overtrading

FOMO is Fear of Missing Out; also known as greed. We have all been there. The market is moving and you want to be in on the action. So instead of making careful, deliberate moves on companies you know really well, you make smaller trades on companies you don't know a lot about, just hoping for a winner.

Statistically speaking, the more you trade per dollar in your portfolio, the poorer your performance—this has been shown time and time again. The most successful traders in the market wait patiently for the perfect opportunity with very high odds of success, and then they make a big move with a high expected return. The losers tend to grasp desperately at whatever looks good at the moment, making too many moves in and out of positions.

Trading too often is a bad strategy for a number of reasons. Not only will the brokerage fees eat away at your profits, but particularly if you are going long on momentum moves during a single day, you are likely taking bigger risks than you have to. The reason for this is that stocks tend to move up much slower than they fall. So if you are long for only a matter of hours, your profits statistically will be slower to come.

Steaming

Anger is not a useful emotion for the trader—it makes you do dumb things. The market isn't personal, but when you find yourself on the wrong side of a trade, it's easy to get pissed off. From a position of resentment or anger towards the anonymous *they* out there, you may unconsciously feel the need to *teach the market a lesson*. Reading this now, the idea may sound ridiculously irrational...and it is...but psychologically when things don't go your way, it can be tempting to lash out at whatever or whomever you feel is responsible for your loss. This is a recipe for disaster.

Gambling Addiction

At its heart, trading is gambling. There is no way around that fact. Sure, there is a price-finding or value-finding purpose behind the endeavor; and you do hope to bring some element of skill to the table, but at the end of the day, you are still placing a bet on a future outcome, and that's gambling.

Winning in the market is so very sweet. Money won is so much sweeter than money earned from a job. Your heart beats faster as you see that chart line turn upward, your inter-day account is in the green, and you are already thinking about what you might buy with your fattened account. When you exit that trade with winnings in tow it is thrilling—a rush.

Like any positive feeling, you will want more of it. You will want to get that feeling again. Be careful though, wanting it a little too much is a sign of addiction. If you are predisposed to addictive behavior, be it drugs or alcohol or sex or whatever, you will likely have to keep tabs on your trading behavior as well. Being addicted to trading will lead to overtrading, and eventually to losses.

Keeping Cool

Rationality is the single trait that will make you money in the market. Being clear-headed and making reasoned decisions time and again is the basic recipe for making money. The cooler you can be when everyone else has his or her hair on fire, the better you will do in the long run. So what can you do to keep cool?

- exercise
- limit caffeine
- get good sleep

- meditate or spend time decompressing
- Be creative. Paint, take photos, sing, dance, whatever.

Stepping Away

One of the biggest advantages you have as an occasional trader is *perspective.* Maintaining that perspective can be a challenge if you start trading more often. Trading on a daily basis, you can lose the independent vantage point that allows you to make rational decisions. Your head gets too far into the market and there can be a tendency to cling too tightly to your beliefs and biases. Being away from the market for long periods of time gives you an advantage over everyone else.

When you get off the trail or come back in from the islands for your two or three days of trading every month, you get to see the market with fresh eyes. You get to re-evaluate positions and question assumptions again from the beginning. The innocence that you bring will help you decide whether recent market moves make sense and when and where there might be opportunity to capitalize when a stock is out of sync with the market.

You've Reached...the Beginning

Your buddy hates his job but won't look for another. Your brother is overweight but can't stop eating junk food. Your mom worries about money but buys a fourth and fifth set of bed sheets with matching towels and can't miss her weekly massage. There might even be a few things about yourself or your life that you don't like, but it seems impossible to change course. Why is it so easy to recognize simple, straightforward solutions to other people's problems, but so hard to see and solve our own? We think there are two reasons:

1. We all operate under assumptions about ourselves, and we are blind to our own problems.
2. Learning something new or changing habits is intimidating, and we are lazy creatures.

If you yearn for adventure or financial independence or both, you can do it—we have no doubt in our minds that you can. If you've read this book from the beginning, we hope that you are at least questioning your assumptions and are a little less intimidated by the changes you can make and the things you can learn to do, and do well.

We never set out to write a book that teaches you exactly how, step by step to make money in the market or head off on that journey around the world. Why? Well that's not really possible. Each of these endeavors is going to involve tens of thousands of decisions that have to be made on a case-by-case basis by you! You will have to use your own judgment each and every time.

It's all up to you, and this is great news.

This personal responsibility stuff is liberating—once you've given up relying on the rest of the world and its ideas, judgments, and assumptions, you are going to hear that little voice in your head more clearly. In fact, it might start shouting at you. Learn to trust that voice, but ignore or question it every time it sounds a bit too cautious. Substitute that caution for skepticism—that's right, question your caution!

In the beginning of anything new, you are going to worry that somewhere down the road, you'll come across a problem that you won't be able to solve. "Even if we get to Suchandsuch Island, we may get pinned down by weather," or, "If I buy that stock, I won't know when to sell it," or, "If I take a few months off to hike the Pacific Crest Trail, I won't be able to find a job when I get back." Don't let an unknowable future keep you stuck in what you *think* is more predictable—it isn't. You have always found a way to take the "next, right step." What makes you think that's going to change?

Focus on what you can control and let the unknowable future take care of itself. Look around yourself today and take inventory of what you do have, right now. See the resources available at this moment, understand what knowledge or understanding is missing and take steps to fill those gaps. Keep learning, but have the wisdom to know when a little more knowledge isn't going to make any difference. Know when it's time to do—and then...do.

If it doesn't work out the way you planned it would (and it won't), then adjust. That's what you've been doing your entire life anyway.

Dream Big Enough

It all starts with a dream. Yours won't match anyone else's so don't go around talking about your dream with friends and family looking for confirmation that it's the right dream. What do *they* know anyway? And be realistic. Don't give yourself a reason not to try. Set the bar too high and you won't feel like it's possible—you'll never do it.

Do not even give a second thought to "failure." What does that even mean? That you didn't do exactly what you said you wanted to? That's ridiculous. Even if you only make it a third of the way around the world on your circumnavigation, do you really think you will look back on all of your adventures and see it as a big waste? Hardly. You are going to savor those memories, and you can always finish the loop sometime down the road if you feel like it.

One Foot at a Time

When you've got a dream in mind, making it happen is simply putting one foot in front of the other—it isn't going to be a long slog. When you cut the cable TV to save that $120 per month, your mindset is going to change. Dropping the Starbucks latte from the budget is going to be very easy and obvious. Then that car is going to look ridiculously out of place in the driveway. Then the driveway is going to seem a little silly. *And why do I have to live so far from my job anyway?* Before you know it, you are going to be asking whether having the job makes any sense in the first place when there might be easier ways to make a bit of cash.

Embrace Risk

We've talked a lot about risk in this book. We hope that we've encouraged you not to simply take *more* risks, but to take *better* risks; smarter risks. Risking some savings or earning potential now to enjoy your time alive a bit more, versus risking your time alive for an unknowable future which is guaranteed to end at some point anyway? Where are the real risks there?

We also hope you've found new ways to minimize risks when they are directly within your control and not bother with the things you can't control.

Hopefully you see now that minimizing your financial need (a.k.a. decreasing your burn rate) means that your market risks go down. No matter what the market does or what happens in your life, the smaller that monthly nut and the more agile your life situation, the more freedom and security you will feel.

The Biggest Challenge

Financially, each and every one of us is going to start from a different place and we all have different needs. That single fact has been the most challenging part about writing this book for us because we know that everyone wants a simple rule for how much to risk, or what the expected return is, or when exactly to buy and sell, or what exactly to buy and sell. Step-by-step instructions, or even thinking a one-size-fits-all solution is possible is the absolute 100% incorrect way of approaching this subject matter.

Why? Because we would be forced to make assumptions about you and the market which would lead you down the wrong path from the very beginning. So if you are disappointed by our lack of specificity, we half-heartedly apologize, but not really. We know the silver bullet is pure fiction.

What We Hope You Learned

If you just finished this book, we hope your eyes and ears are open to opportunities you hadn't considered before. We hope we at least poked some holes in the veil of fear and intimidation that keeps most people doing the same old things that they've always done. If nothing else, we hope that we have done two things with this book:

1. Inspired you to take steps towards getting where you want to be, and
2. Provided at least some partial understanding of the markets and the tools available to you.

We hope that you walk away with a hunger to learn more and a better understanding of the vocabulary so that the other resources out there will make more sense.

Get Out and It Will Work Out

You are smarter than you think you are. You are more resourceful than you assume yourself to be. When push comes to shove you will make the right decision when you need to. Don't get stranded today by living too far out in the future or by following the herd; none of them know which way to go, and that's why they stick together. You have to learn to trust your internal compass—especially when it points you toward living your art.

Don't be afraid to be an outlier, living on the margin—you are going to meet people like yourself. They'll be strong, confident people who trust themselves implicitly, and they'll recognize the same in you—that's why the bonds you form on that final ascent to the mountain peak or at that remote Pacific atoll are so much sweeter and long-lasting than those you have at work or on your neighborhood cul-de-sac. It takes courage to make your dreams come true—it takes courage to live on the margin—and those that have it, and do it, share something that the rest never will.

As you plot and scheme about how to make your dreams come true, remember that making the decision to go is the hardest part. When the trip is over or the journey is complete, you'll look back and see that your assumptions were wrong, you'll recognize how you were forced to adapt, and how in the end, it all worked out.

After you've made that dream a reality, you'll wonder why you spent all those years waiting for the right time or planning the perfect itinerary—your only regret will be that you didn't shed those preconceived assumptions and go earlier. And one day, when a dreamer asks you about how to set out on an adventure like yours, you'll tell them, "Don't wait, go now."

It Starts with an Idea

This book was inspired by a thousand conversations online and in-person. We would never have written this book—and in fact we probably would have never even met had we not followed the advice you find in these pages.

We set off like a couple of fools, and it all worked out.

Made in the USA
Lexington, KY
08 January 2014